A STUDY GUIDE
OF ISRAEL
HISTORICAL - GEOGRAPHICAL

WITH A SUPPLEMENT ON JORDAN

A STUDY GUIDE
OF ISRAEL
HISTORICAL - GEOGRAPHICAL

WITH A SUPPLEMENT ON JORDAN

ARNOLD G. FRUCHTENBAUM
Th.M., Ph.D

POST OFFICE BOX 3723
TUSTIN, CA 92781

ARIEL MINISTRIES

Other Books by the Author

Jesus Was A Jew

A Passover Haggadah for Jewish Believers

Biblical Lovemaking: A Study of the Song of Solomon

Hebrew Christianity: Its Theology, History and Philosophy

Israeolology: The Missing Link in Systematic Theology

Messianic Christology

The Footsteps of the Messiah: A Study of the Sequence of Prophetic Events

Graphic design by Scott Roberts

All Scripture quotations and reference, unless otherwise noted, are from the American Standard Version (ASV), 1901.

Copyright © 1994 by Ariel Ministries
Revised November 1999
ISBN: 0-914863-08-8

Printed in the United States of America

**THIS VOLUME IS DEDICATED TO THE MEMORY OF THE
FRUCHTENBAUM FAMILY.**

To those who died in Poland before the war:

> To my Great-Grandfather, Baruch Simchah Fruchtenbaum

> To my Grandfather, Yitzchak Meir Fruchtenbaum

To those who perished in the Holocaust:

> To my Great-Grandmother, Ittah Leah (Greenbaum) Fruchtenbaum

> To my Great-Uncles, Tzemach Fruchtenbaum
>   and Asher Fruchtenbaum

> To my Great-Aunts, Adah Fruchtenbaum
>   and Chavah (Fruchtenbaum) Zilberstein
>   her husband, Yoseph Zilberstein
>   their two daughters, Gutkah and Frumkah Zilberstein

> To Yadja Fruchtenbaum (the wife of Yaakov Fruchtenbaum)
>   and their son, Simchah Fruchtenbaum

**To those who survived the Holocaust, immigrated to Israel and continued
the family line**:

> To Yaakov Fruchtenbaum
>   his wife, Irka Fruchtenbaum
>   their two daughters, Esther and Ruth Fruchtenbaum

> To Hannah (Fruchtenbaum) Taital
>   her husband Chaim Taital
>   their son, Danl Taital
>   and daughter, Nurit Taital

> To Genya (Fruchtenbaum) Zalmonson
>   her husband, Moshe Zalmonson
>   their daughter, Batya Zalmonson
>   and son, Avi Zalmonson

> To Chumah (Fruchtenbaum) Gadot
>   her husband, Reuben Gadot
>   their daughter, Ruth Gadot
>   their two sons, Amir and Ilan Gadot

To my father, Chaim Fruchtenbaum, and my mother, Adele (Suppes)
Fruchtenbaum, who came to America and where the name continues to be
perpetuated to this day.

HOW TO USE THIS GUIDE

This guide is usable whether you are travelling to and in Israel on your own or if you are part of a group tour with an official guide. This manual will give you information your tour guide may not cover.

This guide has four main parts.

The first section contains some basic information about the Modern State of Israel, followed by a breakdown of the historical and archaeological periods as found on archaeological signs throughout the country. This should be read as you begin your tour of Israel.

Section two begins with a map showing the broad geographical areas as outlined in Deuteronomy 1:6-8 and then covers each specific area. The map will give you an idea in what part of the country you happen to be on any given day. You can then read up on that particular section of the country in the following pages.

Section three lists almost every place in Israel in alphabetical order. As you are heading to your next site, or while you are already there, you can read up on that spot by looking it up in this manual. Since it is in alphabetical order, it will be easy to find. Again, you will find information that your tour guide may not necessarily cover.

Sections four and five are supplemental sections on Jordan. Section four gives you a brief overview of Jordan and section five is an alphabetical listing of places within Jordan similar to section three on Israel.

Please note that every site relevant to Jerusalem will be in the section under "Jerusalem." For example, the Mount of Olives is not listed separately but is in the section under "Jerusalem" and under the subsection, "The Mountains Around Jerusalem."

For your convenience, an index is listed in the back of the book. If you do not find a familiar place listed in the alphabetical sections, look in the index and you will find it there.

Enjoy your time in Israel!

ISRAEL

JORDAN

Israel
The Modern State

I.   GENERAL INFORMATION

A. GOVERNMENT
A republic and a parliamentary democracy which consists of three branches: the legislature (the Knesset); the executive (the government headed by the prime minister); and, the judiciary (the court system). A president elected by the Parliament (Knesset) for a five-year term but with no real power. The real power is held by the prime minister and a cabinet of ministers who are responsible to the Knesset which makes laws and keeps a close watch on all government activities. Members of the Knesset are elected on a proportional-representation basis and represent all the different groups in the Israeli population (including farmers, rabbis, lawyers and Arabs). It is a unicameral house. About 12 political parties with two major blocks: Labor and Likud. Universal suffrage from the age of 18.

B. POPULATION
As of January 1, 1999, approximately 6 million people live in Israel: 4.8 million are Jews, 901,000 are Moslems, 129,000 are Christian and 99,000 are Druze. Other population groups include Circassians (3,000), Samaritans (250) and Bedouins (70,600). Jerusalem is the largest center of population. Tel Aviv is the cultural, commercial and social center of modern Israel even though Jerusalem is the capital. About 3½% of the population live on collective farms. In addition to the population of the State of Israel, there are an additional 1½ million Palestinians in the West Bank and Gaza. The percentage breakdown for the State of Israel is: 80% Jews, 15% Moslems, 2.2% Christians and 1.7% Druze. The Jewish population in the West Bank and Gaza is 154,000.

C. AREA
Before the Six-Day War of 1967, the area was approximately 8000 square miles (the size of Massachusetts), of which 35% was arable, 19% under cultivation, 60% desert and 3% forests. Much has changed since that war. Today Israel is 34,500 square miles (about the size of Maine or Indiana) since the addition of land in the Sinai and on the Golan Heights as well as the West Bank territory. In an effort to reforest their country more than 50 million trees have been planted since 1948. Sinai was returned to Egypt in 1982. On September 13, 1993, Israel and the Palestine Liberation Organization (PLO) signed a Peace Accord and Israel agreed to withdraw from most of the Gaza Strip and Jericho. In subsequent negotiations, Israel has also withdrawn from seven other Arab populated areas: Jenin, Nablus, Tulkarm, Qalqilya, Ramallah, Bethlehem and Hebron.

D. NATURAL RESOURCES
Fisheries (commercial ponds as well as the Sea of Galilee, the Jordan River and the Mediterranean Sea); agriculture including citrus fruits, wheat, barley, olives, cotton, grapes and peanuts; livestock including

sheep, goats, cattle, horses, donkeys; minerals, including copper, iron, potash, phosphates, rock salt, oil and natural gas; **tourism** is big business in Israel!

E. EDUCATION AND WELFARE

The official language is Hebrew, though Arabic is recognized as the official language of Arabs. English is taught in all schools. Education is compulsory for all children ages 5-14. Youth who have not been to compulsory, primary schooling must attend special classes. The Arabs and Jews have separate school systems. The country can boast of several excellent major universities. Israel has a national insurance program for illness, accident and unemployment. The aged and disabled are also provided for through pensions.

F. JEWISH POPULATION ROOTS

The present day Jew in Israel probably comes from one of four backgrounds. ASHKENAZIM (Hebrew for Germany) are Jews who come from central and eastern Europe. They spoke Yiddish, a compound of Hebrew and medieval German, and began coming in the 16th century. In those early days, they settled in Jerusalem, Hebron, Tiberias or Safed. SEPHARDIM (Hebrew for Spain) are Jews from Spain. They began migrating in the 15th century and spoke Ladino, a mixture of Spanish and Hebrew. Up until the 19th century the greatest bulk of people in Israel were the Sephardim. In more recent years, Sephardic Jews have come from the North African countries. They spoke Arabic with an African dialect. A fourth group were the Jews who came from Jewish Oriental communities in Muslim countries like Yemen, Iran and Iraq.

G. MOSLEMS

The biggest minority in Israel are Moslems. They speak a Syrian dialect of Arabic. They have their own state schools, a daily newspaper, "Al Yom" (The Day), some are members in the Knesset and they serve in the police force but not in the army. Moslems are divided by their mode of life. They are villagers or tillers of the soil (most are in this category), townspeople who dwell in their own towns (though a few mix in the big cities) and Bedouins, who live in tents and are breeders of sheep, goats or camels. The Bedouins are the most unique. They are divided into tribes. At the head of each tribe is a Sheik. He is the leader and also the representative in all tribal dealings with government institutions. Their own tribal court is empowered to act in the settlement of their internal disputes. Most live in the Negev and in Sinai, though a few tribes are scattered in the mountains of Galilee.

H. CHRISTIANS

The bulk of the Christian population speaks Arabic and its habits and mode of life are similar to those of its Arab neighbors. They are mostly Greek Orthodox or Catholic. Many of the Catholic orders have erected monasteries and convents on sites venerated in Christian tradition. Within this group there is a small evangelical minority, especially in Nazareth.

I. DRUZE

The Druze religion was founded in Egypt in the 11th century when it split off from the Isma'ili sect of the Shi'ite Moslems. This group accepted the idea that the Caliph al-Hakim bi'amr Allah was the Messiah. In the year 1017, the Caliph proclaimed himself to be the manifestation of God and then turned over all of his earthly duties to his main disciple, Hamra ibn 'Ali ibn Ahmad al-Zuzani. In the year 1021, al-Hakim disappeared and it is believed by historians that he was murdered. The Druze believe that he will someday return as the *mahdi* or redeemer. Hamra, in turn, instructed his disciple, Baha' al-Din, to spread the faith. This he did by writing epistles and sending out missionaries and codifying Druze doctrines. In the year 1043, all proselytizing for the Druze religion ceased and from then on, the Druze increased by natural generation and not by converting people to their religion. As far as their beliefs are concerned, Druze are divided into two groups. The smaller group is the *'Uqqal,* a word that means "The Enlightened." Only these receive full instruction into the Druze religion and they keep it a well-guarded secret. The second group simply includes all the rest who are taught the basic outline of the religion but not the details. But they follow a strict moral and ethical code of behavior. What is known about the beliefs of the Druze is that they believe in the transmigration of souls and that the number of Druze and non-Druze is fixed. This means that every time a Druze dies, another Druze is born. Paradise for the Druze is a vision of God while hell is a failure to attain Paradise. Contrary to Moslems, they do not practice ritual circumcision and do not believe in polygamy or having concubines. Also unlike Moslems, Druze women may own property. Druze reject the five pillars of Islam, but seven duties are binding on all Druze:

1. Recognition of al-Hakim and strict monotheism;

2. The rejection of non-Druze tenets;

3. Rejection of Satan and unbelief;

4. Acceptance of God's acts;

5. Total submission to God;

6. Truthfulness; and

7. Mutual help and solidarity among Druze.

The Druze have simple services on Thursday evenings and initially all of their community affairs are discussed. Then all non-*'Uqqal* leave and the *'Uqqal* remain to pray, study and meditate. Although Druze speak Arabic as a language and their religion is an off shoot of Islam, the Israeli Druze are not considered Arabs. In the 1936 uprising against both British and Arabs, the leader of the Druze, Amin Tarif, proclaimed an "alliance of blood" between the Druze and the Jews and have sided with the Jews ever since. They sided with the Jews in the War of Independence. As of 1957, at the request of the Druze leadership, Druze are drafted into the Israel Defense Forces, while Arabs are exempt because of the problem of dual loyalty. Israeli Druze have been citizens of the state since 1948.

The Druze of the Golan Heights have been under Israeli rule since 1967. They were offered Israeli citizenship in 1970 and while some took the offer, the majority rejected it, probably out of fear that the territory may some day be returned to Syria.

J. CIRCASSIANS

1. Non-Arab Sunni Moslems who are descendants from a group moved here from the Caucasus

   a. Some were forcefully moved here by the Ottoman Turks in the 1870's to help stem the Bedouin attacks

   b. Others moved here to avoid living under Christian rule after 1878 when the Congress of Berlin gave their territory to Russia

2. The Circussians sided with the Israelis in the War of Independence

3. In 1956, they requested military service be made mandatory for them

4. Today they number about 3000 and live in two villages

   a. Rihaniyya - Upper Galilee

   b. Kfar Kama - Lower Galilee

K. SAMARITANS

1. As of January 1995, there were 572 Samaritans. In the fifth century B.C., they numbered over a million and in 1917 only 146.

   a. Males - 311

   b. Females - 261

2. They are about equally divided in two centers

   a. Nablus and Mount Gerizim in the West Bank (Arabic speaking)

   b. Holon in the State of Israel (Hebrew speaking)

3. For all ceremonial and official purpose, they still use the ancient Hebrew script and dialect

4. The Samaritan Religion

   a. Four major principles

      (1) One God: The God of Israel

      (2) One Prophet: Moses

      (3) One Scripture: The Pentateuch

      (4) One Holy Place: Mount Gerizim

   b. The *Taheb* (Returner) - A prophet who is a descendent of Joseph who will appear at the end of days

   c. They celebrate the festivals in the Law of Moses

   d. Four main practices

      (1) Living in the Land of Israel and never leaving it

      (2) Participating each Passover in the sacrifice of the pascal lamb on Mount Gerizim

(3) Observing the Sabbath

(4) Adhering to the laws of purity and impurity

e. Leader: The High Priest

f. Their view of Israel: It is one people comprised of Jews and Samaritans

L. TYPES OF SETTLEMENTS

There are four forms of settlements in Israel. The first are cities; the most significant being Tel-Aviv, Jerusalem and Haifa. The second are *Moshava* or villages. This was the first form of rural Jewish settlements. The third type are *Moshav* or small holder settlements. There, every settler lives separately with his family and tills a plot of land leased to him by the Jewish National Fund while the village privately owns the heavy farming equipment. In the small holder settlement a man is not allowed to hire workers but must work it with his family. The fourth type are *Kibbutz* and *Kevutsa*. They are purely collective. All members live and work together on national land leased to them by the National Fund. There is no private property.

The kibbutz movement is the largest communitarian movement in the world today. The first kibbutz was founded in 1910. By the end of 1991, there were 270 kibbutzim with a population of 129,300.

Each kibbutz is an autonomous unit, socially and economically, but there are strong bonds of co-operation and mutual help between them. These bonds have been formalized in national federations which coordinate the activities of their member kibbutzim and provide them with a wide range of services.

Each kibbutz is a distinct socio-economic entity, based on shared ownership of all property and wealth. In that sense, the kibbutz can be understood most easily as a communal household or as a large home shared by an entire community. The kibbutz is an entirely private domain. The kibbutz community builds its pattern of life around shared social, cultural and economic activities.

The communal kitchen provides food for all of the community and meals are taken in the communal dining-hall. All of the kibbutz population live in housing provided by the kibbutz. While most consumption is collective within the kibbutz framework, there are individual budgets for sake of greater freedom of choice in goods and services for private consumption according to personal taste (toilet articles, clothing, furniture, etc.). Almost all the services needed are provided within the kibbutz and, of course, free of charge.

Economic operations, communally owned and run, make the kibbutz the most complete example of worker ownership and management. Work is a part of the kibbutz way of life and is regarded as a vital means of personal involvement in the life of the community. No cash value is put on it, though, and no salaries are paid. Team-work is stressed, with a minimum emphasis on status differences in role-behavior.

The largest of the national federations is the United Kibbutz Movement, usually referred to by its Hebrew acronym TAKAM, which has slightly over 60% of the total kibbutz population. The next largest is the Kibbutz Artzi, with almost 32% of the population. The third federation is the Kibbutz Dati (orthodox religious) with 6% of the population." Source: *Kibbutz Maagan Flyer*.

M. SUMMARY OF MODERN ISRAELI HISTORY

The British government gave up its mandate over Palestine in May of 1948. The United Nations voted to divide the land between the Arabs and the Jewish people, making Jerusalem an international city shared by all. The Arabs voiced their disapproval of the plan while the Jews were in favor of it. The date was set for May 14, 1948. The world knew that war would immediately break out and the Arab countries were heavily favored to crush the existence of any Jewish state.

On the first night of independence, Tel Aviv was bombed and the Arab armies marched into Israel. The war raged on for a year, finally ending with an armistice between Israel and Jordan, Egypt, Syria and Lebanon. The Arab countries refused to recognize Israel as being anything more than occupied Palestine.

In the summer of 1956, Egypt nationalized the Suez Canal, bringing Israel-Arab tensions to a head. In October of that year, Israel along with Britain and France, attacked Egypt. Israel gained most of the land in the Sinai Peninsula but it was later returned under pressure from the United States. This is known as the Sinai Campaign.

War broke out again in 1967, known as the Six-Day War. Israel gained the Sinai, the West Bank and the Golan Heights east of the Sea of Galilee. Most significant was the gaining of the Old City of Jerusalem. Not since 1948 had the Jews been allowed to come to the Western Wall.

In 1973, Egypt and Syria staged a surprise attack on the Jewish holy day of *Yom Kippur*. The ensuing days proved disastrous for both sides, yet Israel recouped from the surprise attack and maintained its previous borders, with some minor modifications. This is known as the *Yom Kippur* War.

In 1979, Israel and Egypt signed a peace treaty and the Sinai was returned to Egypt in stages, with the final stage completed in 1982.

After repeated attacks by the terrorists of the Palestine Liberation Organization (PLO) in South Lebanon against Israeli settlements in the Galilee, Israel invaded South Lebanon in 1982 in a war against the PLO and Syrian troops occupying Lebanon. Syria was defeated and the PLO infrastructure in South Lebanon was destroyed. The PLO was expelled from South Lebanon and Beirut. Israel withdrew from Lebanon in 1985.

In 1993, there was mutual recognition between Israel and the PLO with Israel agreeing to withdraw from most of the Gaza Strip and Jericho, accomplished in May 1994. A five year period of negotiations is to follow to determine the final status of Jerusalem and the West Bank.

In 1995, further negotiations were conducted concluding with the Oslo II Agreement in which Israel agreed to withdraw from six major West Bank Arab cities and to turn them over to the Palestinian Authority: Jenin, Nablus, Ramallah, Tulkarm, Bethlehem and Qalkilya. The withdrawal process was completed by the end of 1995. A partial withdrawal from Hebron was finalized in 1996. Further withdrawals are presently under negotiation and scheduled for 1998 and 1999.

II. HISTORICAL-ARCHEOLOGICAL PERIODS

A. PALEOLITHIC OLD STONE AGE **700,000 - 9,000 B.C.**

B. THE NEOLITHIC PERIOD **TILL 4500 B.C.**

C. THE CHALCOLITHIC PERIOD **4500-3150 B.C.**

D. THE BRONZE AGE **3150-1200 B.C.**
1. The Early Bronze Age 3100-2200 B.C.
    a. Early Bronze I 3150-2850 B.C.
    b. Early Bronze II 2850-2650 B.C.
    c. Early Bronze III 2650-2350 B.C.
    d. Early Bronze IV 2350-2200 B.C.
2. The Middle Bronze Age 2200-1550 B.C.
    a. Middle Bronze I 2200-2000 B.C.
    b. Middle Bronze IIA 2000-1750 B.C.
    c. Middle Bronze IIB 1750-1630 B.C.
    d. Middle Bronze IIC 1630-1550 B.C.
3. The Late Bronze Age 1550-1200 B.C.
    a. Late Bronze I 1550-1400 B.C.
    b. Late Bronze II 1400-1300 B.C.
    c. Late Bronze III 1300-1200 B.C.

E. THE ISRAELITE PERIOD **1200-587/6 B.C.**
1. Israelite I 1200-1000 B.C.
2. Israelite II 1000-840 B.C.
3. Israelite III 840-587/6 B.C.

F. THE BABYLONIAN PERIOD **587/6-536 B.C.**

G. THE MEDO-PERSIAN PERIOD **536-332 B.C.**

H. THE HELLENISTIC PERIOD **332-63 B.C.**
1. Alexander 332-312 B.C.
2. The Ptolomies 312-198 B.C.
3. The Seleucids 198-167 B.C.
4. The Hasmoneans 167-63 B.C.

I. THE ROMAN PERIOD **63 B.C. - A.D. 324**

J. THE FIRST BYZANTINE PERIOD **A.D. 324-614**

K. THE PERSIAN PERIOD **A.D. 614-629**

L. THE SECOND BYZANTINE PERIOD **A.D. 629-638**

M. THE FIRST MOSLEM PERIOD   **A.D. 638-1099**
   1.   The Ummayyads   A.D. 638-750
   2.   The Abbisids   A.D. 750-877
   3.   The Fatimids   A.D. 877-1071
   4.   The Seljuk Turks   A.D. 1071-1099

N. THE CRUSADER PERIOD   **A.D. 1099-1187**

O. THE SECOND MOSLEM PERIOD   **A.D. 1187-1517**
   1.   The Ayyubids   A.D. 1187-1250
   2.   The Mamelukes   A.D. 1250-1517

P. THE OTTOMAN TURKISH PERIOD   **A.D. 1517-1917**

Q. THE BRITISH MANDATE PERIOD   **A.D. 1917-1948**

R. THE ISRAELI-JORDANIAN PERIOD   **A.D. 1948-1967**

S. THE ISRAELI PERIOD   **A.D. 1967 - PRESENT**

Israel
The Geographical Divisions

THE GEOGRAPHICAL DIVISIONS
based on Deuteronomy 1:6-8

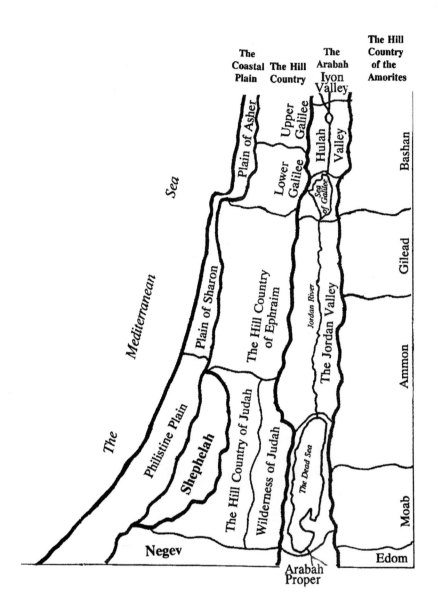

I. THE COASTAL PLAIN

A. THE PLAIN OF ASHER

1. Extends from Rosh Hanikra in the north to Mt. Carmel in the south
2. Size: 5 miles by 20 miles
3. Two Rivers
   a. Belus or Naaman River (Nahar Haman) - Just south of Acco
   b. Kishon River
4. Divided between two tribes
   a. Asher
   b. Zebulun
5. Part of the Ninth Solomonic District - I Kings 4:16
6. Given to Phoenicia by Solomon - I Kings 9:10-14

B. THE PLAIN OF SHARON

1. Extends from Mt. Carmel in the north to the Yarkon River in the south - 60 miles
2. Rivers
   a. Crocodile (Zerka or Blue) - From Dothan and Carmel between Dor and Caesarea
   b. Dead - From Dothan to south of Caesarea
   c. Salt - South of Natanya
   d. Auja - Yarkon
3. Noted for two harbors: Dor and Joppa
4. In New Testament times, a third harbor was added: Caesarea
5. It had a tendency to swamp; causing the Via Maris to move from the coastland, inland, to Aphek
6. In Egyptian records it is mentioned by Thutmose III, Amenhotep II, Shishak and in the Amarna Letters
7. In Assyrian records it is mentioned by Esarhaddon and Tiglath Pileser III
8. Mentioned by Eshmenezer of Sidon
9. The king was killed by Joshua - Joshua 12:18
10. Given to the Tribe of Manasseh - Joshua 17:7-10
11. In David's time, he had herds in Sharon - I Chronicles 27:29
12. Part of the Third Solomonic District - I Kings 4:10-11
13. Destroyed by Shalmenezer IV in 722-721 B.C.
14. Hellenized by Alexander the Great
15. Annexed to the Hasmonian Kingdom by Alexander Yannai
16. The inhabitants in this area began to turn to God under the preaching of Peter - Acts 9:35

17. Declined with the Arab Conquest and turned into swamps

18. Famous flower: The Rose of Sharon (an autumn crocus) - Song of Solomon 2:1

19. In the Prophets: Isaiah 33:9; 35:2; 65:10

20. In this century, the soil was discovered to be excellent for citrus trees and has become the major base for Israel's citrus industry

C. THE PHILISTINE PLAIN

1. Extends from the Yarkon River in the north to Raphia in the south, or more correctly, to Wadi El Arish

2. Rivers

    a. Rubin

    b. Sukerir

    c. Wadi El-Hesi

    d. Wadi Chazzem

    e. Wadi Sheriah

3. Settled by the Philistines in the 12th century B.C. who came from Caphtor (Crete) - Amos 9:7

4. The Philistines established the five cities of the Pentapolis - Joshua 13:3; Judges 3:3; I Samuel 6:16, 18

    a. The Coastline

        (1) Ashdod

        (2) Ashkelon

        (3) Gaza

    b. Inland

        (1) Ekron

        (2) Gath

5. Abraham journeyed through the land of the Philistines - Genesis 21:32-34

6. Moses did not choose to go that way - Exodus 13:17

7. Philistine control retained - Joshua 13:2-3

8. The Ark of the Covenant spent seven months in the Philistine Plain - I Samuel 5:1-6:21 (6:1)

9. David lived in the land of the Philistines - I Samuel 27:1-11; 29:11

10. The head of Saul and his armor was carried into the land of the Philistines - I Samuel 31:9; I Chronicles 10:9

11. Mentioned in David's lament - II Samuel 1:20

12. Subdued by David - I Chronicles 20:4-8

13. Marked the border of Solomon's kingdom - II Chronicles 9:26

14. This is where the Shunammite fled because of the famine -
   II Kings 8:2-3

15. In the Prophets: Jeremiah 25:20; 47:1-7; Ezekiel 16:27, 57; Joel 3:4;
   Amos 1:6-8; 9:7; Obadiah 19; Zephaniah 2:4-7; Zechariah 9:6

II.   THE SHEPHELAH

A. GEOGRAPHICAL INFORMATION

1. The district is made of eolene limestone which separates the Shephelah from the Hill Country, composed of cenomanian limestone

2. The separation between the two types of limestone is by a line of cinonian chalk

A. HISTORICAL INFORMATION

1. It was granted as part of the inheritance of Israel - Deuteronomy 1:7

2. Several kings in the Anti-Gibeonite League were from the Shephelah - Joshua 9:1; 10:28-34

3. Taken by Joshua - Joshua 10:40; 12:8

4. Part of the area given to Judah - Judges 1:9; Joshua 15:33

5. David appointed a supervisor over the sycamore and olive trees - I Chronicles 27:28

6. Solomon planted sycamore trees - I Kings 10:27; II Chronicles 1:15; 9:27

7. Developed by Uzziah - II Chronicles 26:10

8. Taken by the Philistines in the days of Ahaz - II Chronicles 28:18

9. Rebuilt in the return from Babylon - Nehemiah 11:29-30

10. In the inter-testamental period it was occupied by Edomites who were later forced to convert to Judaism

11. In the Prophets: Micah 1:10-16; Obadiah 19

12. The Shephelah was cut through by five valleys which led to Jerusalem and so the cities along these valleys were often fortified

    a.   The Valley of Ayalon

        (1) Gezer

        (2) Ayalon

        (3) Beth Horon

    b.   The Valley of Sorek

        (1) Timna

        (2) Zorah

    c.   The Valley of Elah

        (1) Socoh

        (2) Azekah

    d.   The Valley of Zephathah (Beth Guvrin)

        (1) Mareshah

        (2) Moresheth Gath

    e.   The Valley of Lachish - Lachish

III. THE HILL COUNTRY

NOTE: *The Upper Galilee and Lower Galilee notes are both combined and listed under Lower Galilee*

A. UPPER GALILEE

B. LOWER GALILEE

1. It is divided between Upper Galilee (3,000 to 4,000 feet) and Lower Galilee (1,500 feet)

   a. Upper: Litani River (Leontes) to Valley of Beth Hakerem - Famous for olive trees

   b. Lower: Valley of Beth Hakerem to the Hills of Samaria

2. Part of the land that Moses saw before his death - Deuteronomy 34:2

3. Part of the northern confederacy against Joshua - Joshua 11:2

4. Area was captured by Joshua - Joshua 11:1-15

5. Settled by the Tribes of Asher, Zebulun, Issachar and Naphtali - Joshua 20:7; 21:32; I Chronicles 6:76

6. Later parts of it were given to Hiram - I Kings 9:10-14

7. Taken by Tiglath Pileser III - II Kings 15:29

8. Taken by Aristobulus I and made part of the Hasmonean Kingdom

9. Isaiah gave a unique prophecy concerning Galilee (Isaiah 9:1-2) which was fulfilled in the ministry of Jesus (Matthew 4:12-16, 23)

10. Herod was tetrarch of Galilee - Luke 3:1

11. Area of Jesus' ministry

    a. Matthew

       (1) 2:22

       (2) 3:13

       (3) 4:12, 23, 25

       (4) 17:22

       (5) 19:1

       (6) 21:11

       (7) 26:32, 69

       (8) 27:55

       (9) 28:7, 10, 16

    b. Mark

       (1) 1:14, 28, 39

       (2) 3:7

       (3) 6:21

       (4) 9:30

       (5) 14:28

(6) 15:41

(7) 16:7

  c. Luke

    (1) 2:4, 39

    (2) 4:14, 44

    (3) 5:17

    (4) 8:26

    (5) 17:11

    (6) 23:5-6, 49, 55

    (7) 24:6

  d. John

    (1) 1:43

    (2) 4:3, 43, 45, 47, 54

    (3) 7:1, 9, 41, 52

12. Area of Apostolic Ministry: Acts

  a. 1:11

  b. 9:31

  c. 10:37

  d. 13:31

13. Galilee was an area which the Jews began to settle as a result of the Zionist movement

14. The first settlement in Upper Galilee was Rosh Pinna (1882) and in Lower Galilee it was Ilania (1899)

C. THE HILL COUNTRY OF EPHRAIM

1. Size: 40 x 50 miles

2. Heavily wooded - Joshua 17:15-18

3. Part of the land that Moses saw - Deuteronomy 34:2

4. Taken by Joshua at the fall of Ai - Joshua 8:1-35

5. The Anakim were cut off from here - Joshua 11:21

6. Settled by the Tribes of Ephraim and Manasseh - Joshua 17:14-18

7. Contained Shechem, one of the cities of refuge - Joshua 21:21; I Chronicles 6:67

8. Home of Joshua - Joshua 19:49-50

9. Burial place of Joshua - Judges 2:9

10. Eleazer was buried here - Joshua 24:33

11. It revolted against Cush Rishathaim - Judges 3:27

12. Home of Deborah - Judges 4:5

13. Revolted against Midian - Judges 7:24

14. Home of Tola, one of the Judges of Israel - Judges 10:1

15. Where the story of Micah and the Levite took place - Judges 17:1-18:26

16. The Tribe of Dan passed through here on their migration to the north - Judges 18:2

17. Home of the Levite and his concubine - Judges 19:1, 18

18. Home of the man who took the Levite in - Judges 19:16

19. Home of Samuel the Prophet - I Samuel 1:1

20. Saul searched for his asses - I Samuel 9:4

21. Hiding place for Jews during Philistine occupation - I Samuel 14:22

22. Home of Sheba who led the second revolt against David - II Samuel 20:21

23. The First Solomonic District - I Kings 4:8

24. Mentioned in Gehazi's lie - II Kings 5:22

25. Abijah made his speech to Jeroboam condemning him for his failure to obey - II Chronicles 13:4-12

26. Asa cleansed the cities he took in this area - II Chronicles 15:8

27. Marked the northern area of Jehoshaphat's evangelistic campaigns - II Chronicles 19:4

28. Foreigners were settled into this area by Assyria - II Kings 17:26

29. In the Prophets - Jeremiah 4:15; 31:6; 50:19

D. THE HILL COUNTRY OF JUDAH

1. Size: 50 x 20 miles

2. Part of the area that Moses saw - Deuteronomy 34:2

3. United against Joshua - Joshua 9:1

4. Taken by Joshua - Joshua 10:1-14, 36-39

5. The Anakim were cut off - Joshua 11:21

6. Sections given to the Tribe of Levi - Joshua 21:11

7. The fortified cities in the Hill Country were destroyed by Sennacherib - II Kings 18:13

8. It was developed by Jotham - II Chronicles 27:4

9. Home of Elizabeth and Zacharias - Luke 1:65

E. THE WILDERNESS OF JUDAH

1. From Wadi Kelt in the north to the Negev in the south

2. Size: 15 x 50 miles

3. Area where the Benjaminites were defeated - Judges 20:42, 45, 47

4. Some of David's hiding places during the flight from Saul - I Samuel 23:14-26:3; Psalm 3:superscription

5. Part of David's flight from Absalom - II Samuel 17:16

6. Uzziah built towers in the Wilderness - II Chronicles 26:10

7. It was a place of refuge for the Maccabees under Jonathan in the years 160-155 B.C.

8. Area where John the Baptist grew up - Luke 1:80

9. Where John received his call - Luke 3:2

10. Site of the preaching of John the Baptist - Matthew 3:1-4; 11:7; Mark 1:3-4; Luke 3:4; 7:24; John 1:23

11. The 40 days of fasting and the first temptation of Jesus - Matthew 4:1-4; Mark 1:12-13; Luke 4:1

12. The home of over sixty monasteries which developed since the fourth century, especially Greek Orthodox; a number of which continue to exist to this day

   a. St. George - Originally called Cosiba, it was rebuilt in the nineteenth century

   b. Karantal (Quarantal) - A nineteenth century monastery built near the remains of Douka, founded in 340 B.C. by Chariton, the father of Judean Desert monasticism

   c. Theodosius - The largest in the Judean Desert, built in the fifth century and measures 221 feet by 328 feet

   d. Mar Saba - The burial place of Saint Sabas who founded ten different monasteries

F. THE NEGEV

1. Basic Facts

   a. Average rainfall: 5-8 inches

      (1) Twelve inches in the North

      (2) Almost zero in the Eilat area

   b. Western Negev - Flat, dusty plain slashed with wadis

   c. Eastern Negev - Mountainous terrain composed of flint, limestone, chalk, dolomite and granite

2. One of the homes of Abraham - Genesis 12:9; 13:1; 20:1; 21:14; 20-21

3. Where Ishmael grew up - Genesis 21:14; 20-21

4. Major area of the Wilderness Wanderings - Numbers 10:12; 12:16; 13:3, 26; Judges 11:16, 18; 14:1-45

5. The 12 spies were sent to the Land from here - Numbers 13:17, 22, 29

6. Part of the area seen by Moses - Deuteronomy 34:2

7. Taken by Joshua - Joshua 11:16

8. Taken by the Tribe of Judah - Judges 1:9

9. Settled by the Tribes of Judah and Simeon - Judges 1:16

10. Raided by David while he abode in Ziglag - I Samuel 27:10

11. Elijah fled here from Jezebel - I Kings 19:4-7

12. Taken by the Philistines in the days of Ahaz - II Chronicles 28:18

13. In the Prophets - Obadiah 19

14. Civilization development

    a. Nabatean

    b. Roman

    c. Byzantine - 100,000 people

15. Jewish settlement began with Negba in 1939 and in 1943 with Revivim, Gevulot and Beit Eshel

16. 1946 - Eleven more settlements established all in one day: Yom Kippur

17. 1948 - 26 total settlements

18. 160 mile pipeline from Sea of Galilee supplies water for Negev settlements

19. Today - Sixty percent of the land area of Israel but only 10 percent of the population

20. The *Makteshim* - The Negev is pockmarked by three craters which may have been caused by the destruction of Sodom and Gomorrah

    a. *Hamaktesh Hakatan* - The Little Crater
       (1) Approximately three by five miles

       (2) Drained by Wadi Hatzera which runs into Wadi Zin

       (3) The rim rises 250 feet above the floor

       (4) Uniqueness: It is almost perfectly circular with steep walls

    b. *Hamaktesh Hagadol* - The Big Crater

       (1) Approximately four by eight miles

       (2) The rim is 250 feet above the floor

       (3) Has steep slopes on top but gentle sloping on the bottom

       (4) Contains fossils of coral reefs, sea lilies and sea urchins

    c. *Maktesh Ramon* - The Great Crater

       (1) Approximately five by 25 miles

       (2) The rim rises 375 feet above the floor

       (3) Subdivided into two valleys by Mount Ardon

          (a) The Ardon Valley - Drained by Wadi Nekarot via Wadi Haririm, Wadi Geled and Wadi Hotit

          (b) The Mahmal Valley

       (4) It has steep slopes on top and gentle slopes on the bottom

       (5) Contains a great variety of geological phenomena

IV. THE ARABAH

A. THE IYON VALLEY (AYOUN)

1. Border between Israel and Phoenicia and Aram (Syria)

2. Biblical Valley of Mizpah - Joshua 11:3, 8

3. The city was smitten by Ben Hadad - I Kings 15:20;
   II Chronicles 16:4

4. The city was taken by Tiglath Pileser III - II Kings 15:29

5. In 1948, the valley became part of Lebanon

6. One of four sources for Jordan River, the Baragit or Ayoun flows
   through here

   a. Also known as *Hatanur*, meaning "oven" because one of the
      high waterfalls has formed the shape of a chimney in the rock

   b. The Ayoun River begins in Lebanon but flows into Israel

   c. The waterfalls of the Ayoun River

      (1) The Ayoun Falls - About 30 feet high

      (2) The Mill Falls - About 65 feet high and named after the
          nearby flour mill

      (3) The Cascade Falls - Double falls about 30 and 15 feet high

      (4) The Oven Falls - About 30 feet high

B. THE HULAH VALLEY

1. Size: About 20 miles long and four-five miles wide

2. Descends from 600 feet above sea level to 180 feet above sea level

3. Guarded by Abel Beth Maacah on the north and Hazor on the south

4. The northern side which is now the Israel-Lebanon border is 1200
   feet above sea level

5. The Lake of Hula was drained in 1957

6. The four head waters of the Jordan River flow through this valley

   a. Banyas or Hermon River - 122 million cubic meters

   b. Dan River - 252 million cubic meters

   c. Hatzbani or Snir River - 117 million cubic meters

   d. Iyon River - Eight million cubic meters

7. A total of 1,480 million cubic meters of water drains into this valley
   every year

8. In the *Talmud* it is known as Hulata

9. In the *Midrashim* it is called Hulat Antokhia

10. Settled by the Tribes of Dan and Naphtali

11. First modern Jewish settlement began in 1883 with the village of
    Yesod Ha-Maalah

C. THE SEA OF GALILEE

1. Measurements

    a. 13 miles long

    b. 5 to 8 miles wide

    c. 32 miles around

    d. 150 feet deep (varies 60-156 ft.)

    e. 630 feet below sea level - The lowest sweet water lake in the world

2. Names

    a. The Sea of Chinnereth (Kinneret) - Numbers 34:11; Joshua 11:2; 12:3; 13:27

    b. The Lake of Gennesaret - Luke 5:1

    c. The Sea of Tiberias - John 6:1; 21:1

    d. The Sea of Galilee - Matthew 4:18; 15:29

3. Marked the eastern border of the Land - Numbers 34:11

4. Marked the boundary of the Transjordanian Tribes - Deuteronomy 3:17; Joshua 12:3; 13:27

5. Major area of Jesus' ministry - Matthew 4:18; 15:29; Mark 1:16; 7:31

6. Site of the drowning of the pigs - Mark 5:1-20; Luke 8:26-39

7. Jesus frequently crossed this sea - Matthew 8:23; Mark 8:10; Luke 8:22; John 6:1

8. The miracle of the stilling of the waters - Matthew 8:23-27; Luke 8:22-25

9. Jesus walked on the water - Matthew 14:22-33; John 6:16-21

10. Miracle of the enormous catch - Luke 5:1-11

11. Miracle of Peter's fish - Matthew 17:24-27

12. Jesus gave Peter his lesson on feeding the sheep - John 21:1-23

13. Jesus' Ministry

    a. 19 of 32 parables

    b. 25 of 33 miracles

14. The rabbis teach: The Lord created seven seas but the Sea of Gennesaret is His delight

15. The sudden storms on the sea are called *Sharkia*, Arabic for "east"

16. Key Cities

    a. Tiberias

    b. Migdal-Magdala (Tarichae)

    c. Caparnaum

    d. Chorazin

    e. Bethsaida

    f. Gergasa

    g. Gamla

       h. Hippos-Susita

       i. Kinneret

   17. The Fishing Industry

      a. Contains 18 species, 10 of which are commercially important

      b. The edible fish fall into three main categories

        (1) Musht - Five species including St. Peter's fish

        (2) Biny (Barbels) - Three species of the carp

        (3) Sardines - Two species

      c. It contains catfish which cannot be eaten by Jews and so they are not as commercially important

D. The Jordan Valley

1. Extends from the Sea of Galilee to the Dead Sea
2. Distance of 70 miles
3. 4-14 miles wide
4. The Zor
   a. 100-150 feet lower than main valley
   b. 600 feet to two miles wide
5. River bed within Zor is 90-200 feet wide
6. Fed by other rivers
   a. From east: Yarmuk and Jabbock
   b. From west: Nahr Jalud and Wadi Faria
7. Place where Lot settled - Genesis 13:10-11
8. Israelite encampment before crossing the Jordan River - Numbers 31:12; 33:50; 35:1; Deuteronomy 1:1
9. Part of the area that Moses was allowed to see - Deuteronomy 34:3
10. Area of Jewish settlement - Deuteronomy 4:46, 49
11. Involved in the defeat of Ai - Joshua 8:14
12. Part of the northern confederacy against Joshua - Joshua 11:2
13. Defeated and taken by Joshua - Joshua 11:6-8
14. Eastern part of it was given to Gad - Joshua 13:27
15. The route for murderers of Ishbosheth - II Samuel 4:7
16. Solomon made his furniture for the Temple - I Kings 7:46; II Chronicles 4:17
17. Area where Elijah hid - I Kings 17:3-5
18. Area of John the Baptist's ministry - Matthew 3:5; Luke 3:3; John 1:28
19. Where Zedekiah was captured - II Kings 25:4-5; Jeremiah 39:4-5; 52:7-8
20. A section of it known as "The Pride of the Jordan" was once the abode of many lions: The Zor - Jeremiah 12:5; 49:19; 50:44; Zechariah 11:3
21. In the Psalms: 42:6

E. THE DEAD SEA

1. It has a number of names given in the Scriptures

   a. The Salt Sea - Genesis 14:3; Deuteronomy 3:17

   b. The Eastern Sea - Joel 2:20; Ezekiel 47:18

   c. The Former Sea - Zechariah 14:8

   d. The Sea of the Arabah - Deuteronomy 3:17; II Kings 14:25

   e. Arabic

      (1) Bahr Lut - Sea of Lot

      (2) Bahr el-Mivet - Dead Sea

   f. Greek and Roman - Lake Asphatites

2. The basic measurements

   a. 48 miles long

   b. 11 miles wide - Average 9½ miles

   c. 124 miles around

   d. 189 square miles on the surface

   e. It is 1,292 feet below sea level

   f. It is 1,319 feet deep

   g. The bottom is 2,600 feet below sea level

3. Divided by The Lishon (the "Tongue") which, in biblical times, crossed over the entire Dead Sea and divided it in two, though today it only protrudes about two-thirds of the way

4. Area of the battle of the five kings against the four - Genesis 14:1-12

5. Border of the Transjordanian tribes - Deuteronomy 3:17; Joshua 12:3

6. When Israel crossed the Jordan River, its waters were cut off from entering the Dead Sea - Joshua 3:16

7. It marked the southern and eastern border of the land of settlement - Numbers 34:3, 12

8. Taken by Israel - Joshua 12:3

9. Beginning of the southern border - Joshua 15:2

10. East border of the Tribe of Judah - Joshua 15:5

11. East border of the Tribe of Benjamin -Joshua 18:19

12. The southern border of the Land was restored under Jeroboam II - II Kings 14:25

13. In the Kingdom, the Dead Sea waters will be healed and will have and contain life - Ezekiel 47:6-12

14. Today it is very rich in minerals

    a. Potassium chloride - 2 billion metric tons

    b. Magnesium bromide - 980 million metric tons

    c. Sodium chloride - 11 billion metric tons

    d. Magnesium chloride - 22 billion metric tons

    e. Calcium chloride - 6 billion metric tons

    f. Gypsum - 81 million metric tons

F. THE ARABAH PROPER

1. 110 miles long, 6-12 miles wide

    a. Begins at 1,292 feet below sea level

    b. After 62 miles, it rises to 650 feet above sea level

    c. Highest point above sea level is at Jebel er Rishe

    d. After 48 miles, it descends to sea level

2. Borders

    a. The mountains of Edom on the east change colors during the day from light pale in the morning to pink, red and purple in the evening

    b. The Negev Hills in the west made up limestone and flint ridges

3. Area of the battle of the five kings against the four - Genesis 14:1-12

4. Cities of the Arabah destroyed - Genesis 19:1-29

5. Part of the Wilderness Wanderings - Deuteronomy 1:1; 2:8

6. Part of the area that Joshua took over - Joshua 11:16; 12:1-3

7. Taken by Israel - Deuteronomy 1:7; 3:10, 17; 4:49

8. Eastern border of the Land - Joshua 18:18

9. David defeated the Syrians - II Samuel 8:13

10. David defeated the Edomites - I Chronicles 18:10-13; Psalm 60: superscription

11. Route of the Queen of Sheba

12. Amaziah defeated the Edomites - II Kings 14:7; II Chronicles 25:11

13. First Jewish settlement: Yotvatah - 1948

G. THE RED SEA

1. Israelite crossing from Egypt - Exodus 13:18; 14:1-31; 15:4, 22; Numbers 33:8; Deuteronomy 11:4; Joshua 2:10; 4:23; 24:6; Judges 11:16; Nehemiah 9:9-11; Psalms 106:7, 9, 22; 136:13, 15; Acts 7:36; Hebrews 11:29

2. One of the borders of the Promised Land - Exodus 23:31

3. Area of the Wilderness Wanderings - Numbers 14:25; 21:4; 33:10-11; Deuteronomy 1:1, 40; 2:1

4. King Solomon's ships - I Kings 9:26

5. Part of Armageddon - Jeremiah 49:21

V. THE HILL COUNTRY OF THE AMORITES

A. BASHAN (GOLAN HEIGHTS)

1. From a root meaning "fruitful plain" or "smooth plain"

2. Extends from Mount Hermon in the north to the Yarmuk River in the south - About 35 miles and about 725 square miles

3. 1,600-3,000 feet above sea level

4. Bashan - Four sections

    a. Jetur

    b. Golan - The only part within Israel

    c. Hauran

    d. El Leja

5. The Golan is a flat, basaltic plateau with many rows of extinct volcanos

6. During the Early Bronze Age (3150-2200 B.C.), it was used as a burial site marked to this day by large stone slabs known as dolmens

7. Taken by Israel - Numbers 21:33; 32:33; Deuteronomy 1:4; 3:1-11; 4:47; 29:7; Joshua 9:10; 11-12; 12:1-6; 13:31; Nehemiah 9:22; Psalms 135:11; 136:20

8. Mentioned in conjunction with Dan - Deuteronomy 33:22

9. Portions were given to the Tribe of Manasseh - Deuteronomy 3:13; Joshua 13:29-30; 17:1-6; 21:6, 27; 22:7; I Chronicles 5:23; 6:62

10. Further settled by members of the Tribe of Gad -
I Chronicles 5:11-12, 16

11. The city of Golan was situated here as a Levitical City - Joshua 21:27

    a. Believed by some to be present day Dabura

    b. Dabura may have been the capital of the Jewish Golan during the Roman and Byzantine periods

12. The city of Golan was also one of the six Cities of Refuge -
Deuteronomy 4:43; Joshua 20:8; I Chronicles 6:71

13. Frequently served as a buffer zone between Israel and Aram (Syria)

14. It served as the Sixth Solomonic District - I Kings 4:13, 19

15. A disputed area between Israel and the Arameans (Syria) and eventually taken from Israel by Hazael when Jehu was king -
II Kings 10:32-33

16. Geshur - Located in the Southern Golan between the eastern shore of the Sea of Galilee and west of the fertile plains of Bashan along the major trade routes (The King's Highway)

    a. Area taken by Moses was on the border of Geshur -
    Deuteronomy 3:14; Joshua 12:5; I Chronicles 2:23

    b. Israel failed to dispossess the Geshurites - Joshua 13:11, 13

    c.   Home of Maacah, the daughter of King Talmai, the wife of David and mother of Absalom and Tamar - II Samuel 3:3; I Chronicles 3:2

    d.   Place where Absalom fled after killing his half-brother Amnon - II Samuel 13:37-38; 14:23, 32; 15:8

    e.   Geshur, along with Aram (Syria) conquered 60 towns from the sons of Machir, the father of Gilead - II Samuel 15:8; I Chronicles 2:23

    f.   Ancient sites in the land of Geshur

        (1) Mitham Leviah

            (a) Meaning: The Enclosure of the Lioness

            (b) Was once a densely populated city from the Early Bronze Age (3100-2200 B.C.)

        (2) Rogem Hiri (Rujm el-Hiri)

            (a) Contains five huge stone circles with 125,000 cubic feet of stone, some weighing as much as 5.5 tons, dating back to 3000 B.C. but the exact purpose is unknown

            (b) Meaning of Arabic name: Stone Heap of the Wild Cat

            (c) Modern Hebrew name: *Galgal Refayim*, Giants' Circles

            (d) Also contains large dolmen fields

        (3) Tel Soreg

            (a) Cave dwellers from the Middle Bronze Age I (2200-2000 B.C.)

            (b) Continued habitation until the Hellenistic Period when it was overshadowed by Hippos and Aphek

        (4) Tel Hadar

            (a) The major Geshurite royal stronghold

            (b) Inhabited during the Middle and Late Bronze Ages, it reached its height during the Israelite Period

            (c) This was probably the city to which Absalom fled

17. Noted for its rams - Deuteronomy 32:14

18. Noted especially for its bulls - Psalm 22:12; 68:15; Jeremiah 50:19; Ezekiel 27:6; 39:18; Amos 4:1; Micah 7:14

19. In the Psalms: 68:22

20. In the Prophets: Isaiah 2:13; 33:9; Jeremiah 22:20; Nahum 1:4; Zechariah 11:2

21. Hellenistic Period (332-63 B.C.)

    a.   Judah Maccabee defends the Jews of Bashan and Golan

    b.   Conquered by Alexander Yannai in 83-81 B.C.

    c.   Iturians, an Arab tribe, settled in the Northern Golan

22. During the Roman Period (63 B.C. - A.D. 324) it was heavily settled by both Jews and Greeks

23. New Testament Times - Included five provinces that made up the Tetrachy of Philip, the son of Herod the Great

    a. Iturea - The Greek form for Jetur; in the extreme north and included Mount Hermon

        (1) Jetur was a son of Ishmael - Genesis 25:15

        (2) Fought against the Tribes of Reuben, Gad and the Half-tribe of Manasseh - I Chronicles 5:19

        (3) During the Assyrian Period, the Itureans moved north from Gilead to the Golan around Mount Hermon and became known for herding, mountain agriculture, robbing and smuggling

        (4) After remaining nomadic for six centuries, during the second half of the second century B.C., they founded a strong kingdom establishing their capital at Chalsis

        (5) According to Josephus, the Hasmonean King Aristobulus I (104-103 B.C.) made war against the Itureans and forced many of them to convert to Judaism

        (6) The height of the Iturean Kingdom was reached under King Ptolemy Mennaeus - 85-40 B.C.

        (7) During the Hellenistic and Roman Periods, the Jews and Itureans had friendly relations

        (8) Area was conquered by Rome and made part of the Roman Empire in 63 B.C.

        (9) Zenodorus was the last independent Iturean ruler (30-20 B.C.) who was deposed by the Roman governor of Syria

        (10) In the New Testament, it is recorded that Philip, the son of Herod the Great, became the Tetrarch of Iturea - Luke 3:1

        (11) The Itureans disappear in the seventh century A.D. but some believe that the modern Druze are the descendants of the Itureans

        (12) Iturean Sites

            (a) Khirbet Zemel - Near the Druze town of Bukata

            (b) Tel el-Hawarit - Between the Druze towns of Ein Kinya and Masadeh

            (c) Khirbet Ra'abaneh - At the edge of Odem Forest

            (d) Bab el-Hawah - North of Kibbutz Merom Golan

            (e) Har Senaim - Near Moshav Neve Ativ

            (f) The Lost City - Near Mount Agass

    b. Gaulanitis - Greek for Golan, today known as the Golan Heights

    c. Trachonitis - The modern El Leja covering the territory between Southern Golan and Damascus comprising a volcanic plateau

    d. Auranitis - Greek form for Hauran located south of Trachonitis

    e. Batanea - Greek form for Bashan but as a province located between Gaulanitis to the west, Trachonitis to the north and Auranitis to the east

24. Byzantine Period (A.D. 365-638)

    a. Jewish and Christian settlements exist side by side

    b. As many as one million Jews lived here in about one hundred towns

    c. Thus far, 25 synagogues have been discovered

    d. Had a large population of Messianic Jews

    e. With the Arab conquest, the settlements were abandoned and nomads prevail - Out of 173 Byzantine sites, only 14 continued to exist

25. During the Crusader Period (1099-1291), it served as a border area between the Crusader Kingdom and the Emirate of Damascus

26. During the subsequent Moslem Period, it was sparsely populated and mostly by Bedouins but roads and caravanesarais were built

27. During the Ottoman Turkish Period (1517-1917), permanent settlements were built composed of Bedouin, Magreb, Circassian, Alawite, Druze and Turkoman

28. In the early days of Zionism, there were some early settlements in this area but they were abandoned

    a. The first settlement was Bnei Yehudah in 1885 by settlers from Safed but it was abandoned after two years

    b. The settlers resettled in Bir a-Shagum

29. After World War I the area became part of the British Mandate but in 1923 was given to Syria under the French Mandate and Bir a-Shagum was abandoned after 32 years when two members were murdered

30. In 1948, after the Syrians were defeated, they fortified the Golan Heights and used it for periodic shelling of Jewish settlements in the Hulah Valley

31. During the Six Day War, it was the major scene of battle in the last two days of that war

32. The Arab and Circassian population fled in 1967 and today it is occupied by the Druze in four towns in the northern part

    a. Ein Kinya - The smallest and the oldest of the four by several centuries

    b. Majdal Shams - Established by Druze from Galilee in the 18th century and the largest of the four

    c. Bukata - Established about a century ago by two families from Majdal Shams after a family dispute

    d. Masada - Also established by residents of Majdal Shams about a century ago

33. Since 1967, many *kibbutzim* and *moshavim* have been established

34. In the Yom Kippur War, the Syrians retook most of the Golan but lost it again in the Israeli counter attack

35. Population and settlement today

    a. Before the Six Day War in 1967, it had a population of 40,000

    b. After the war, 6,400 of the original population stayed behind

    c. Current population is 30,000

        (1) 13,000 Jews

        (2) 17,000 Druze

    d. There are 33 Jewish settlements

        (1) One city - Katzrin

        (2) 27 *kibbutzim*

        (3) Five *moshavim*

B. GILEAD

1. Name comes from a root meaning "rugged land"

2. From the Yarmuk River in the north to the Jabbock River in the south

3. Area of the flight of Jacob from Laban - Genesis 31:21, 23, 25

4. The buyers of Joseph came from here - Genesis 37:25

5. Area taken and settled by the Transjordanian tribes - Numbers 32:1-42; Deuteronomy 2:36; 3:10, 5-16; 4:43; Joshua 12:1-6; 13:11; 22:9, 13, 15, 32

6. Part of the area was given to the Tribe of Manasseh - Numbers 32:39-40; Joshua 13:31; 17:1-6; I Chronicles 27:21; Psalm 60:7; 108:8

7. Another part was given to the Tribe of Gad - Numbers 32:33-36; Joshua 13:24-28; I Chronicles 5:14-16; 6:80

8. Area of Ramoth, a City of Refuge - Joshua 20:8; 21:38

9. Members of the Tribe of Reuben also settled here - I Chronicles 5:1-10

10. Settled by the family of Jair - I Chronicles 2:21-23

11. Part of the area that Moses saw - Deuteronomy 34:1

12. Did not participate in Barak's revolt - Judges 5:17

13. Where the fearful went after leaving Gideon - Judges 7:3

14. Home of Jair, one of the judges of Israel - Judges 10:3-5

15. Home of Jephthah, one of the judges of Israel - Judges 11:1; 12:7

16. Ephraim defeated here under Jephthah - Judges 12:4-7

17. Participated in the Anti-Benjaminite War - Judges 20:1

18. Part of the Saul and Jonathan Philistine War - I Samuel 13:7

19. Saul's body was brought here and burned and the bones buried - I Samuel 31:11-13

20. Ishbosheth ruled over the northern tribes of Israel from here - II Samuel 2:8-10

21. The war between David and Absalom occurred here - II Samuel 17:24-19:10

22. Home of Barzillai - II Samuel 17:27; 19:31; I Kings 2:7; Ezra 2:61; Nehemiah 7:63

23. Included as part of David's census - II Samuel 24:6

24. Home of some of David's men of valor - I Chronicles 26:31

25. The northern section was part of the Sixth Solomonic District - I Kings 4:13

26. The southern section was part of the Twelfth Solomonic District - I Kings 4:19

27. Home of Elijah the Prophet - I Kings 17:1

28. Area where Ahab was killed at Ramoth Gilead - I Kings 22:1-36

29. Where Jehu was anointed King of Israel - II Kings 9:1-15a

30. Area taken by Hazael from Jehu - II Kings 10:32-33

31. Participated in Pekah's revolt against Pekahiah - II Kings 15:25

32. Taken by Tiglath Pileser III - II Kings 15:29

33. Famous for its medical balm - Jeremiah 8:22; 46:11

34. The goats of Gilead - Song of Solomon 4:1; 6:5

35. In the Prophets: Jeremiah 22:6; 50:19; Ezekiel 47:18; Hosea 6:8; 12:11; Amos 1:3, 13; Obadiah 19; Micah 7:14; Zechariah 10:10

36. Area of Perea of the New Testament

C. AMMON

1. From the Jabbock River in the north to the Arnon River in the south - Numbers 21:24

2. Northern section known as the Mishor, a root meaning "Tableland"

    a. Also called the Tableland of Moab - Deuteronomy 3:10

    b. Part of the Transjordanian conquest of Israel - Joshua 13:9, 16

    c. Area of Balaam's prophecies - Numbers 23-24

    d. Near by Moses was buried - Deuteronomy 34:6

3. The origin of the Ammonites - Genesis 19:38

4. Taken by Israel - Numbers 21:24; Deuteronomy 3:11; Joshua 12:2

5. Sections will always belong to Ammon - Deuteronomy 2:19, 37

6. Half of the territory was given to the Tribe of Gad - Deuteronomy 3:16; Joshua 13:10, 25

7. Along with Moab, it oppressed Israel - Judges 3:13

8. Defeated by Jephthah - Judges 10:6-12:3

9.   Subdued by Saul - I Samuel 11:1-11; 12:12; 14:47

10. Subdued by David - II Samuel 8:12, 17; I Chronicles 18:11

11. Home of one of David's mighty men - I Chronicles 11:39

12. Revolted against David and was defeated - II Samuel 10:1-19;
     I Chronicles 19:1-20:3

13. Capital was besieged and destroyed in the Urijah incident -
     II Samuel 11:1-12:31

14. Solomon built a temple for the god of Ammon - I Kings 11:1, 5, 7, 33;
     II Kings 23:13

15. The mother of Rehoboam was from Ammon - II Chronicles 12:13

16. It warred against King Jehoshaphat - II Chronicles 20:1-23

17. Home of the mother of Zabad, one of the killers of Joash -
     II Chronicles 24:26

18. Subdued by Jotham - II Chronicles 27:5

19. Subdued by Uzziah - II Chronicles 26:8

20. Raided Judah in the days of Jehoiakim - II Kings 24:2

21. Involved in the conspiracy in the murder of Gedaliah: Ishmael sent by
     King Baalis - Jeremiah 40:11-41:15

22. Tobiah came from there - Nehemiah 2:10, 19; 4:3; 13:1-9

23. Tried to influence the returnees from Babylon against rebuilding -
     Nehemiah 4:7

24. Jews intermarried with Ammonites - Ezra 9:1; Nehemiah 13:23

25. Anti-Israel - Psalm 83:7

26. In the Prophets: Isaiah 11:14; Jeremiah 9:26; 25:21; 27:3; 49:1-6;
     Ezekiel 21:20, 28; 25:1-10; Daniel 11:41; Amos 1:13-15;
     Zephaniah 2:8-9

27. Finally brought to an end by Judah Maccabbee

D. MOAB

1.   From the Arnon River in the north to the Zered River in the south -
     Numbers 21:13-15; Judges 11:18

2.   The origin of the Moabites - Genesis 19:37; I Chronicles 1:4

3.   Hadad the Edomite smote Midian in the Field of Moab - Genesis 36:35

4.   Took note of the Red Sea Crossing - Exodus 15:15

5.   Moab's refusal to allow Israel to pass through forced Israel to walk
     around their land - Numbers 21:11-30; Deuteronomy 2:9, 11, 29;
     Judges 11:15, 18; II Chronicles 20:10

6.   Israel camped in the Fields of Moab - Numbers 26:1-63; 31:12;
     33:44-50; 35:1; 36:13

7.   Hired Balaam to curse Israel - Numbers 22:1-24:17; Joshua 24:9-10

8.   Israel's sin in Moab - Numbers 25:1

9. Moses died in the land of Moab - Deuteronomy 34:1-8

10. Members of the Tribe of Judah had possessions in Moab - I Chronicles 4:22

11. Some Benjaminites were born there - I Chronicles 8:8

12. Oppressed Israel - Judges 3:12-30; Joshua 13:32; I Samuel 12:9

13. Israel worshipped the gods of Moab - Judges 10:6

14. Not claimed by Israel - Judges 11:15-25

15. The family of Naomi went to live here and it was the home of Ruth - Ruth 1:1-22; 2:2, 6, 21; 4:3, 5, 10

16. Subdued by Saul - I Samuel 14:47

17. David hid his family here during his flight from Saul - I Samuel 22:3-5

18. Subdued by David - I Chronicles 18:1-2; II Samuel 8:2, 12

19. Benaiah, one of David's mighty men, killed men of Moab - II Samuel 23:20; I Chronicles 11:22

20. One of David's mighty men came from here - I Chronicles 11:46

21. Solomon's intermarriage and worship - I Kings 11:1, 7, 33; II Kings 23:13

22. Rebelled against Israel after the death of Ahab - II Kings 1:1

23. Warred with Judah and Israel - II Kings 3:4-27

24. Warred against Jehoshaphat - II Chronicles 20:1-23

25. Home of the mother of Jehozabad, one of the killers of Joash - II Chronicles 24:26

26. Raided Israel in the days of Joash - II Kings 13:20

27. Raided Judah in the days of Jehoiakim - II Kings 24:2

28. From here the Jews returned to Mizpah - Jeremiah 40:11-12

29. Jews intermarried with the Moabites - Ezra 9:1; Nehemiah 13:23

30. In the Psalms - 60:8; 83:6; 108:9

31. In the Prophets -
Isaiah 11:14; 15:1-16:14; Jeremiah 9:26; 25:21; 27:3; 40:11; 48:1-47; Ezekiel 25:8-11; Daniel 11:41; Amos 2:1-2; Micah 6:5; Zephaniah 2:8-9

E. EDOM

1. From the Zered River in the north to the Red Sea in the south

2. The origin of the Edomites - Genesis 25:30; 32:3; 36:9; I Chronicles 1:43-54

3. Settled by the descendants of Esau - Genesis 36:1-43

4. Took note of the Red Sea crossing - Exodus 15:15

5. Refused passage to Israel in the Wilderness Wanderings - Numbers 20:14-23; 21:4; 33:37; Judges 11:17-18

6. Part of Balaam's prophecy - Numbers 24:18

7. A border of the Promised Land - Numbers 34:3; Joshua 15:1, 21

8. Part of Deborah's prophecy - Judges 5:4

9. Subdued by Saul - I Samuel 14:47

10. Home of Doeg - I Samuel 21:7; 22:9, 18, 22; Psalm 52: superscription

11. Subdued by David - II Samuel 8:14; I Chronicles 18:11-13

12. Solomon controlled the port area - I Kings 9:26; II Chronicles 8:17

13. Solomon intermarried with Edomites - I Kings 11:1

14. Revolted against King Solomon - I Kings 11:14-22

15. Joined Israel and Judah against Moab - II Kings 3:8-26

16. Had no king but a deputy - I Kings 22:47

17. Revolted against Judah in the time of Joram - II Kings 8:20-22; II Chronicles 21:8-10

18. Joined the Ammonites and Moabites in the war against Jehoshaphat - II Chronicles 20:10, 23

19. Defeated by Amaziah - II Kings 14:7, 10; II Chronicles 25:11-19

20. Judah worshipped the gods of Edom - II Chronicles 25:20

21. Defeated Judah under Ahaz - II Chronicles 28:17

22. Jews returned from Edom to Mizpah - Jeremiah 40:11

23. In the Psalms - 60:superscription, 8-9; 83:6; 108:9-10; 137:7

24. In the Prophets -
Isaiah 11:14; 34:1-15; 63:1; Jeremiah 9:26; 25:21; 27:3; 40:11; 49:7-22; Lamentations 4:21-22; Ezekiel 25:12-14; 32:29; 35:15; Daniel 11:41; Joel 3:19; Amos 1:6, 9-12; 2:1; 9:12; Obadiah; Malachi 1:4

25. The Edomites later moved into the Negev and the area was renamed Idumea

26. Herod the Great was Idumean

VI. THE SINAI

A. GEOGRAPHY

1. Geographically divided into three key sections

   a. The Northern Plain

      (1) Composed of sand dunes

      (2) The key road: Via Maris

   b. The Central Highlands - A high plateau (4,000 feet above sea level)

      (1) Roads

         (a) The Way of Shur

         (b) Deir el Haj

      (2) Passes

         (a) The Gidi Pass

         (b) The Milta Pass

   c. The Southern Mountains

      (1) Mount Serbal

      (2) Mount Katherine (Katharina)

      (3) Mount Sidmor

      (4) Mount Sinai (Jebel Musa)

2. The Sinai Peninsula is shaped in a triangular form

   a. The northern border: Mediterranean Sea

   b. The western border: Gulf of Suez

   c. The eastern border: Gulf of Eilat (Aqaba)

3. It connects Asia with Africa by means of the Via Maris

B. HISTORY

1. Area of the early years of the Wilderness Wanderings - Exodus 19:1-2

2. It was the major scene of the Sinai Campaign of 1956 and the southern front of the Six-Day War in 1967

3. The capital of the Sinai is El Arish

Israel
The Specific Places

NOTE: *The primary Hebrew name comes first (with a few exceptions). The Arabic name is in parenthesis. Other names (Greek, Aramaic, alternate Hebrew names or otherwise) follow the hyphen.*

ABEL BETH MAACAH (ABEL EL-KEMAH)

1. Meaning: "Meadow of the House of Oppression"
2. Guarded the Hulah Valley on the south and the Iyon Valley on the north
3. Along a major trade route
4. Involved in the revolt of Sheba - II Samuel 20:14-22
5. Smitten by Ben Hadad at Asa's request - I Kings 15:20; II Chronicles 16:4
6. Fell under Tiglath Pileser III - II Kings 15:29
7. Roman Times - Known as Abila

ABEL MEHOLAH

1. Part of the route by which the Midianites fled from Gideon - Judges 7:22
2. Part of the Fifth Solomonic District - I Kings 4:12
3. Home of Elisha the prophet - I Kings 19:16

ACCO - PTOLEMAIS - ACRE

1. In Egyptian records, it is mentioned in the Execration Texts, the First Campaign of Thutmose III and the Amarna Letters
2. City was given to Tribe of Asher but Asher failed to take it - Judges 1:31
3. Part of the area given to Hiram by Solomon - I Kings 9:11-13
4. Taken by two Assyrian monarchs: Sennecherib and Ashurbanipal
5. In 333 B.C., it fell to Alexander the Great and the citizens welcomed him
6. In 261 B.C., it fell under Egyptian sovereignty and was renamed Ptolemais after Ptolemy II Philadelphus
7. In 219 B.C., it fell under Syrian sovereignty
8. In 145 B.C., Jonathan Maccabee was tricked, taken prisoner and later executed
9. When Pompey made it part of the Roman Empire in 65 B.C., it became a Roman colony where army veterans were settled and built a Roman naval base
10. Here Herod the Great and Octavian met together and made their peace
11. Paul spent one day here - Acts 21:7
12. In A.D. 66, it was sacked by the Jews in reprisal for the slaughter of the Jews in Caesarea and so the First Jewish Revolt began
13. The Romans made their headquarters here for the war in the First Jewish Revolt

14. Pliny credits Acco with discovering the art of glass-making

15. By the year 190, it had its own bishop

16. In the Byzantine Period, it became largely Samaritan and was named Samaritiki

17. Taken in the Persian Conquest in 614

18. In A.D. 636, it became part of the Arab Conquest

19. In 1104, the Crusaders took it under Baldwin who renamed it Saint Jean d'Acre after Joan of Arc and the city often was called Acre - The Crusaders also turned it into a naval base

20. After the Crusader stronghold of Jerusalem fell to the Arabs, it became the Crusader capital and main port for the Mediterranean and various orders set up their centers

    a. The Knights Templars

    b. The Teutonic Order

    c. Order of Saint Lazarus

    d. The Order of the Knights of Saint John - Hospitallers

21. Contrary to their normal practice, they allowed Jews to live here

22. In 1187, it was taken by Saladin

23. In 1191, it was retaken by the Crusaders under Richard the Lionhearted of England and Philip Augustus of France

24. In 1192, it became the capital of the Crusader Kingdom since Jerusalem was not retaken

25. In 1291, it became the last Crusader stronghold to fall to Sultan Khalil el-Ashraf (Mameluke); out of 12,000 knights, only seven survived

26. It laid in ruins until 1749 when the fortifications were built by Bedouin Sheikh Dehar el-Omar - He also invited Jews to settle in the city

27. In 1775, Ahmed Pasha the Albanian (El Jazzar) rebuilt the city with its splendor

28. He also built the Turkish Aqueduct that brought water from the Kabri Stream to Acco

29. El Jazzar was able to withstand the Napoleonic siege of 1799

30. In 1814 Suleiman Pasha became the ruler of Acco and totally rebuilt the aqueduct and it is the aqueduct that is mostly visible today

31. During the British Mandate Period, the Citadel was used as the British prison where many of the Jewish freedom fighters such as Jabotinsky were imprisoned and others were hung

32. In 1947, Jewish commandos breached the walls of the fortress freeing both Jewish and Arab prisoners

33. In 1948, it was one of the three strategic cities of Galilee which fell to Jewish forces - Captured in May 1948

34. Today it is a city of 40,000 with about two-thirds being Jewish

35. The Aqueducts of Acco

    a. There are a total of three aqueducts

        (1) Helenistic

        (2) El-Jazzar

        (3) Suleiman Pasha

    b. They gathered water from four springs in the Kabri vicinity

        (1) Ein Shefa - The most bountiful spring which originated with Aphek-Asher

        (2) Ein Giah

        (3) Ein Shayara

        (4) Ein Zuph

36. Things to see

    a. El Jazzar Mosque

    b. El Jazzar Fortress - Used by the British as a prison and place of execution for Jewish underground fighters

    c. Saint John's Crypt

    d. The Khan El-Umdan

    e. The Old Testament Tel (Tel el-Fukhkhar)

        (1) Crusaders called it Toron

        (2) From here, Richard the Lionhearted set out to conquer the city

        (3) Also called Napoleon's Hill - From here he also tried to conquer the city but failed

        (4) From this hill, Israeli forces launched their attack on the city in 1948

    f. The Crusader Subterranean City

    g. The Harbor

    h. The Walls - Built by El-Jazzar

37. The Aqueduct

    a. Built by Ahmed Jazzar Pasha (El Jazzar) to bring water from the Kabri River to Acco

    b. Destroyed by Napoleon during his siege of Acco

    c. Rebuilt by Suleiman Pasha

    d. It is 13 miles long

ACHSHAPH

1. Part of the northern confederacy against Joshua - Joshua 11:1

2. Defeated by Joshua - Joshua 11:6; 12:7, 20

3. City of the Tribe of Asher - Joshua 19:25

ACHZIV

1. A city given to the Tribe of Asher - Joshua 19:29

2. However, it was one of the cities the Tribe of Asher failed to capture - Judges 1:31

ADORAIM (DURA)

1. Fortified by Rehoboam - II Chronicles 11:9

2. Taken by John Hyrcanus in 125 B.C. as part of his conquest of Idumea

ADULLAM

1. The Judah and Tamar incident occurred here - Genesis 38:1-30

2. The king was killed by Joshua - Joshua 12:15

3. Given to the Tribe of Judah - Joshua 15:35

4. It served as one of the hiding places of David - I Samuel 22:1-2; II Samuel 23:13; I Chronicles 11:15

5. Fortified by Rehoboam - II Chronicles 11:7

6. Resettled in the return from Babylon - Nehemiah 11:30

7. In the Prophets - Micah 1:15

AI

1. Closely associated with the town of Bethel and stated to be east of Bethel - Genesis 12:8; Joshua 7:2

2. Defeated the Israelites - Joshua 7:2-5

3. Later defeated by Joshua - Joshua 8:1-29; 9:3; 10:1-2

4. The king was killed by Joshua - Joshua 12:9

5. Taken by Sennecherib - Isaiah 10:28

6. Resettled in the return from Babylon - Ezra 2:28; Nehemiah 7:32; 11:31

ANATOTH (ANATA)

1. Levitical City of the Tribe of Benjamin - Joshua 21:18; I Chronicles 6:60

2. Home of Abiezer, one of David's mighty men - II Samuel 23:27

3. Home of Abiathar who sided with Adonijah and was later expelled to the same city - I Kings 2:26-27

4. Home of Jehu, one of David's mighty men - I Chronicles 12:3

5. Home of Abiezer, leader of one of the 24 Levitical courses - I Chronicles 27:12

6. Destroyed by Sennecherib - Isaiah 10:30

7. Home of Jeremiah - Jeremiah 1:1; 29:27

8. God judged the men of Anatoth who conspired against Jeremiah - Jeremiah 11:18-23

9. Jeremiah was ordered to purchase a field signifying that the Jews would return - Jeremiah 32:6-25

10. Resettled in the return from Babylon - Ezra 2:23; Nehemiah 7:27; 11:32

APHEK - ANTIPATRIS (ABU FUTRUS)

1. Mentioned in the Campaign of Thutmose III and the Execration Texts
2. City on the Via Maris
3. The king was killed by Joshua - Joshua 12:18
4. Key rallying point for the five Philistine kings
   a. Against Samuel - I Samuel 4:1
   b. Against Saul - I Samuel 29:1
5. The Ark of the Covenant was captured by the Philistines (third stopping point) - I Samuel 4:5-11
6. David was sent back by the Philistines from here - I Samuel 29:1-11
7. It became a border point between Judea and Samaria
8. Herod the Great rebuilt the city in 35 B.C. and renamed it Antipatris after the name of his father
9. Paul was brought here from Jerusalem on the way to Caesarea - Acts 23:31
10. The Crusaders built a fortress here called "The Castle of the Silent Springs," reused by the Turks and its ruins are visible to this day
11. The springs in this area are the source of the Yarkon River and were used by the British to bring water to Jerusalem

APHEK - ASHER

1. Given to the Tribe of Asher - Joshua 19:30
2. Control retained by Canaanites - Joshua 13:4; Judges 1:31
3. Remains of a Crusader fortified flour mill
   a. During the Crusader period produced most of the flour for Acco
   b. Continued to operate until 1925
   c. The fortification on the roof dates from the 1936-1939 Arab disturbances

APHEK - BASHAN (FIQ)

1. Site of the war between Ahab and Ben Hadad and here the Syrians were defeated - I Kings 20:26-30
2. Syrians were defeated here by Joash of Israel - II Kings 13:17

ARAD

1. King of Arad attacked Israel at Mount Hor - Numbers 21:1-4; 33:40
2. The king was killed by Joshua - Joshua 12:14
3. Settled by Kenites - Judges 1:16
4. Destroyed by Shishak and recorded in his annals - I Kings 14:25-28; II Chronicles 12:1-9
5. Archaeological excavations uncovered a counterfeit holy of holies that was destroyed in the time of Hezekiah - II Kings 18:4; II Chronicles 31:1

6. Also found were the Arad Ostraca - Two hundred clay shards from various periods of the Judean Kingdom

   a. Over one hundred written in Hebrew

   b. About ninety written in Aramaic

   c. One mentions "the House of Jehovah"

   d. One mentions Edom and the King of Judah

   e. Seventeen letters written to Eliashiv ben Ashiahu the commander of the fortress in 586 B.C.

7. Continued to exist as a fortified city throughout the Persian, Hellenistic, Roman and Byzantine Periods

8. The excavation evidence at Tel Arad showed a number of corresponding elements with Scripture

   a. The Lower City is Canaanite

      (1) Settled as early as fourth millennium B.C.

      (2) It reached its peak about 3000 B.C.

      (3) The material culture was highly developed as testified by the public buildings, the temple-cultic center and the many tools found there

      (4) Water was collected by run-off into a large reservoir found in the center of the city

      (5) Surrounded by a wall which was 7.9 feet high

   b. The Upper City is Israelite

      (1) The fort was built by Solomon - The walls measure 180 feet long and 164 feet wide

      (2) The fort was rebuilt by Jehoshaphat - II Chronicles 19:4

      (3) The water tunnel was built by Jehoash - II Kings 12:1-18; II Chronicles 24:13-26

      (4) Rebuilt by Uzziah - II Chronicles 26:10

      (5) Rebuilt by Jotham - II Chronicles 27:4

      (6) It was destroyed under Ahaz by Edom - II Chronicles 28:17

      (7) Rebuilt by Hezekiah - II Chronicles 32:1-3

      (8) Rebuilt by Josiah - II Chronicles 34:6

      (9) Final destruction by Nebuchadnezzar

9. A small citadel was established during the Persian Period

10. Another was erected during the Hellenistic Period - Destroyed in the third century B.C.

11. Later, a Roman and Byzantine citadel stood here

12. After the Arab conquest in the seventh century, it served as a Khan

13. Destroyed in the eighth century

14. Modern Arad was established in 1961 about five miles east of the tel

THE ARBEL

1. Imposing mountain honeycombed with caves
   a. About 540 feet above sea level
   b. About 1,140 feet above the Sea of Galilee
2. Possibly biblical Beth Arbel - Hosea 10:14
3. During the Maccabean Period, it was a place of refuge for the Jews
   a. Fortified by Judah Maccabee
   b. Captured by the Selucid general Bacchides
4. In 38 B.C. Herod cleared out the area of Parthians and Jewish rebels thus restoring Roman rule over Galilee
   a. Herod lowered soldiers in baskets to the mouth of the caves and then slaughtered the rebels with arrows and fire brands
   b. Many chose to die by jumping rather than surrender
5. The traditional tombs of Seth, Levi, Simeon and Dinah are located here
6. The Arbel Synagogue - A fourth century synagogue facing south toward Jerusalem but the entry is on the east; the only Galilean synagogue known with such a design
7. The Arbel Fortress - Along the Cliffs of the Arbel now marked by one lone tree

ARNON RIVER (WADI EL-MUJIB)

1. Served as the border between Ammon and Moab - Numbers 21:13; 22:36
2. Taken by Israel - Numbers 21:13-28; Deuteronomy 2:24-37; 3:1-17; 4:48; Judges 11:13, 22-26
3. The City of Moab where Balaam and Balak met was at this border - Numbers 22:36
4. The southern point of the Tribe of Reuben - Deuteronomy 3:16; Joshua 13:16
5. It served as one of the Israelite encampments - Deuteronomy 2:24-36; Numbers 21:13-26; Judges 11:18
6. The southern limit of what Hazael took from Jehu - II Kings 10:32-34
7. In the Prophets - Isaiah 16:2; Jeremiah 48:20

ASHDOD (ISDUD) - AZOTUS

1. On the Via Maris
2. Home of the Anakim - Joshua 11:22
3. A city given to the Tribe of Judah - Joshua 15:46-47
4. The Philistines, however, retained control - Joshua 13:1-3
5. It was the fourth stopping point of the Ark of the Covenant - I Samuel 5:1-7; 6:17
6. Destroyed by Uzziah - II Chronicles 26:6
7. Destroyed by Sargon II - Isaiah 20:1

8. It served as a threat to the returnees from Babylon - Nehemiah 4:7; 13:23-24

9. In the Prophets: Isaiah 20:1; Jeremiah 25:20; Joel 3:4-8; Amos 1:8-9; Zephaniah 2:4; Zechariah 9:6

10. Besieged for 29 years by Pharaoh Psammeticus (633-609 B.C.) before falling

11. Renamed Azotus in the Hellenistic Period

12. Plundered first by Judah Maccabee (163 B.C.) and later by Jonathan Maccabee (148 B.C.)

13. Philip the Evangelist traveled through here - Acts 8:40

14. Ashdod Yam (Minat el-Qala) was the seaport for the city of Ashdod which was inland

15. This is as far as the Egyptian Army came in 1948

16. The modern city of Ashdod was built in 1957 near ancient Ashdod Yam and has a population of 65,000

17. Today, Ashdod is the second major port of Israel and is part of the Eilat-Ashdod oil pipeline

ASHKELON (MAJDAL)

1. Mentioned in the Amarna Letters

2. Taken by Ramses II in 1280 B.C.

3. Retained by the Philistines - Joshua 13:1-3; I Samuel 6:17

4. It was taken by Judah, though Judah did not maintain control - Judges 1:18

5. Samson killed 30 men to repay his part of the vow of the riddle - Judges 14:19

6. Part of the lament of David - II Samuel 1:20

7. In the Prophets: Jeremiah 25:20; 47:5-7; Amos 1:8; Zephaniah 2:4, 7; Zechariah 9:5

8. Surrendered to the Assyrians in 734 B.C.

9. During the Hellenistic Period, it became an important seaport

10. The Hasmoneans tried and failed to capture the city

11. The birthplace of Herod the Great, who rebuilt the city

12. In the Byzantine period, Jews were the only minority group allowed the free practice of their religion

13. In 1153, the Crusaders took the city, destroyed the Jewish community and built a strong stone wall

14. Taken by Saladin in 1187

15. In 1270, it was destroyed by the Saracens under Sultan Baybars and abandoned until 1948

16. In 1948, it was used as an Egyptian Army base during its invasion of Israel but conquered by Israeli forces in Operation Ten Plagues on November 5, 1948

17. The modern city is built as of 1948 with the present population standing at 56,300

ATLITH

1. A Crusader fort built in 1217-18 as the Castle of the Pilgrims - *Castrum Peregrinorthm* or *Chateau des Pélerins*

2. The Knights Templars resorted to this city after the loss of the Dome of the Rock

3. The last Crusader fortress to fall on August 14, 1291; simply abandoned after Acco fell

4. Six weeks later the castle was dismantled by the Mamelukes

AVDAT - OBODA

1. First mentioned on the Peutingcrian Table from the fourth century B.C. stating that Oboda was on the main road from Aila (Eilat) to Jerusalem and also in the Nitzanna Papyri of the sixth century

2. One of the three and the main Nabatean-Byzantine city of the Negev in the area of the Wilderness of Zin situated on a hill about 1,860 feet above sea level

3. The total settlement period lasted from the fourth century B.C. until the seventh century A.D.

4. Linked the central Negev with Edom (Petra) and Northern Arabia and the Mediterranean (Gaza)

   a. The caravan route known as the Spice Route which brought herbs, spices, perfumes and treasures from the Arabian Peninsula to Gaza by way of Petra and the Negev

   b. From Avdat, the roads branched off to Mamshit, Nitzanna and to Gaza

5. It began as a Nabatean settlement in the fourth century B.C. and continued until A.D. 106 when it became Roman and later Byzantine when the Nabateans were Christianized - One of three such cities

6. The Nabatean name of Oboda is named after King Obodas II (30-9 B.C.) who was buried here and was considered a god

7. The Byzantines built two churches, one over the Temple of Zeus

8. The peak of its prosperity was during the Byzantine Period: fourth through seventh century

9. The Byzantines retained control until 634 when it was destroyed in the Arab invasion

10. Things to see

    a. Roman Burial Caves - 22 double caves containing four inscriptions, all of them of women

b. Roman Tower - A defense tower containing an inscription: "With good luck, Zeus-Obodas help Eirenaios, who built this tower from its base in the year 188 (A.D. 294) with the help of Ouailos the builder from Petra and Eutichos"

c. The City Fortress - Byzantine Period serving as place of refuge in times of danger

d. The Temple Square - Religious center throughout the Nabatean, Roman and Byzantine Periods

e. The Wine Press - Byzantine Period

f. The Church Square

(1) Monastery

(2) Two Byzantine Churches - Burned in 636 in the Moslem invasion

(a) The Northern Church

i. Built in the middle of the fourth century using stones from the Nabatean Temple

ii. Contains a well-preserved baptistry

(b) The Southern Church - The Church of Saint Theodore

i. Built in the fifth century

ii. Contains the graves of Jewish believers

a) "Tobias the Blessed"

b) "Zachary, Son of John, buried in the Martyrium of St. Theodoros" - Dated December 19, 541

g. The Caves of the Saints - Contains inscriptions of prayers to Saint Theodoros for protection from witchcraft and the evil eye

h. The Bathhouse - Supplied by a nearby well which is about 200 feet deep

i. The Roman Villa - Reconstructed private house dating from the Roman Period

j. The Roman-Byzantine Quarter - The residential section with a street and private homes on each side and containing conduits to catch rain water and conduct it to cisterns

k. Rammaliya Cisterns - Nabatean water holes hewn into rock

l. The Nabatean Farm - Reconstructed and using Nabatean techniques to raise wheat, barley, almonds, apricots and pistachios

AZEKAH

1. Part of the area where Joshua defeated the Anti-Gibeonite league - Joshua 10:10-11

2. Given to the Tribe of Judah - Joshua 15:35

3. Part of the area of the camp of the Philistines against Saul in the Valley of Elah - I Samuel 17:1

4. Fortified by Rehoboam - II Chronicles 11:9

5. Mentioned in the inscriptions of Sargon II which reads: "I returned a second time to the land of Judah. The city of Azekah is a stronghold which is situated in the midst of the mountains, located on a mountain range like a pointed dagger, it was like an eagle's nest and rivaled the highest mountains and was inaccessible even for siege ramps and for approaching with battering rams it was too strong."

6. Destroyed by Nebuchadnezzar - Jeremiah 34:7

7. Mentioned in conjunction with the Babylonian destruction among the inscriptions found in the Lachish Letters which reads: "And may my lord know that we are watching for the signal fires of Lachish according to all the signs which my lord has given, because we cannot see Azekah."

8. Resettled after return from Babylon - Nehemiah 11:30

AZMAVETH (HIZMA)

1. It was a city founded by the descendants of Saul - I Chronicles 8:36

2. Rebuilt after the return from Babylon - Ezra 2:24; Nehemiah 7:28

3. Home of the Temple Singers - Nehemiah 12:28-29

BARAM (BIRIM)

1. An important city of the Mishnaic-Talmudic Period

2. Until 1948 it was a Maronite Christian village' now abandoned

3. Two second-third century synagogues with the larger being best preserved

    a. It measures about 45 by 60 feet

    b. Like others in the area, it faces south toward Jerusalem

    c. Unlike others, it had a portico composed of six columns and it also had a well

    d. It has three portals with a lintel engraved with wreaths, vines and grape clusters

    e. The eastern portal has an Aramaic inscription reading, "The builder is Elazar bar Yodan"

    f. The lintel of the smaller synagogue has an inscription reading, "Peace in this place and all of Israel. Yosef Halevi ben Levi made this lintel. May there be a blessing on his deeds."

4. One of the traditional tombs of Esther

BEEROTH (BIREH)

1. One of the cities of the Gibeonite League - Joshua 9:17

2. Given to the Tribe of Benjamin - Joshua 18:25

3. Home of the murderers of Ishboseth - II Samuel 4:2-9

4. Home of Naharal, Joab's armor bearer - II Samuel 23:37; I Chronicles 11:39

5. Rebuilt in the return from Babylon - Ezra 2:25; Nehemiah 7:29

BEERSHEBA (TEL ES-SABA)

1. Situated about 900 feet above sea level at a point where four wadis come together: Besor, Gerar, Hevron (Hebron) and Beersheba

2. Remains found as early as the Calcolithic Period

3. After a period of 2,000 years of non-settlement, it was settled in the Israelite Period first built by David and continued for 500 years until it was destroyed by the Babylonians

4. Site of Abraham's well - Genesis 21:22-32

5. Possibly the site where Isaac was born - Genesis 21:1-5

6. The site of the Sanctuary of the Everlasting God and here the tamarisk tree was planted - Genesis 21:33

7. Hagar and Ishmael went out from Beersheba into the wilderness - Genesis 21:14-19

8. Became the home of Abraham - Genesis 22:19

9. The site of Isaac's well and altar - Genesis 26:23-33

10. Home of Jacob - Genesis 28:10

11. Jacob returned here from Haran and from this place he went to Egypt - Genesis 46:1, 5

12. Given to the Tribe of Judah - Joshua 15:28; I Chronicles 4:28

13. One of the Judean cities given to the Tribe of Simeon - Joshua 19:2; I Chronicles 4:28

14. The two sons of Samuel served as judges here - I Samuel 8:2

15. Southern limit of David's census - II Samuel 24:7

16. Elijah left his servant here while fleeing from Jezebel - I Kings 19:3

17. Southern point of Jehoshaphat's evangelistic campaigns - II Chronicles 19:4

18. Zibia, the wife of Ahaziah, came from Beersheba - II Chronicles 24:1

19. Home of the mother of Jehoash - II Kings 12:1

20. Southern point of Josiah's reformations - II Kings 23:8

21. Southern point of the Judean return from Babylon - Nehemiah 11:30

22. Rebuilt in the return from Babylon - Nehemiah 11:27-30

23. Noted for having an idolatrous shrine - Amos 5:5; 8:14

24. During the Hellenistic Period, it was taken by John Hyrcanus when it was (at that time) part of Idumea

25. The history of the tel ends with the Early Arab Period

26. Marked off as the southern point of settlement of the Land as seen in the expression, "From Dan to Beersheba" - Judges 20:1; I Samuel 3:20; II Samuel 3:10; 17:11; 24:2, 15; I Kings 4:24-25; I Chronicles 21:2; II Chronicles 30:5

27. The modern town, several miles away from the tel, began in 1900 when it was the regional headquarters of the Turkish Army

28. In the initial battles of the War of Independence, it was taken by the Egyptian Army but recaptured by Israelis in Operation Ten Plagues

29. Today, it is Israel's fourth largest city and serves as the capital of the Negev with a total population of 154,000 people (2,000 in 1917). It was exclusively Arab until 1948 when it quickly became predominantly Jewish

30. Every Thursday, it hosts the weekly Bedouin market

31. Tel Beersheba - Things to see

   a. City wall

   b. City gate

   c. Well

   d. Homes made of mud brick

   e. Four-horned altar

   f. Store houses

Belvoir - Kochav Hayarden

1. Names

   a. French name - "Beautiful View"

   b. Hebrew name

      (1) "Star of the Jordan"

      (2) After a former Jewish settlement in the area

2. Built on same site as Fort Agrippina in Roman times

3. 1,400 feet above the Jordan Valley

4. Crusader castle of the 12th century occupied by the Knights Hospitallers and built over a period of 21 years (1168-1189)

5. Taken by Saladin in January 1189 after an 18-month siege and the knights were permitted to leave, alive, for Tyre

   a. This was one and half years after the Battle of the Horns of Hattin showing the strength of the fortress

   b. Belvoir held even after the fall of Crusader Jerusalem, Acco and Safed

   c. After eighteen months, the Moslems made a breach on the eastern wall leading to the surrender of the fortress

6. Partially destroyed in 1219 and then totally destroyed in 1227 by the governor of Damascus to prevent the Crusaders from retaking it and using it as a stronghold

7. In the 18th century, an Arab village was established here and named *Keochav al-Hava* meaning, "The Star of the Winds"

8. Taken by Israeli forces in May 1948 and successfully defended against Iraqi attacks

9. The fortress was excavated in 1966-1968

BENOT YAAKOV BRIDGE

1. Name means "Daughters of Jacob" due to a tradition that Jacob and his household crossed here
2. On the Via Maris where it crosses the Jordan River
3. Border between Bashan and Israel
4. Border between the Tetrachies of Philip and Herod Antipas
5. Border between the Crusaders and the Moslems
6. In 1799, Napoleon blocked this bridge to keep reinforcements from reaching Acco
7. During World War I the defeat of the Turks at this bridge opened up the way to take Damascus
8. During World War II the Vichy French were crushed at this bridge
9. One of the bridges destroyed by the Haganah in the "Night of the Bridges Campaign" in June 1946
10. In 1948, it became the border point between Israel and Syria
11. During the Six-Day War, it was one of the entrance points by which Israel entered Syria

BETAR (BATTIR)

1. A city that served as Bar Cochba's last stand and where he was killed by the Romans in 135 A.D.; ending the Second Jewish Revolt
2. In Arabic, the tel is known as *Khirbet el Yahud,* The Ruin of the Jews

BETH ALPHA

1. The ancient city is located today at Kibbutz Hephzibah
2. It contains the remains of a sixth century synagogue with a well-preserved mosaic floor
3. The mosaic floor contains three panels which pictures the Ark of the Covenant, the signs of the zodiac and the sacrifice of Isaac

BETHANY (EL-AZARIEH)

1. The name means "the house of the poor one"
2. First settlement began in the Persian Period - Sixth century B.C.
3. Home of Mary, Martha and Lazarus - Luke 10:38-42; John 11:1, 18
4. The resurrection of Lazarus occurred here - John 11:35-44
5. The feet of Jesus were washed here - John 12:1-8
6. Home of Jesus during the Passion Week - Matthew 21:17; 26:6; Mark 11:11-12; 14:3; Luke 19:29; John 12:1
7. It was near this city that the Ascension took place - Luke 24:50-51
8. The Church of Saint Lazarus - Greek Orthodoxy

BETH DAGON (BEIT JANN)

1. Given to the Tribe of Asher - Joshua 19:27

2. The highest village in the country

3. Today, it is a Druze village of 6000

BETHEL (BEITIN)

1. The second most mentioned town in the Bible, second only to Jerusalem

2. Known originally as Luz - Genesis 28:19

3. Close to Ai - Joshua 7:2; 8:9, 12, 17; 12:9

4. Place of Abraham's altar when he first came into the Land - Genesis 12:8

5. Abraham returned here from Egypt - Genesis 13:3-4

6. Jacob had his famous dream here - Genesis 28:10-22; 31:13

7. Jacob returned here from Haran - Genesis 35:1-16

8. Deborah, Rebekah's nurse, was buried here - Genesis 35:8

9. Jacob's name was changed to Israel here - Genesis 35:9-10

10. Taken in conjunction with Ai - Joshua 8:1-17

11. The king was killed by Joshua - Joshua 12:16

12. Border town between the Tribe of Ephraim (Joshua 16:1-2; I Chronicles 7:28) and the Tribe of Benjamin (Joshua 18:13; 21:22)

13. Taken by the House of Joseph - Judges 1:22-29

14. It served as the place for council for the Benjaminite War - Judges 20:18, 26, 31; 21:2, 19

15. Home area for the prophetess, Deborah - Judges 4:5

16. Major area of Samuel's ministry - I Samuel 7:16

17. Altar to God was erected here and Saul met three men going there - I Samuel 10:3

18. Served as Saul's military camp - I Samuel 10:3; 13:2

19. One of the cities where David sent his spoils - I Samuel 30:27

20. Jeroboam's southern religious sanctuary - I Kings 12:26-33

21. Here, the incident of the man of God with his warning against Jeroboam took place - I Kings 13:1-32

22. Home of Hiel, who rebuilt Jericho - I Kings 16:34

23. Taken by Abijah from Jereboam - II Chronicles 13:19

24. One of the cities which contained the School of the Prophets - II Kings 2:2-3

25. The Elijah and Elisha episode took place in this city - II Kings 2:2-3

26. The two bears ate the children making fun of Elisha here - II Kings 2:23-24

27. Survived Jehu's reform - II Kings 10:29

28. Became the home of the priest who taught the Gentiles of Samaria - II Kings 17:28

29. Josiah brought the ashes of idols which were burned in Kidron here - II Kings 23:4

30. Josiah destroyed the altar of the golden calf - II Kings 23:15-20

31. Rebuilt in the return from Babylon - Ezra 2:28; Nehemiah 7:32; 11:31

32. In the Prophets: Jeremiah 48:13; Hosea 10:15; 12:4; Amos 3:14; 4:4; 5:5-6; 7:10-17

33. It was from this city that representatives were sent to Zechariah concerning the question of fasting - Zechariah 7:1-14

34. Developed during the Hellenistic period and in 160 B.C. it was fortified by Bacchides

35. In A.D. 69, taken by Vespasian and rebuilt as a Roman town which flourished until the Arab conquest

BETH GUVRIN (BETH JIBRIN) - BETAGABRIS - ELEUTHEROPOLIS (FOR ADDITIONAL INFORMATION, SEE "MARESHAH")

1. First mentioned by Josephus as a city destroyed by Vespasian in A.D. 68

2. Located by ancient Mareshah which it replaced when the former was destroyed in A.D. 40 by the Parthians

3. Became a Jewish settlement from A.D. 70 through the Byzantine Period in A.D. 640 with leading rabbis living here in the third and fourth century

   a. Remains of a Jewish synagogue

   b. Remains of a Jewish cemetery

4. In A.D. 200, under Septimus Severus the Romans turned it into a city and named it Eleutheropolis - The City of the Free

5. Became an administrative capital covering the territory from Beth Shemesh, in the north, and Beersheba, in the south, and from the Mediterranean, in the west, and the Dead Sea, in the east

   a. Water supplied by two aqueducts

   b. Five roads with Roman milestones led to the city from all directions

6. During the Byzantine Period (A.D. 324-640), many Churches and Monasteries flourished here with a population of 15,000

   a. The key church was the Church of Saint Anne - Preserved in the Arabic name of Santahanna

   b. Rebuilt during the Crusader Period

   c. Remains visible to this day

7. During the Arab Period (A.D. 640-1099), it became the capital of the South and a major producer of limestone

8. The Crusaders built a small fortified city in 1136 and added more churches

9. Until the War of Independence, a small Arab village stood here

10. Captured by the Egytian Army in June 1948 but retaken by Israeli forces on October 27, 1948 in Operation Yoav

11. Kibbutz Beth Guvrin established in May 1949

12. The Bell Caves - a total of 63 limestone bell-shaped caves

   a. Created by both nature and ancient quarrying during the Arab Period 7th-10th century by Arabic-speaking Christians

   b. The soft cinonian chalk was used to make limestone plaster or cement and building stones

   c. The park contains sixty such caves with about eight hundred others awaiting excavation and restoration

BETH HAKEREM - RAMAT RACHEL

1. City of the Tribe of Judah - Joshua 15:59b (LXX)

2. The palace of Jehoiakim was built here - Jeremiah 22:13-19

3. It served as a fire signal town for possible invasions against Jerusalem - Jeremiah 6:1

4. Rebuilt in the return from Babylon and members of the city helped to rebuild the Dung Gate - Nehemiah 3:14

BETH HORON (BEIT UR)

1. Guarded the Beth Horon Road, the easiest approach to Jerusalem from the coast

2. There were two Beth Horons: Upper Beth Horon (Beit Ur El Faka) and Lower Beth Horon (Beit Ur Et Tahta)

3. Part of the area of the Anti-Gibeonite League flight - Joshua 10:10-11

4. Levitical City for the Tribe of Ephraim - I Chronicles 6:68

5. Built by the daughter of Ephraim - I Chronicles 7:24

6. Upper and Lower Beth Horon served as the border of Ephraim - Joshua 16:3 (Lower) and Joshua 16:5 (Upper)

7. Lower Beth Horon served as the border of Benjamin - Joshua 18:13-14

8. Levitical City - Joshua 21:22; I Chronicles 6:68

9. Through this area, the Philistines sent one of their three expeditionary forces - I Samuel 13:18

10. Upper and Lower Beth Horon were both fortified by King Solomon - I Kings 9:17; II Chronicles 8:5

11. Smitten by the men of Ephraim - II Chronicles 25:13

12. In 166 B.C., Judah Maccabee defeated the Syrian army under Seron

13. In 160 B.C., Judah Maccabee defeated the Syrians under Nicanor

14. Cestius Gallus was harassed by the Zealots and killed here on his retreat from Jerusalem in A.D. 66

BETHLEHEM OF GALILEE

1. Given to the Tribe of Zebulun - Joshua 19:15

2. Home of Ibzan, one of the judges of Israel - Judges 12:8-10

BETHLEHEM OF JUDAH

1. Its origin is recorded in I Chronicles 2:51, 54

2. On the road to Bethlehem, Rachel was buried - Genesis 35:16-20; 48:7

3. City given to the Tribe of Judah - I Chronicles 4:4

4. Home of Micah's Levite - Judges 17:1-13

5. Home of the Levite's concubine and where he went in search of her - Judges 19:1-9, 18

6. The story of the Book of Ruth occurs here - Ruth 1:1, 2, 19, 22; 2:4; 4:11

7. Home of David - I Samuel 16:18; 17:58; 20:6, 28

8. David was anointed king here - I Samuel 16:1-13

9. From here, David went to the Valley of Elah - I Samuel 17:12-18

10. Home of Joab, Abishai and Asahel - II Samuel 2:32

11. Asahel was buried here - II Samuel 2:32

12. The story of Bethlehem's well - II Samuel 23:14-17; I Chronicles 11:16-19

13. Home of Elhanan, one of David's mighty men - II Samuel 23:24; I Chronicles 11:26

14. Fortified by Rehoboam - II Chronicles 11:6

15. Many of the Jews fled here after Gedaliah was killed - Jeremiah 41:17

16. Rebuilt after the return from Babylon - Ezra 2:21; Nehemiah 7:26

17. Place prophesied for Messiah's birth - Micah 5:2; John 7:42

18. The birth of Jesus - Matthew 2:1-12; Luke 2:1-20

19. The slaughter of the babes of Bethlehem - Matthew 2:16-18

20. During the Byzantine Period, Jews were forbidden to live here

21. Jerome translated the Latin Vulgate here

22. Taken by the Crusaders in 1100 - returned in the Crusader-Moslem Wars and rebuilt

23. Destroyed by the Turks in 1244 and again rebuilt

24. Today, it is an Arab town of 35,000 residents both Christian and Moslem

25. Things to see

    a. The Church of the Nativity - Sits over ancient Bethlehem

        (1) Present church was built by Justinian in the sixth century

        (2) It sits over the Byzantine church built in 325

        (3) Spared in the Persian invasion of 614 because of the three magi pictured on the mosaic floor

        (4) In 1101, Baldwin I was consecrated here and in 1121, Baldwin II

(5) In the Turkish Period, the doorway was reduced to its present size

(6) Place of birth marked by a silver star

(7) Inside the Nativity Grotto hang 53 lamps

b. Milk Grotto

c. Shepherd's Field

d. Tomb of Rachel

e. Mar Elias Monastery

(1) Traditional site where Elijah rested after fleeing from Jezebel

(2) First built in the sixth century

(3) Present structure dates from 12th century

f. Davidic Well - Believed to be the well of II Samuel 33:16

g. Bethlehem Bible College - Evangelical school, training Arab believers for ministry throughout the Middle East

BETHPHAGE

1. The name means "the house of figs"

2. Jesus received the colt, the foal of an ass, upon which He rode to Jerusalem - Matthew 21:1-7; Mark 11:1-7; Luke 19:29-35

BETHSAIDA

1. Meaning - House of Fishing

2. Located on the east side of the Jordan River where it enters the Sea of Galilee

3. Rebuilt by Tetrarch Herod Philip in A.D. 30 and named Julias where he built a mausoleum in which he was buried in A.D. 36

4. Home of Philip, Peter and Andrew - John 1:44; 12:21

5. The blind man was healed here - Mark 8:22-26

6. The disciples were sent to this point after the feeding of the 5,000 - Mark 6:45

7. A place of retreat for Jesus - Luke 9:10

8. One of three cities which Jesus cursed - Matthew 11:21-22; Luke 10:13-14

9. Josephus was wounded here in clash with the Romans in A.D. 66

10. In the First Jewish Revolt, the Romans destroyed the city and it was never rebuilt thereafter

BETH SHEAN (TEL EL-HUSAN) (BEISAN) - SCYTHOPOLIS (TEL IZTABBA)

1. Controlled the Beth Shean Pass connecting the Jordan Valley and the Jezreel Valley

2. In Egyptian records it is mentioned in the Execration Texts, the Campaign of Thutmose III, the Amarna Letters and the Campaign of Seti I

3. Given to the Tribe of Manasseh - Joshua 17:11; I Chronicles 7:29

4. Not taken by Joshua and retained by the Canaanites - Joshua 17:12-16; Judges 1:27-28

5. Taken by the Philistines - I Samuel 31:7

6. Saul's body was fastened on the walls of Beth-Shean - I Samuel 31:8-12; II Samuel 21:12

7. Part of the Fifth Solomonic District - I Kings 4:12

8. Destroyed by the Assyrians in 732 B.C.

9. Resettled by Greeks and renamed Scythopolis and became the largest city of the Decapolis

10. In 143 B.C., Jonathan Maccabee tried to halt the Syrians and agreed to negotiations, only to be tricked and captured

11. In 104 B.C., it was taken by the sons of John Hyrcanus and the inhabitants were given the choice to convert to Judaism or leave. The majority chose to leave and the city became Jewish again and returned to the name of Beth Shean

12. In 63 B.C., with Pompey and the Romans, it was rebuilt and it became the capitol of the ten cities of the Decapolis and was again renamed Scythopolis; the only city of the Decapolis west of the Jordan

13. In the First Jewish Revolt in A.D. 66, Vespasian made the city the winter camp for the 5th and 10th Legions

    a. Many Jews of Scythopolis sided with Romans against the Jews

    b. Later, 13,000 Jews of Scythopolis were slaughtered by the Greek residents of the city

14. Jews lived here during the Mishnaic Period during which time it became a major industry in linen and textiles

15. Scythopolis began to prosper during the reign of Hadrian (A.D. 117-138) and attained its greatest status under Antonius Pius (A.D. 138-161) and Marcus Aurelius (A.D. 161-180)

16. City grew and prospered under the Byzantines and made the capital of Palestina Secunda - Had a pluralistic society of Pagans, Jews, Christians and Samaritans, each with their own houses of worship

    a. The gladiator games were stopped

    b. The theatre, bath houses and fountains continued to function

17. With the Arab Conquest, the Omayyad Dynasty (A.D. 661-750) made it a regional capital

18. Began to decline with the Abbasid Dynasty (A.D. 750-950) which made Tiberias its capital but it did become a center for wine making in spite of Moslem prohibition against it

19. City was destroyed on January 18, 749 by an earthquake and slowly abandoned

20. Crusaders built a fortress on top of the tel which was destroyed by Sultan Baybars in 1263

21. In the 19th century it became only a small village of 200 people - Settled by many Egyptians after the land was conquered by Egyptian ruler Muhammad Ali in 1830

22. At the time of the British Conquest in 1918, it had

    a. 1,710 Moslems

    b. 250 Christians

    c. 40 Jews - Immigrants from Kurdistan and other Arab countries

23. Became a base for Arab raiders against Jewish settlements until the town was taken by the Haganah on May 12, 1948 without a fight

24. Today it is the largest preserved Roman-Byzantine city in the country

25. The Jewish Sages used to say: "If the Garden of Eden is in the land of Israel, then its gate is at Beth-Shean." (Rabbi Simeon Ben Lachish - Talmud:Eruvim, 19a)

26. Population Growth

    a. Roman Period - 15,000 - 20,000

    b. Byzantine Period - 40,000 - 50,000

    c. Today - 15,000

27. Things to see

    a. Old Testament Tel (Tel el-Husan)

        (1) Over 20 cities

        (2) About 150 feet above the ground and yet about 340 feet below sea level

        (3) Destroyed by Tiglath Pileser III in 732 B.C.

        (4) After that only a temple to Zeus was built on top of the tel

    b. New Testament City (Tel Iztabba)

        (1) Roman Amphitheater - For games and gladiator fights seating 7000 but discontinued when Christianity arrived

        (2) Largest ancient bathhouse - 1½ acres (one of six Roman bath houses in the city)

        (3) The Roman Round Temple - The Cult of Dyonysius

        (4) The Nymphaeum - Fountain with aqueducts

        (5) The Valley Street: Byzantine street and quarter

(6) The Roman-Byzantine Theater - Main cultural center with a seating capacity of seven thousand people and used for dramas, comedies and pantomimes

(7) The Tyche Mosaic - Sixth century mosaic of the goddess of Good Fortune

(8) Palladius' Street: The Colonnaded Street - From the theater to the Town Center and the tel running northeast and southwest

(9) Sylvanus Street - Running northwest and southeast

(10) The Basilica - Main civic building of the Roman city

(11) The Roman Portico

(12) The Tetrapylon - Foundations of four pillars which once held statues

(13) The Agora - Large open square market

(14) Two Synagogues: One Jewish (containing a mosaic floor with Aramaic and Greek inscriptions) and one Samaritan

(15) Christian Churches and Monasteries with mosaic floor

(16) The Roman Bridge - Crossing the Harod River

   c. Crusader Fort - Built for eye contact with the Fortresses of Belvoir and Mount Tabor

BETH-SHEARIM

1. After the Bar Cochba Revolt failed, it became a center of Judaism along with Sepphoris

2. For a while it served as the seat of the Sanhedrin

3. Judah Hanasi codified the Mishnah (the Oral Law) here in A.D. 220 and is buried here, though his grave has not been found and soon became a desirable place for Jewish burial since Jerusalem was off-limits

4. The two sons of Judah Hanasi (Rabbi Simeon and Rabbi Gamaliel) were buried here and their tomb has been found

5. Site of a Jewish Necropolis - A vast network of 26 subterranean catacombs that served as the major burial place for world Jewry during the third and fourth century when the Mount of Olives was no longer available

   a. Contains relief-ornamented sarcophagus

   b. Many inscriptions in Hebrew, Aramaic and Greek

   c. Drawings of biblical scenes

   d. Drawings of Jewish symbols - Not all known as to their meaning

   e. The largest catacombs contained 400 tombs

6. Also discovered: A synagogue, an oil press and a basilica

7. Destroyed by the Romans in A.D. 351 by Emperor Gallus and disappeared from history

8. During the 19th century, a small Arab village was established on the site named *Shech Abreq*

9. Rediscovered in 1936

10. Nearby is a statue of Alexander Zaid - One of the founders of the Hashomer killed by Arabs in 1938

BETH SHEMESH (EIN SHAMUS)

1. Northern border of Judah - Joshua 15:10

2. Given to the Tribe of Dan - Joshua 19:41

3. Levitical City - Joshua 21:16; I Chronicles 6:59

4. After the Tribe of Dan departed from the area, the city was given to Judah - II Chronicles 6:59

5. Seventh stop of the Ark of the Covenant - I Samuel 6:9-21

6. Second Solomonic District - I Kings 4:9

7. Jehoash, king of Israel, defeated Amaziah, the king of Judah - II Kings 14:11-14; II Chronicles 25:20-24

8. Captured by the Philistines in the days of Ahaz - II Chronicles 28:18

BETH YERACH

1. Name means: House of the Moon

2. A large Canaanite city dating from 2500 B.C. with massive city walls and with the largest ancient storage silos ever found with a capacity of storing 1500 tons of wheat

3. Abandoned around the time of the Israelite Conquest (1400 B.C.) and not rebuilt until the Persian Period (sixth to fourth centuries B.C.)

4. During the Hellenistic Period, it was renamed Philoteria, named after the sister of Ptolemy II Philadelphis

5. During the Roman Period, it was given the status of a free city and named Ariah

6. During the Byzantine Period, it had a bath house, synagogue and church

7. Church was destroyed in the Moslem Invasion and a winter palace was built in its place

8. It was later abandoned and remained desolate for about a thousand years

9. The land was bought by Jews in 1905 hoping to build villas but this goal was not achieved

10. Today, the site contains two institutions

    a. Beth Yerach Regional High School

    b. Oholo Teacher Training Seminary

BETH-ZUR

1. The origin is mentioned in I Chronicles 2:45

2. Given to the Tribe of Judah - Joshua 15:58

3. Fortified by Rehoboam - II Chronicles 11:7

4. Rebuilt in the return from Babylon and the inhabitants helped to rebuild the Jerusalem wall - Nehemiah 3:16

5. In 165 B.C., Judah Maccabee defeated the Syrians under Lysias

6. Maccabees built a fortress and the defeat of the Syrians opened the way to Jerusalem

7. In 162 B.C., Lycias captured the city after he defeated Judah Maccabee at Beth-Zechariah, forcing the Maccabees to withdraw to Gophna

8. In 150 B.C., it was retaken by Simon Maccabee

BIRZAVITH (BIR ZEIT)

1. City is mentioned in I Chronicles 7:31 simply stating that Malchiel was the father of Bir Zeit

2. In 162 B.C., Bacchides killed the leaders of the Hasidim and so the revolt continued

3. In 161 B.C., Judah Maccabee gathered his forces for the Battle of Eleasa in which he was killed

BROOK BESOR

Here, David left his men to stay with their things - I Samuel 30:9-10, 21-25

THE BROOK OF EGYPT (WADI EL ARISH)

1. Marked the southern boundary of the Land - Numbers 34:5

2. Marked the southern boundary of Judah - Joshua 15:4, 47

3. Marked the southern boundary of the Solomonic Kingdom - II Chronicles 7:8

4. Marked the southern point of the Babylonian conquest in the days of Jehoiakim - II Kings 24:7

5. It will mark the southern border of the Millennial Kingdom - Ezekiel 47:19; 48:28

BURMA ROAD

1. Built to bypass Latrun Fort and the Shaar HaGai Pass controlled by the Arab forces in the War of Independence

2. Built between June 2-10, 1948

3. Completed only one day before the cease-fire of June 11, 1948

4. It helped break the siege of Jerusalem and helped to retain the Jewish side of the city under Israeli control

CAESAREA

1. The city was built by Herod the Great in honor of Augustus Caesar on the older site of Strato's Tower in 22 B.C. and called it Caesarea Maritama

   a. Strato's Tower was built during the Hellenistic Period about 250 B.C. by the Phoenicians to service their ships sailing between Sidon and Egypt

    b.   It was annexed to Judah by Alexander Yannai in 96 B.C.

       (1) Inhabitants were given the choice to convert to Judaism or leave - most chose to leave

       (2) It was then settled by Jews

       (3) After the conquest by Rome under Pompey, he again paganized the city

2. It then became the Roman and Byzantine capital and seat of government and all Roman procurators made their headquarters here

3. The Roman aqueduct was built by the Sixth and Tenth Legions to bring water from the Zerka (Shuni) River and Nahal Taninim at Mount Carmel and the Kabara Springs to the city of Caesarea

4. Hadrian built a second aqueduct along side the Herodian to increase the water supply

5. Home of Philip the Evangelist - Acts 8:40; 21:8

6. Paul stopped off here on the way to Tarsus - Acts 9:30

7. Cornelius and his house were converted here and became the first Gentiles in the church - Acts 10:1-48; 11:11

8. Agrippa I died here - Acts 12:19-23

9. Paul stopped off at Caesarea on the way to Jerusalem - Acts 18:22

10. Paul stayed at Philip's home in Caesarea - Acts 21:8-16

11. Paul was imprisoned here - Acts 23:22-35

12. Paul had a total of three judgments

    a.   Under Felix - Acts 24:1-27

    b.   Under Festus - Acts 25:1-22

    c.   Under Agrippa II - Acts 25:23-26:32

13. Paul left for Rome from Caesarea - Acts 27:1

14. In A.D. 60, the Jews of Caesarea were killed which helped to trigger the revolt later

15. In A.D. 66, the revolt began in Caesarea when 20,000 Jews were killed in one day

16. In A.D. 70, Titus made 2,500 Jewish prisoners of war fight wild beasts

17. In A.D. 132-135, it became the major supply port for the Romans against the Bar Cochba Revolt and where Rabbi Akiba, the spiritual leader of the revolt, was executed

18. It became the base for two early Gentile church leaders: Eusebius and Origin

19. In A.D. 195, the decision to observe Easter on a Sunday was made here

20. Home of the talmudic rabbis: Hoshaya and Abbahu

21. Emperor Justinian made it the capital of Palestina Prima and oppressed both the Jewish and Samaritan inhabitants - Finally led to a Samaritan revolt that burned down much of the city in A.D. 555.

22. Became Moslem in 639 and went into a decline

23. 1101 - Crusader King Baldwin took the city and put all residents to the sword

24. Under the Crusaders, the city revived it's status

25. 1187 - Taken by Saladin after his victory at the Horns of Hattin and all Christian inhabitants were either killed or sold into slavery

26. 1191-1192 - Retaken by Crusaders in the Third Crusade

27. 1252 - Walls were rebuilt and fortified by Louis IX of France as part of the Sixth Crusade

28. 1265 - Taken by Sultan Baybars and went into a steady decline again

29. 1291 - Destroyed by Mameluks and ceases to exist

30. In 1878, a village was founded on the site by Moslem immigrants from Bosnia and remained until 1948

31. Today, it is a wealthy neighborhood with a golf course

32. Things to See

   a. Roman Aqueduct - Built by Hadrian which brought water from the Shuni Springs as needed for a growing population

   b. The Roman Theater - The oldest in Israel with a seating capacity of 3,500 and where a dedicatory inscription was found reading: "Pontius Pilate, the prefect of Judea, has dedicated to the people of Ceaserea a temple in honor of Tiberius"

   c. The Amphitheater - Measuring about 300 feet long and 180 feet wide used for athletic and gladiator games

   d. The Temple of Augustus - Built by Herod using the same dimensions as those of the Temple of Jerusalem

   e. Byzantine Bath House

   f. Hippodrome - Measuring about 900 feet long and 150 feet wide it could seat about 15,000 and used for chariot racing

   g. Byzantine Forum with statues, one of which is believed to be that of Hadrian

     (1) This was the fourth north-south street added to the three built by Herod

     (2) A mosaic inscription at the foot of the stairs reads: "The Commander Flavius Strategius built the wall and the stairs and the apse at public expenditure in the days of Procurator Flavius Entolis in the tenth indication in a good hour."

   h. The Crusader City - Only about ten percent the size of the Roman-Byzantine City

   i. Crusader Church - The Cathedral of Saint Peter

     (1) Severely damaged by Saladin in 1187

     (2) Reconstructed and rededicated in 1218

j. The Synagogue

   (1) The first century synagogue was the site of a quarrel between Jews and Greeks that helped spark the First Jewish Revolt in A.D. 66.

   (2) The third century synagogue has a mosaic floor containing the names of priestly families

   (3) New synagogues were built in the fourth and fifth centuries

   (4) Abandoned in the eight century

CAESAREA PHILIPPI - PANEAS (BANYAS)

1. Known as Baal Hermon - Judges 3:3; I Chronicles 5:23

2. Known as Baal Gad - Joshua 11:17; 12:7

3. Given to the Tribe of Manasseh - I Chronicles 5:23

4. During the Hellenistic Period, it was the worship center of the god Pan and the Nymphs and renamed Paneas; there are five niches in the cliff which are the remains of the temple of the Greek god

5. The modern Arabic name, Banyas, originates from its Greek name

6. In the year 198 B.C., the Seleucids under Antiochus III defeated Ptolemy IV and so took control of all Judea

7. Augustus Caesar gave the city to Herod the Great who built a temple there in honor of Caesar

8. Enlarged by Philip, Herod's son, and so named Caesarea Philippi

9. Renamed Neronias, in honor of Nero, by Agrippa II

10. Here, Peter made his confession and the coming of the church was prophesied - Matthew 16:13-28; Mark 8:27-30

11. City flourished during the Roman, Byzantine, Arab, Crusader and Mameluke Periods

12. Lost its importance during the Ottoman Turkish Period

13. Site of the 30-foot high Banyas Waterfall and the perennial Hermon River, one of the four sources of the Jordan River which flows all year round

  a. The Hermon River has three tributaries which dry up in the summer

   (1) Nahal Saar

   (2) Nahal Sion

   (3) Nahal Gouta

  b. The river itself exits from the western side of the mount on which Nimrod Castle sits

  c. Ein Banyas (the Spring of Banyas) originally gushed out of the cave at the base of Mount Hermon but now emerges from below the cave and flows to the Banyas Waterfall

  d. About five miles from its source, it joins the Dan River to become the Jordan River

14. The Banyas Cave measures about 45 feet high and 60 feet wide

15. The white building above the cave marks the grave of Nebi Khader - Arabic name for Elijah the Prophet

16. Nearby the Banyas Caves are the ruins of Herod Phillip's palace

17. Other remains include Herodian city remains, a Roman bridge and Crusader structures

18. The nearby Matruf Mill is the only water-powered flour mill left in Israel still in operation

19. Talmudic Legend: If ever the waters turn red, it will mean the coming of the Messiah

CANA (HIRBET QANA)

1. The actual site is located in the Valley of Iphtael now known as the Valley of Beth Nephtoa seven miles north of Nazareth

2. In Egyptian sources, it is mentioned in the Execration Texts and the Amarna Letters

3. Mentioned by Tiglath Pileser III in Assyrian records

4. Home of Nathaniel - John 21:2

5. Jesus' first miracle - John 2:1-11

6. The second miracle of the healing of the nobleman's son - John 4:46-54

CAPERNAUM

1. Began in the second century B.C. and continued until the Arab invasion of the seventh century A.D.

2. Here, Herod Antipas kept a military garrison of Roman soldiers under a centurion

3. Home of Peter and Andrew - Mark 1:29

4. Jesus visited the city immediately after the wedding at Cana - John 2:12

5. Home of the nobleman - John 4:46

6. Jesus made His headquarters here - Matthew 4:12-13; 9:1; Luke 4:23

7. Roman garrison town headed by a centurion who was responsible for building the Jewish synagogue - Matthew 8:5-13; Luke 7:1-10

8. Jesus often preached in the synagogue here and in one case cast out a demon - Matthew 8:14-15; Mark 1:21-27; Luke 4:31-37

9. Peter's mother-in-law was healed here - Mark 1:30-31; Luke 4:38-39

10. Jesus healed the palsied man here - Matthew 9:1-8

11. Matthew had his office as tax collector here - Matthew 9:9

12. Sermon on the bread of life was preached here - John 6:16-59

13. The paralytic was healed here - Mark 2:1-12

14. The story of the *shekel* and the fish - Matthew 17:24-27

15. Dispute over who was the greatest - Mark 9:33-37

16. One of the three cities cursed by Jesus - Matthew 11:23-24; Luke 10:15-16

17. The present synagogue was built about A.D. 300 or later but sits on the foundation of the first century synagogue

18. An inscription found here in a synagogue reads: "Alphaeus the son of Zebedee, the son of John made this column. On him be blessing."

19. Town where Jews and Messianic Jews co-existed as late as A.D. 400 as reported by Egeria, a nun who visited between 381-384 - The white limestone synagogue was very close to the Byzantine Church

20. Town abandoned in the seventh century and rediscovered in the nineteenth century when the site was bought and excavated by the Franciscans

21. The Church of the Seven Apostles

    a. Red domed, Greek Orthodox Church in Capernaum next to the property owned by the Roman Catholic Church

    b. Built in 1931 to establish a Greek Orthodox preschool in Capernaum which up to then had been only Catholic

    c. Named in honor of Seven Apostles who came from or lived in Capernaum

CARMEL

1. Given to the Tribe of Judah - Joshua 15:55

2. The Monument of Saul was erected here after the victory over Amalek - I Samuel 15:12

3. The Nabal incident occurred here - I Samuel 25:2-42

4. Home of Abigail and Nabal - I Samuel 25:2-5; II Samuel 2:2; 3:3; I Chronicles 3:1

5. Home of Hezrai, one of David's might men - II Samuel 23:35; I Chronicles 11:37

CASTEL (EL QASTEL)

1. Believed to be Mount Ephron of Joshua 15:9, a border point between Judah and Benjamin

2. Had a fortress on the summit during the Roman Period

3. Crusaders built a fortress called *Castellum Belveer*

4. One of the three bottlenecks controlling the road to Jerusalem in 1948

5. After changing hands more than once, it was taken by Israeli forces on April 9, 1948 opening the road to Jerusalem

6. Chronology of battle

    a. April 1-3 - Palmach conquers Castel

    b. April 5 - Arabs recaptured Castel but the Etzion Brigade in a counter attack recaptured it again

    c. April 7 - Arab Commander Abd Elkader El Husseini takes command of Arab forces

    d. April 8 - Arab Commander killed with a burst from a sub-machine gun

       (1) Arabs thinking Commander was taken prisoner attack and the Palmach retreats from Castel

       (2) Arabs fail to exploit success and leave battle for Old City to attend Commander's funeral

    e. April 9 - Palmach takes Castel for the final time

CHASTELET CASTLE

1. Crusader Castle built by French Crusaders overlooking the Benot Yaakov Bridge

2. Guarded the road from and to the bridge

3. Conquered by Saladin in 1179

    a. Captured by digging a tunnel under the main tower and setting it on fire

    b. All one thousand inhabitants were killed and their bodies thrown into the cistern

    c. The citadel was then dismantled

CHORAZIN/CHORAZIM

1. A city first established in the first century

2. One of the three cities cursed by Jesus - Matthew 11:21-22; Luke 10:13-14

3. Noted in the Talmud as a place where good wheat was grown

4. Site of a black basalt synagogue containing the Seat of Moses dating from the third-fourth century

    a. The stone chair contained the inscription: "This is the Chair of Moses"

    b. During this period, the population stood at about 5,000

5. Was in ruins by end of fourth century

6. Rebuilt at the end of the fifth or beginning of the sixth century

7. It survived the Arab Conquest in the seventh century and had a period of growth but destroyed in the eighth century

8. Settlement was renewed in the 13th century and had continuous occupation until the beginning of the 20th century

DABERETH (DABURIYYA)

1. City of the Tribe of Zebulun - Joshua 19:12

2. Levitical City - Joshua 21:28; I Chronicles 6:72

DAN (TEL EL KHADDI)

1. Abraham overtook the five kings here - Genesis 14:14

2. Northern limit of what Moses saw - Deuteronomy 34:1

3. Originally known as Laish, it was taken by the Tribe of Dan and renamed - Joshua 19:47; Judges 18:1-31

4. One of the two cultic centers under Jeroboam involving the worship of the golden calf - I Kings 12:28-33

5. Taken by Ben Hadad at Asa's request - I Kings 15:20; II Chronicles 16:4

6. It survived Jehu's reform - II Kings 10:29

7. It became a synonym for the northern boundary of the Land, as seen in the expression "from Dan to Beersheba" - Judges 20:1; I Samuel 3:20; II Samuel 3:10; 17:11; 24:2, 15; I Kings 4:25; I Chronicles 21:2; II Chronicles 30:5

8. It usually was the first city to fall whenever there was an invasion from the north - Jeremiah 8:16

9. In the Prophets: Jeremiah 4:15; 8:16; Ezekiel 27:19; Amos 8:14

10. It became a commercial center - Ezekiel 27:19

11. The Arabic name is Tel el Khaddi, which means "the Hill of the Judge" and preserves the original meaning of Dan (Hebrew for "Judge"). The Arabic name for the spring is 'Ain el-Kadi

12. At Tel Dan was found the city gate, the temple to the golden calf built by Jeroboam and the oldest known reference to the House of David from an inscription of Hazael, King of Damascus, boasting of his victory over both the King of Israel and the King of the House of David

13. Also discovered was the first known *chutzot* (like that mentioned in I Kings 20:34), a marketplace outside a city wall established by the conquering power (in this case, Syria) to sell the conquering power's products with the income going to that power

14. The tel was finally deserted in the Roman Period when Ceasarea Philipi became the center of the region

15. The Dan River

    a. One of the four sources of the Jordan River - Both its largest and most important

    b. Unique to the Dan River is the source: An aquifer fed by rain and melting snow from Mount Hermon

    c. The source consists of two groups of springs: The first group contains five springs west of Tel Dan; the second and main group of springs comes from the northwest corner of Tel Dan

DEBIR (RABUD)

1. Its former name was Kiryat Sepher - Joshua 15:15; 21:15; Judges 1:11
2. Conquered by Joshua - Joshua 10:38-39
3. The Anakim of Debir were cut off - Joshua 11:21-22
4. The king of Debir was killed - Joshua 12:13
5. Judah destroyed Debir under Caleb - Joshua 15:15-17; Judges 1:11-15
6. Southern border city for the Tribe of Judah - Joshua 15:7
7. Given to the Tribe of Judah, especially the family of Caleb - Joshua 15:15-20, 49; 21:15
8. Levitical City - Joshua 21:15; I Chronicles 6:58

DEGANYA

1. It was the first kibbutz established in 1909-1911 by ten men and two women
2. Served as a Palmach base in the War of Independence
3. Within the kibbutz is the remains of a Syrian tank which was part of the Syrian invading force that invaded in 1948 but was repulsed by molotov cocktails

DOR - TANTURA (KHIRBET EL-BURJ)

1. In Egyptian records, it is found in the Tale of Wen-Amon
2. Part of the northern Canaanite alliance against Joshua - Joshua 11:2
3. Defeated by Joshua - Joshua 11:1-9
4. The king was killed by Joshua - Joshua 12:23
5. Given to the Tribe of Manasseh - Joshua 17:11; I Chronicles 7:29
6. Manasseh, however, failed to drive the Canaanites out - Joshua 17:12; Judges 1:27
7. Part of the Fourth Solomonic District under his son-in-law Abinadab - I Kings 4:11
8. Captured by Ashmenezer, a fifth century king of Sidon
9. Conquered by Alexander Yannai in the Hasmonean Period
10. Destroyed in the fourth century but rebuilt in the seventh century
11. During the Crusader Period, it was a Crusader castle called Castellum Merle
12. During the Ottoman Turkish Period, the Arab village of Tantura was located here
13. In 1794, the forces of Napoleon landed for the siege of Acco and from here he left again for Egypt
14. In 1948, 500 Egyptian commandos tried to invade Israel from this point but none survived

Eglon (Tel Hasi)

1. In Egyptian records, it is mentioned in the Execration Texts

2. One of the cities of the Anti-Gibeonite League - Joshua 10:3, 5, 23

3. Destroyed by Joshua - Joshua 10:34-37

4. The king was killed by Joshua - Joshua 12:12

5. Given to the Tribe of Judah - Joshua 15:39

Eilat (Ailah) (Aqaba)

1. It was often mentioned with the town of Ezion Geber - Deuteronomy 2:8; I Kings 9:26; II Chronicles 8:17

2. It was one of the stopping points in the Wilderness Wanderings - Deuteronomy 2:8

3. It served as a Solomonic port - II Chronicles 8:17-18

4. It was rebuilt and restored to Judah under Azariah or Uzziah - II Kings 14:22; II Chronicles 26:2

5. Taken by Rezin, king of Assyria - II Kings 16:6

6. In Roman times, it was called Aila and the Roman Tenth Legion was stationed there

7. Was the base of a Jewish tribe with whom Mohammad made a treaty

8. During the Moslem Period, it was a crossroads for pilgrimages to Mecca from Egypt, Africa and the Israeli Coast

    a. Main Road: *Dareb el-Haj* , The Pilgrim's Way

    b. Minor Road: *Dareb el-Aza*, The Gaza Way

9. Conquered by Crusaders in 1116 by King Baldwin I with a small force of 40 knights

    a. This action separated the two large Moslem centers of Cairo and Damascus

    b. Moslems wishing to make a pilgrimage to Mecca had to pay a toll tax

    c. Baldwin also built a fortress here later reused by the Mamelukes

10. Reconquered by Saladin in 1170 after he transported parts of ships on camel back by way of the *Dareb el-Haj*

11. In 1182, Reynald de Chatillon, the Crusader ruler of Transjordan, tried to do the same and, after an initial success, the venture ended with the death of all the knights

12. The fort was built by Sultan Nasir about 1320 and rebuilt by the last of the Mameluke Sultans, Qanush el-Ghuri in 1505

13. Area was largely abandoned except by Bedouins until the late Turkish Period

14. Taken by the British in World War I by Lawrence of Arabia

15. In 1925, it became part of the Emirate of Transjordan

16. Biblical Eilat is now Aqaba in Jordan

17. Modern Eilat was built by the British around an old Police Station called Umm Rashrash

    a. Originally, the Arab name was Ailah

    b. In the 15th century, the name was changed to Aqaba

18. It was taken by Israel in Operation Uvda in March 1949

19. It was the Egyptian blockade to the Port of Eilat in May 1967 that led to the Six-Day War

20. Eilat Today

    a. It is Israel's most southern city with a population of 26,000

    b. Serves as Israel's third major port next to Haifa and Ashdod - Israel's only access to the Indian and Pacific Oceans

21. Things To See

    a. In Israeli Eilat

        (1) Coral Beach - With snorkeling gear

        (2) Coral World Underwater Observatory

        (3) Taba - The border between Israel and Egypt

        (4) Amram Pillars - Five towering pillars carved out by nature

        (5) Ein Netafim - A droplet spring attracting many ibex

        (6) The Red Canyon - A gorge cut through red sandstone

        (7) Umm Rashrash Police Station - Captured in 1949 at the end of the War of Independence around which modern Eilat was built

        (8) Ein Evrona and the Dorr Palms - The most northern point these palms are found

        (9) Timna Park - The site of ancient copper mines

            (a) The Arches - Natural stone arches

            (b) The Chariots - Ancient rock drawings showing ox-drawn chariots and soldiers

            (c) The Mushroom - Natural formation from red sandstone and nearby an ancient copper smelting plant

            (d) Solomon's Pillars - Carved by natural erosion

            (e) Temple to the goddess Hathor - The goddess of love, music, dance, cats, cows and miners

    b. In Jordanian Aqaba

        (1) The Crusader Castle - Now a museum

        (2) Ezion Geber - Tel Khalaifah

        (3) Wadi Rum

Ein Avdat

1. Beginning of the Wadi Zin that leads to the Wilderness of Zin

2. Separates the Central Negev from the Northern Negev Highlands

3. Home of the ibex: The wild goats of Psalm 104:18

Ein Dor (Indur)

1. City of the Tribe of Manasseh - Joshua 17:11

2. Canaanite control retained - Joshua 17:12

3. The incident with Saul and the Witch of Ein Dor took place here - I Samuel 28:5-25

4. Involved either in the collapse of the Midianites or in the death of Sisera - Psalm 83:9-10

Ein Eglaim (Ein Fashka)

1. It is prophesied as a place for future fishing when the future healing of the Dead Sea takes place - Ezekiel 47:10

2. Place where the Essenes of Qumran grew their food

Ein Ganim (Jenin)

1. City of the Tribe of Issachar - Joshua 19:21

2. Levitical City - Joshua 21:29

3. The point where Ahaziah fled from Jehu - II Kings 9:27

4. Today it is an Arab town with a population of 35,000

Ein Gedi (Tel el-Jurn)

1. Contains a total of four springs: Ein Gedi, Ein Nahal Arugot, Ein Nahal David and Ein Shulamit

2. History goes back to the Chalcolithic Period (3000 B.C.) with a temple from that period

3. Identified by some as the Hazazon-Tamar of Genesis 14:7

4. City of the Tribe of Judah - Joshua 15:62

5. One of the confrontations between David and Saul occurred here - I Samuel 23:29-24:22

6. Camp of the Moabites, Ammonites and Meunites when they came up against Jehoshaphat - II Chronicles 20:2

7. The name means "Spring of the Kid" and it was noted as an oasis for wild goats - Song of Solomon 1:14

8. Famous for growing aromatic and medicinal plants like the henna - Song of Soloman 1:14

9. During the Babylonian Period, it became part of Idumea

10. Taken by John Hyrcanus during his campaigns in Idumea in 125 B.C.

11. In Roman times, it had a large Jewish population and was famous for its wine and dates

12. On Passover night in A.D. 70, the Sicarri, under Elazar ben Yair, raided and killed 700 residents to obtain supplies for Masada

13. Administrative district under Bar Cochba in A.D. 132-135 - Nearby is the Cave of Letters where the Bar Cochba letters were found and frequently mentioned in the letters

14. Had continuous settlement through the Persian, Hellenistic, Roman, Byzantine and Early Moslem Periods ending in the 6th-7th century

15. In subsequent centuries it became known as a wild place inhabited by Bedouins

16. It was one of the last areas taken by Israel in the War of Independence

17. Settled by the new state on March 10, 1949

18. The Kibbutz was established in 1956

19. It will be a key spot for fishing during the Messianic Kingdom - Ezekiel 47:10

EIN GEV

1. The first Jewish fishermen village in Israel and the first Jewish settlement on the east side of the Sea of Galilee, established in 1937 and now catches about 350 tons of fish a year

2. The statue in the kibbutz is in memory of the Syrian retreat during the War of Independence - Inspired by a member who concealed her pregnancy in order to remain and fight and died in the battle for the kibbutz

EIN HAROD (EIN J'ALUT)

1. Served as both a camp and testing ground of Gideon - Judges 7:1-7

2. Served as the camp of Saul in his campaign against the Philistines - I Samuel 29:1

3. Home of Shammah, one of David's mighty men - II Samuel 23:25

4. Home of Elikah, one of David's mighty men - II Samuel 23:25

5. In the twelfth century it was the scene of several battles between the Crusaders and the Moslems

6. In 1260, the Mamelukes defeated the Mongols

7. The modern kibbutz of Ein Harod was established in 1920

8. Over the spring are the tombs of Yehoshua and Olga Henkin, who acquired the land from the Arabs. Yehoshua Henkin is known as the "Redeemer of the Land"

9. In the late 1930's, British officer Orde Charles Wingate trained the young members of the *Palmach* to fight Arab bands in his "Night Squads"

10. Ein Harod remained a training base for the *Palmach*, the elite fighting unit of the *Haganah,* up until the War of Independence

EIN SHEMESH

1. Also known as the Apostles' Fountain
2. Marked the northern border of Judah - Joshua 15:7
3. Marked the southern border of Benjamin - Joshua 18:17

EKRON (TEL MIQNE)

1. The city was retained by the Philistines - Joshua 13:1-3
2. Border city between the Tribes of Judah (Joshua 15:11) and Dan (Joshua 19:43)
3. City of the Tribe of Judah - Joshua 15:45-46
4. Briefly taken by Judah but lost again - Judges 1:18
5. The sixth stop of the Ark of the Covenant - I Samuel 5:10-12; 6:16-17
6. Subdued by Samuel - I Samuel 7:14
7. It marked the point of the flight of the Philistines after the death of Goliath - I Samuel 17:52
8. Ahaziah desired to inquire concerning his health of Ekron's god - II Kings 1:1-3, 6, 16
9. Taken by Sargon II and later by Sennecherib
10. Destroyed by Alexander the Great - Zechariah 9:5-7
11. In the Prophets - Jeremiah 25:20; Amos 1:8; Zephaniah 2:4

EMMAUS (IMWAS)

1. In 165 B.C., Judah Maccabee, in two stages, defeated the Syrian army under Gorgias
2. The place of one of the post-resurrection appearances of Jesus - Luke 24:13-32
3. Served as the Roman camp of the Fifth Macedonian Legion during the First Jewish Revolt
4. Also served as a base for Arab armies in their conquest of the Land in A.D. 639

ESHTAOL

1. The origin is found in I Chronicles 2:53
2. Border town between Judah and Dan - Joshua 15:33
3. Originally given to the Tribe of Dan - Joshua 19:41
4. Area of the activities of Samson - Judges 13:25
5. Area of Samson's burial - Judges 16:31
6. From Eshtaol, spies were sent out to find a new place to live - Judges 18:2, 8, 11

ESHTEMOA (SAMUA)

1. City of the Tribe of Judah - Joshua 15:50; I Chronicles 4:17, 19

2. Levitical City - Joshua 21:14; I Chronicles 6:57

3. One of the cities to which David sent spoils of the Amalekites - I Samuel 30:28

EZION GEBER (TEL KHALAIFAH)

1. One of the stops in the Wilderness Wanderings - Numbers 33:35-36; Deuteronomy 2:8

2. Port city for the ships of Solomon - I Kings 9:26-28 (10:11, 22); II Chronicles 8:17-18

3. Port for the ships of Jehoshaphat and here they were broken - I Kings 22:48; II Chronicles 20:35-37

GAMLA

1. According to the Talmud, this was a fortified walled city since the days of Joshua

2. Disappeared after the Bronze Age but populated by Jews during the Hellenistic Period

3. The Hasmonian Alexander Yannai (Jannaeus) captured the city from its Hellenistic rulers

4. Herod the Great settled Jews there to populate the frontier regions of his kingdom

    a. Home of Yehudah of Gamla, who founded the Zealot Movement about 40 B.C. to free Israel from Rome

    b. His grand-nephew was Elazar ben Yair, who led the last stand of Masada

5. The city had only one small path that led to it from the surrounding mountains - The same one used today

6. The city wall was constructed under the direction of Josephus

7. In the First Jewish Revolt, it was besieged by Agrippa II for seven months who then gave up

8. Last Jewish stronghold in Bashan to fall to Vespasian after a one month siege

    a. The first entry by the Romans was beaten back but in the second a few days later, the Romans were able to overcome the defenders

    b. According to Josephus, only one thousand women survived

9. The city was forgotten until rediscovered in 1968

10. Remains

    a. Oldest known synagogue

        (1) Built during Herods' lifetime

        (2) It is the only synagogue uncovered in Israel known to be built within city limits while the Temple was still standing

    b. Roman assault ramp

    c. City wall

    d. Residential houses

11. The area contains many dolmens

    a. Table-like stone structures used for burial in the Middle Bronze Age

    b. Those are about 200 dolmens in the Gamla area and another 200 elsewhere in the Golan

12. The Gamla Waterfall is the highest in the country - About 150 feet high

13. Nearby is *Deir Quruh*, which means "Monastery of the Youth"

    a. Remains of a Byzantine Church

    b. The Greek inscription reads: "The God of Gregorius redeems and is merciful. Amen."

    c. Contains an ancient olive press

14. The area also contains a large population of Griffon Vultures which are seen flying over the ruins

GATH (TEL ES SAFI) - TEL ZAFIT

1. Home of the Anakim - Joshua 11:22

2. Philistine control retained - Joshua 13:1-3; I Samuel 6:17

3. Inhabitants were defeated by Benjamin but Benjamin did not hold control - I Chronicles 8:13

4. Responsible for killing a number of the members of the Tribe of Ephraim - I Chronicles 7:20-21

5. Fifth stopping place of the Ark of the Covenant - I Samuel 5:8-9

6. Subdued under Samuel - I Samuel 7:14

7. Home of Goliath - I Samuel 17:4, 23

8. One of the cities of the flight of the Philistines after the death of Goliath - I Samuel 17:52

9. Place where other members of Goliath's family were killed - II Samuel 21:18-22; I Chronicles 20:4-8; Psalm 34:superscription, 56

10. One of the places of refuge for David while he fled from Saul

    a. First occasion pretending to be mad - I Samuel 21:10-15

    b. Second occasion pretending to change sides - I Samuel 27:1-12

11. Part of David's lament - II Samuel 1:20

12. Origin of one of David's musical instruments - Psalm 8; 81; 84 (superscriptions)

13. Taken by David - I Chronicles 18:1

14. The Ark of the Covenant was in the home of Obed-Edom, a Gittite for three months - II Samuel 6:10-12; I Chronicles 13:13-1

15. Six hundred men of David's private guard were Philistines from Gath - II Samuel 15:18-22; 18:2

16. Fortified by Rehoboam - II Chronicles 11:8

17. Servants of Shimei flee to here - I Kings 2:39-41

18. Taken by Hazael - II Kings 12:17

19. Destroyed by Uzziah - II Chronicles 26:6

20. In the Prophets: Amos 6:2; Micah 1:10

GATH HEPHER (MASHHAD)

1. City of the Tribe of Zebulun - Joshua 19:13

2. Home of Jonah - II Kings 14:25

GAZA

1. In Egyptian records, it is mentioned by Thutmose III in the Amarna Letters and in the Taanach Letters

2. Mentioned in the Table of Nations - Genesis 10:19

3. Generally considered as the southern point of the Land of Canaan

4. Original inhabitants of Gaza were displaced by the Caphtorim - Deuteronomy 2:23

5. Home of the Anakim - Joshua 11:22

6. Southern point of Joshua's conquest - Joshua 10:41

7. Given to the Tribe of Judah - Joshua 15:47

8. However, the Philistines retained control - Joshua 13:1-3; I Samuel 6:17

9. It may have been taken briefly by Judah but was regained by the Philistines - Judges 1:18

10. During the period of the Judges, it marked the southern point of Midianite control - Judges 6:4

11. Samson carried away the gates of the city wall - Judges 16:1-4

12. Samson was imprisoned and eventually died here - Judges 16:21-30

13. Southern point of Solomon's dominion - I Kings 4:24

14. Smitten by Hezekiah - II Kings 18:8

15. Subdued by Tiglath Pileser III

16. Subdued by Sargon II

17. Destroyed by Sennecherib

18. Destroyed again by Pharaoh Necho - Jeremiah 47:1-7

19. Its destruction by Alexander the Great was prophesied - Zechariah 9:5

    a. Alexander the Great took it after a two month siege

    b. He dragged the governor of the city around the city behind his chariot until he died

    c. 10,000 inhabitants were put to death

    d. The rest of the inhabitants were sold into slavery

20. In the Prophets: Jeremiah 25:20; 47:1-7; Amos 1:6-7; Zephaniah 2:4

21. During the Hellenistic Period, it changed hands many times between the Ptolemies of Egypt and the Seleucids of Syria

22. Taken by Alexander Yannai in 96 B.C.

23. It eventually was taken by Cleopatra of Egypt but given to Herod the Great by Rome

24. However, officially it remained a free city

25. During the New Testament period, it became known as Gaza the Desolate - Acts 8:26 (Probably as viewed from New Gaza)

26. During the Byzantine Period, it flourished with a large Jewish population

27. It fell to Arab control in A.D. 634

28. During the Crusader Period, it became a fortified port

29. Taken by Saladin in 1170

30. Shabbetai Tzvi, a false messiah, married a prostitute in order to fulfill a minor messianic prophecy of the tradition of the rabbis in 1665

31. Captured by Napoleon in 1799

32. The Jews left Gaza in 1929 as a result of the Arab riots

33. After the 1948 war, it was the only Philistine city not under Israeli control

34. In 1956, in the Sinai Campaign, it fell to Israel but Israeli forces were forced to withdraw due to American pressure

35. In 1967, it fell to Jewish control again as a result of the Six-Day War

36. Today, the City of Gaza, along with the Gaza Strip, has an Arab population of 720,000, of which 450,000 are refugees since 1948. There are 5,000 Jewish settlers in the Gaza Strip scattered among 16 settlements

37. In 1993, Israel agreed to withdraw from Gaza by April 13, 1994 and give it full autonomy under the Palestine Liberation Organization (PLO) as part of the "Gaza-Jericho first" agreement before granting autonomy to the West Bank

GEBA (JABA)

1. City of the Tribe of Benjamin - Joshua 18:24; I Chronicles 8:6

2. Levitical City - Joshua 21:17; I Chronicles 6:60

3. Part of the vicinity of the war against the Benjaminites - Judges 20:33

4. Original inhabitants were descendants of Ehud - I Chronicles 8:6

5. Part of the area of the conflict of Jonathan against the Philistines - I Samuel 13:3-14:46

6. Jonathan destroyed the Philistine garrison, thus beginning the war - I Samuel 13:3

7. Second conflict in this area - I Samuel 14:5-15

8. Part of the area of the fighting between David and the Philistines - II Samuel 5:25

9. Part of the northern border of Judah - II Kings 23:8; Zechariah 14:10

10. Fortified by Asa with the stones of Rama - I Kings 15:22;
    II Chronicles 16:6

11. Marked the northern boundary of Josiah's reforms - II Kings 23:8

12. Taken by Sennecherib - Isaiah 10:29

13. Rebuilt after the return - Nehemiah 7:30; 11:31; Ezra 2:26

14. Home of the Temple Singers - Nehemiah 12:28-29

15. It is to be the northern limit of the area made like the Arabah during
    the Millennium - Zechariah 14:10

16. In the Prophets: Isaiah 10:29; Zechariah 14:10

GEDARA (UMM QEIS)

1. One of the ten cities of the Decapolis

2. It was the capital of a district called Gedaritis which included Perea

3. Controlled an area that included Gergasa - Matthew 8:28; Mark 5:1;
   Luke 8:26

4. Though located in Gilead on the other side of the Yarmuk River, its
   harbor was located at Tel Samra (Haon) on the Sea of Galilee

5. Conquered by Antiochus the Great in 218 B.C.

6. Taken by the Hasmonean, Alexander Yannai, in 98 B.C.

7. Taken for Rome by Pompey in 65 B.C. who also had the city rebuilt

8. It became one of the seats of the five Jewish Councils set up
   by Gabinius

9. The Emperor Augustus Caesar gave it to Herod the Great

10. It was destroyed by Vespasian

11. During the Byzantine Period (fourth-seventh centuries), it flourished
    and served as an episcopal seat

12. Contains the remains of three theaters, a temple, a colonnaded street
    and basilica

GERAR (TEL ABU HAREIRA) - TEL HAROR

1. Southern boundary of the land of the Canaanites - Genesis 10:19

2. Incident between Abraham and Abimelech occurred here -
   Genesis 20:1-8; 21:22-34

3. Home of Isaac - Genesis 26:1, 17

4. Incident between Isaac and Abimelech occurred here -
   Genesis 26:6-11, 26-31

5. Limit of Asa's pursuit of the Ethiopians - II Chronicles 14:13-14

6. Taken by John Hyrcanus in 125 B.C. in his campaign against Idumea

GERGASA (KURSI)

1. The healing of the Gergasene demoniac and the drowning of the pigs occurred here - Mark 5:1-20

2. The site of the Talmudic Kurshi viewed as a center of idol worship

3. Remains of the largest known Byzantine monastery in the Holy Land measuring about 450 by 370 feet

    a. First mentioned by St. Sabas in 491 and probably dates from the fifth century

    b. Damaged in the Persian Invasion of 614

    c. Rebuilt but destroyed by an earthquake and fire in the eighth century and by the ninth century ceased to be a place of Christian pilgrimage

    d. The baptistry was built in 585 and the Greek inscription reads: "In the time of the most God beloved Stephenos the priest and abbot was made the mosaic of the photisterion in the month of December, fourth indication, in the time of the pious and Christ-beloved our King Mauricius first Consulate"

    e. The crypt on the south side of the church held the remains of thirty elderly monks

    f. The north side of the church has a good example of a mill stone and an olive press

    g. After the Church was abandoned in the eighth century, the Moslems defaced that part of the mosaic floor that had images of man and animal and used the remains as homes and storage rooms

    h. Rediscovered accidently in 1969-1970 as a new road was being built and opened to the public in 1982

4. A chapel was excavated on the hill overlooking the monastery which was paved with three separate layers of mosaics marking the place where the demoniac lived among the tombs

GEZER

1. Key city on the Via Maris - It is seven hundred feet above sea level and has a good view in every direction

2. It also controlled the road that branched off from the Via Maris to Jerusalem

3. In Egyptian records, it is mentioned by Thutmose III, in the Amarna Letters and the Merneptah Stele

4. The army of Gezer was defeated by Joshua - Joshua 10:33

5. The king was killed by Joshua - Joshua 12:12

6. Border city of Ephraim - Joshua 16:3; I Chronicles 7:28

7. However, the Philistines retained control - Joshua 16:10; Judges 1:29; I Chronicles 7:28

8. Levitical City - Joshua 21:21; I Chronicles 6:67

9. Here, David smote the Philistines - II Samuel 5:25; I Chronicles 14:16; 20:4

10. Given as a dowry to Solomon by the King of Egypt - I Kings 9:15-16

11. Fortified by Solomon and became one of his three chariot cities - I Kings 9:15-16

12. During the Hellenistic Period, the Syrians fled here after their defeat at Emmaus

13. Later, it became a Maccabean stronghold after being taken by Simon Maccabee in 142 B.C.

14. Things to see

   a. The Gezer High Place - Ten monumental stones from the Canaanite Period (1600 B.C.)

   b. The Canaanite Tower and wall (1600 B.C.)

   c. Middle Bronze Gateway

   d. The Solomonic Gate - The best preserved in all Israel

   e. The underground water tunnel

      (1) It is 25 feet down

      (2) It is 140 feet long

   f. Burial Chambers

GIBEAH (TEL EL-FUL)

1. City of the Tribe of Benjamin - Joshua 18:28

2. Scene of the famous crime of the Benjaminites - Judges 19:10-20:48

3. Home of Saul - I Samuel 10:26; 15:34; 22:6; 23:19; 26:1

4. The first capital of Israel - I Samuel 11:4

5. Jonathan's military camp - I Samuel 13:2

6. Saul's military camp after Gilgal - I Samuel 13:15-16; 14:2

7. Camp of Jonathan's forces - I Samuel 14:3

8. The watchmen from here saw Jonathan's activity against the Philistines - I Samuel 14:16

9. Seven sons of Saul were hung here in revenge for the slaughter of the Gibeonites - II Samuel 21:1-6

10. Home of Ittai, one of David's mighty men - II Samuel 23:29

11. Home of Ahiezer and Joash, two of David's mighty men - I Chronicles 11:31; 12:3

12. Home of Micaiah, the wife of Jeroboam and the mother of Abijah - II Chronicles 13:2

13. Sennecherib destroyed this city - Isaiah 10:29

14. According to Josephus, Titus spent the night here before reaching Jerusalem for the final siege in A.D. 68

15. In the Prophets: Isaiah 10:29; Hosea 5:8; 9:9; 10:9

GIBEON (JIB)

1. Leading city of the Gibeonite League - Joshua 9:3-17

2. Referred to as a great city - Joshua 10:2

3. City of the Hivites - Joshua 11:19

4. The Anti-Gibeonite War - Joshua 10:1-43

5. City of the Tribe of Benjamin - Joshua 18:25; I Chronicles 8:29; 9:35-37

6. Levitical City - Joshua 21:17

7. Home of Ishmaiah, one of David's mighty men - I Chronicles 12:4

8. Part of the area where David defeated the Philistines -
   I Chronicles 14:10

9. Men of Joab defeated the men of Abner here - II Samuel 2:12-29

10. Asahel was killed here - II Samuel 3:30

11. Joab killed Amasa here - II Samuel 20:4-9a

12. It was Saul's attempt to destroy this place that brought about the
    death of his other sons - II Samuel 21:1-9

13. The Tabernacle abode here in David's and Solomon's time -
    I Chronicles 16:39; 21:29; II Chronicles 1:3-4, 13

14. Solomon prayed for wisdom here - I Kings 3:4-15; 9:2;
    II Chronicles 1:3, 6-13

15. Home of Hananiah the Prophet - Jeremiah 28:1

16. Where Ishmael and the captives of Mizpah were caught -
    Jeremiah 41:11-16

17. Rebuilt after the return from Babylon - Ezra 2:20; Nehemiah 7:25

18. Members of this city helped to rebuild the wall - Nehemiah 3:7

19. In the Prophets: Isaiah 28:21; Jeremiah 28:1; 41:12, 16

GILOH (BEIT JALLA)

1. City of the Tribe of Judah - Joshua 15:51

2. Home of Ahithophel, David's advisor who sided with Absalom -
   II Samuel 15:12; 23:34

3. Ahithophel committed suicide - II Samuel 17:23

4. Home of Eliam, one of David's mighty men - II Samuel 23:34

GIMZO (JIMZU)

1. Taken by the Philistines in the days of Ahaz - II Chronicles 28:18

2. Home of famous mishnaic rabbi - Nathan of Gimzo

GUSH HALAV (GISH)

1. The most important city in Upper Galilee in the ancient world

2. Home of Yochanan, one of the leaders in the First Jewish Revolt
   against Rome in A.D. 66

3. Last city to fall in Galilee during this First Jewish Revolt

HAIFA

1. It is a conglomeration of two Hebrew words, *Hof Yaffe*, which means "beautiful coastline"

2. Israel's third largest city with a population of 253,000 with a ten percent Arab population

3. Israel's largest main port

4. Its history only begins to date from the third century

5. In 1100, it was taken by the Crusaders who slaughtered the Jewish and Arab population

6. In 1251, it was destroyed by the Mamelukes

7. Present city owes its origin to Sheik Dahr al-Omar Zahar who built a castle here in 1761

8. Taken briefly by Napoleon in 1799

9. Briefly ruled by Ibraham Pasha of Egypt (1831-1840)

10. Main growth occurred during the British Mandate Period

11. City taken by Israeli forces just as the British were leaving

12. Reputation as a city that works: "While Jerusalem prays and Tel Aviv plays, Haifa works."

13. Home of two major academic institutions

    a. Technion

    b. University of Haifa

14. Home of Israel's only subway

15. Things to see

    a. The Bahai Shrine

    b. The Illegal Immigration Museum

    c. Elijah's Cave - Where by tradition, Elijah trained his disciples

    d. Stella Maris and the Carmelite Monastery

       (1) Originally, there stood a Byzantine Monastery destroyed by the Pessianu in 614

       (2) During the Crusader Period, a new Greek Monastery was built and named after Saint Margaret

       (3) Destroyed by the Arabs except for its chapel

       (4) On this site, the modern Stella Maris was built

       (5) Looted by Turks in 1914 and in May 1915 Turkish soldiers destroyed the monument in memory of Napolean's soldiers - The monument was restored after the British took Haifa in September 1918

HALHUL

1. City of the Tribe of Judah - Joshua 15:58

2. By Jewish tradition, it is the burial place of Gad and Nathan

HAMMAT

1. There are a total of seventeen hot springs in Hammat
2. The hot springs were known for their healing quality since Canaanite times
3. Fortified city of the Tribe of Naphtali - Joshua 19:35
4. Levitical City - Joshua 21:32
5. Site of Tiberias Hot Springs used since Roman times who built the first spas here. New spas built in the 18th and 19th centuries
6. City was inhabited during the Roman, Byzantine and Omayyad Periods
7. Several synagogues on top of each other were found
8. The Severus Synagogue - Synagogue from the fourth century and destroyed in the fifth century with mosaic floor containing the signs of the Zodiac, the sun-god, Helias and the four winds
   a. Severus was one of the founders of the synagogue with close ties with the presidents of the Sanhedrin when it was based in Tiberias
   b. The mosaic floor also contains inscriptions in Hebrew, Aramaic and Greek
   c. Also contains a mosaic of the Holy Ark and the seven branched lampstand
9. Above is the tomb of Rabbi Meir Baal Hanes, a miracle working disciple of Akiba

HAMMAT GADER (EL HAMMA)

1. Noted for its four mineral hot springs, containing sulfur and potassium, especially during Roman times
   a. Built by the residents of Gedara in the early second century
   b. The second largest in the Roman Empire and popular with Rabbi Judah Hanasi and frequented by Jews, Romans, Greeks and Christians
   c. Named two of the springs after gods of love
      (1) Eros - God of sexual love
      (2) Anteros - God of mutual love
2. Seven pools (including the Lepers' Pool) connected by halls (including the Hall of Niches) and walkways with three different types of pools
   a. The Frigidarium - Cold water pool
   b. The Tepidarium - Medium or luke-warm pool
   c. The Caldarium - Hot water pool
3. Had a Roman theater which sat two thousand people

4. Saint Epiphanius, a fourth century Jewish Christian monk, complained that both men and women bathed together and said: "Satan is working at Hammat Gader"

5. Containing the remains of a synagogue from the fifth century with a mosaic floor and five Aramaic inscriptions containing the names of donors

6. Destroyed by an earthquake but rebuilt by the Arabs in the seventh century

7. Fell into disuse from the ninth century until recent modern times

8. Site of the railroad bridge that connected Damascus and Haifa; blown up in the "Night of the Bridges" on June 16-17, 1946. One of ten bridges blown up by the Palmach to impede British movement

9. Although given to Israel in 1948, it was impossible to defend and it was taken by the Syrians

   a. Annexed by Syria in 1950

   b. Israel sent a police patrol to protest the annexation but it was attacked by the Syrians and seven of the Israeli policemen were killed

10. Retaken by Israel during the Six-Day War in 1967 and is now used as an Israeli spa and an alligator, cayman and crocodile farm

    a. Resort was built in 1967 but destroyed by terrorists in 1969

    b. Rebuilt by Golan kibbutzim in 1977

HAZOR

1. The largest tel in the country covering a total of 205 acres with 21 layers of cities

   a. The Upper City - Thirty acres

   b. The Lower City - 175 acres

2. City on the Via Maris

3. In Egyptian records it is mentioned in the Execration Texts, in the Amarna Letters, by Thutmose III, Amenhotep II and Seti I

4. It was a Canaanite royal city and the leader of the northern confederacy against Joshua - Joshua 11:1-5

5. Destroyed by Joshua - Joshua 11:10-13

6. King killed by Joshua - Joshua 12:19

7. City of the Tribe of Naphtali - Joshua 19:36

8. Canaanite city that oppressed Israel after the judgeship of Ehud - Judges 4:2, 17

9. Taken by Barak - Judges 4:23-24

10. Army of Hazor led by Sisera - I Samuel 12:9

11. One of the three key cities fortified by Solomon - I Kings 9:15

12. The water system was built by Ahaz who also built those of Gezer and Megiddo

13. Destroyed by Tiglath Pileser III in 732 B.C. - II Kings 15:29

14. In 144 B.C., it was taken by Jonathan Maccabee after defeating the army of Demetrius II

15. The water tunnel is ninety feet long

HEBRON (EL KHALIL)

1. The origin is in I Chronicles 2:42

2. It was founded seven years before Zoan (Tanis). One of the oldest cities of Egypt - Numbers 13:22

3. Its original name was Kiryat Arba - Joshua 14:14-15; 15:54; 21:11

4. One of the places where Abraham erected an altar - Genesis 13:18

5. Home of Abraham and Isaac - Genesis 35:27

6. Sarah died here - Genesis 23:2, 19

7. Joseph went out from Hebron to seek his brothers - Genesis 37:14

8. Area of the cave of Machpelah where the three fathers and mothers were buried

    a. Sarah - Genesis 23:17-20

    b. Abraham - Genesis 25:8-10

    c. Isaac - Genesis 35:28-29

    d. Rebecca - Genesis 49:31

    e. Leah - Genesis 49:31

    f. Jacob - Genesis 50:13

9. Area that the twelve spies of Israel went into - Numbers 13:22

10. One of the cities of the Anti-Gibeonite League - Joshua 10:3, 5

11. Taken by Joshua - Joshua 10:35-37

12. Anakim was cut off from this city - Joshua 11:21

13. The king was killed by Joshua - Joshua 10:23; 12:10

14. Part of Caleb's inheritance - Joshua 14:13-15; 15:13-14; Judges 1:20

15. Levitical City - Joshua 21:11, 13; I Chronicles 6:55-57

16. City of Refuge - Joshua 20:7

17. The Tribe of Judah fought against it - Judges 1:10

18. Samson carried the gates of Gaza to Hebron - Judges 16:1-3

19. One of the cities to which David sent spoils of the Amalekites - I Samuel 30:31

20. David's capital during his reign over Judah - II Samuel 2:1-5:13 (2:1, 3, 11, 32; 3:2, 5, 19, 20, 22, 27; 4:1, 8, 12; 5:1, 3, 5, 13); I Kings 2:11; I Chronicles 11:1-3; 29:27

21. Joab returned here after fighting with Abner - II Samuel 2:32

22. Abner was killed here - II Samuel 3:27-29

23. Abner was buried here - II Samuel 3:32

24. Ishboseth's head was buried and his murderers killed here - II Samuel 4:12

25. Some of David's sons were born here - I Chronicles 3:1-4

26. David was made king over all Israel in Hebron - I Chronicles 11:1-3; 12:23, 38

27. Absalom began his revolt against David here - II Samuel 15:7-12

28. Fortified by Rehoboam - II Chronicles 11:10

29. Rebuilt after the return from Babylon - Nehemiah 11:25

30. In 125 B.C., it was taken by John Hyrcanus in his campaign against Idumea

31. It is the site of the Pool of Birkat es Sultan, perhaps the same pool as in II Samuel 4:12

32. Jews continued to live here after A.D. 70

33. Jews were expelled from here by the Crusaders in 1100

34. Jews return but the Jewish community wiped out by the Arab riots of 1929 and 1936

35. Jews return after the Six-Day War

36. Today it is an Arab city of 83,000

37. Things to see

    a. Abraham's Terebinth - In the courtyard of the Russian Church built in 1871

    b. Cave of Machpelah - Herodian structure with Mameluke additions

    c. Glass Blowing Factory

HERODIUM

1. Area where Herod defeated Antigonus

2. One of the three fortifications of Herod the Great

3. The town built in this area was known as Herodia

4. Herod the Great is buried here

5. Used by Jewish forces during the Bar Cochba Revolt

6. Last known use was during the Byzantine Period

HILL OF MOREH

1. Part of the Via Maris

2. The camp of the Midianites was here - Judges 7:1

HIPPOS (KAL'AT EL-HUSN) - SUSITA

1. The Aramaic and Greek names mean "mare" and the Arabic name means "fortress of the horse"

2. Towers over one thousand feet above the Sea of Galilee

3. First settled by the Greek Seleucids around 250 B.C.

4. One of the ten cities of the Decapolis which contained a population of 10,000-20,000 and contained the cardo, nymphaeum, theater and an aqueduct bringing water in from fifteen miles away since it had no natural water source

5. Captured by Alexander Yannai in 80 B.C.

6. Taken by Pompey in 63 B.C.

7. Augustus gave it to Herod and when he died, it was annexed to the Province of Syria

8. Had a Jewish community during the Second Temple Period with strong trade relations with Tiberias

9. In the First Jewish Revolt, the Gentile residents slaughtered the Jewish population

10. One of the first cities to accept Christianity, it has the remains of five Byzantine churches

11. Residents would sail to Tiberias on Sabbaths and Jewish holy days to harass the Jews

12. Baptistry inscribed with date - A.D. 591

13. Conquered by the Moslems in A.D. 635

14. A large part of the city, including its aqueduct system ,was destroyed by an earthquake in A.D. 747; causing the city to be abandoned

15. During the Middle Ages, it was called Susiya - Retained by the Arab name

16. During the War of Independence, the tel was used by the Syrians to shell Kibbutz Ein Gev until the kibbutzniks took it from behind and so became a border point from 1948 to 1967

HORNS OF HATTIN

1. An extinct volcano 1,038 feet above sea level

2. Site of the City of Madon, one of the cities of the Hazor confederacy - Joshua 11:1

3. The king was killed by Joshua - Joshua 12:19

4. It was the place where Saladin defeated the Crusaders on July 4, 1187

   a. Crusaders were encamped at Zippori (Sepphoris)

   b. Saladin brought his army to the southern part of the Sea of Galilee and began moving toward Galilee and the Horns of Hattin

   c. He sent a force to attack the Crusader Castle in Tiberius which led the Crusader army out of Zippori to the rescue

   d. Upon arrival at the Horns of Hattin, the Crusaders were attacked and defeated

   e. This led to the subsequent fall of Crusader castles all over the country and eventually Jerusalem

  f. Crusaders remained in the country for another century but the glory of their kingdom had passed

  g. The battle was between Saladin and Guy of Lusignon

   (1) 20,000 Crusaders were killed

   (2) 30,000 were taken prisoner

 5. The holy place for the Druze religion which venerates Jethro, the father-in-law of Moses, known as Nabi Shuweib - His tomb is believed by the Druze to be located here

 6. The Protestant site of the Mount of Beatitudes

IBLEAM (I'BILLIN)

1. A town given to the Tribe of Asher but possessed by Manasseh - Joshua 17:11

2. Manasseh failed to drive out the Canaanites from this town - Judges 1:27

3. Mentioned as a nearby town where Jehu killed Ahaziah, the king of Judah - II Kings 9:27

JABBOCK RIVER - NAHR EZ ZARQA

1. Enters Jordan at Succoth (South) and Adam

2. Border between Gilead and Ammon - Numbers 21:24; Deuteronomy 3:16; Joshua 12:2

3. Jacob crossed this river - Genesis 32:22

4. It was part of the Israelite Conquest - Numbers 21:24; Deuteronomy 2:37; Joshua 12:1-6; Judges 11:13, 22

5. Border between the Tribes of Gad and Reuben - Deuteronomy 3:12, 16

JAFFA - JOPPA

1. On the Via Maris, at the point where it turned due east to Aphek

2. Mentioned in Egyptian records as a city conquered by Thutmose III

3. Given to the Tribe of Dan - Joshua 19:46

4. Solomon's harbor for the Cedars of Lebanon - II Chronicles 2:16

5. Jonah tried to flee from the presence of the Lord - Jonah 1:3

6. Conquered by Sennacherib

7. Ezra's port for the Cedars of Lebanon - Ezra 3:7

8. Darius I of Persia ceded the city to Eshmunazar, king of Sidon, who turned it into a Phoenician colony

9. Taken by Alexander the Great - 333

10. When Antiochus Epiphanes came to plunder Jerusalem, he drowned 200 Jews here

11. Burned by Judah Maccabee in 163 B.C. for drowning Jews

12. Jonathan and Simon Maccabee took it in 147 B.C. and made it a port city for the Hasmonian kingdom

13. Simon Maccabee took it again in 143 B.C.

14. In 64 B.C., Pompey separated it from Judah but it was returned to Judah in 30 B.C. by Augustus

15. Taken by Herod in 37 B.C. but, because of loyalty to the Hasmoneans, bypassed rebuilding it and made Caesarea the major port

16. The story of Peter and Tabitha - Acts 9:36-42

17. Home of Simon the Tanner, the place of Peter's vision - Acts 9:43-10:23, 32; 11:5-13

18. Destroyed by Vespasian - Rebuilt as a Roman city and renamed Flavia Joppa

19. Between the two Jewish revolts, the Jewish community was revived and participated in the Diaspora Revolt

20. During the Byzantine Period, the Jewish community suffered periodic massacres

21. During the Moslem Period, Jaffa became the port city of the provincial capital of Ramlah

22. The Jewish community suffered destruction during the Crusader Period

23. During the Mameluke Period, it became the chief point of entry for travelers and pilgrims of all religions

24. During the Ottoman Turkish Period, especially 1600-1880, a number of Christian religious institutions and hostels were built

25. 1799 - Napoleon took the city and slaughtered 2,000 POW's who were Arabs and Jews — The regiment that was responsible caught leprosy and all but seven died

26. Jaffa's fortifications were rebuilt by British General Sidney Smith

27. In 1820, there was a revival of the Jewish community with the building of a synagogue and hostel by Isaiah Ajiman of Constantinople

28. In 1832, Jaffa was conquered by Egypt under Mohammed Ali but the Turks recaptured the city from him in 1842

29. In 1864, the walls of Jaffa were dismantled

30. In 1910, it became part of Tel Aviv

31. On March 28, 1917, the Turks expelled the Jews of Jaffa as well as Tel Aviv but Jews returned after the British conquest

32. During the Arab riots of 1936-1939, the British closed the port to Jewish immigration

33. It was an Arab city until May 1948 when the majority fled, leaving an Arab minority that became citizens of the State

34. Things to see

    a. House of Simon the Tanner (Traditional)

    b. Saint Peter's Church of the Pravoslavs - Tomb of Tabitha (Traditional - Greek Orthodox)

    c.   Saint Peter's Church and Franciscan Monastery - The Tabitha miracle (Traditional - Roman Catholic)

    d.   Old City Streets

    e.   Excavations

    f.   The Jaffa Port

    g.   The Jaffa Port Lighthouse - Built in 1936

    h.   Immanuel House - Messianic center and hostel built in 1866 and run by the Anglican Church

        (1) Originally built by Armenian Gentile visionaries (157 of them) and called themselves The Church of the Messiah and came to prepare for the return of the Jewish Messiah

        (2) In 1871, the property was sold to Templars, a German group who believed themselves to be the people of God and used it as a school

        (3) In 1878, it was sold to a Russian baron named Platon von Ustinov who enlarged the building and used it as:

           (a) A hospital for Jews of the first *Aliyah* (1879-1883)

           (b) Later, his relatives used it as a hotel (1895-1914)

        (4) It was purchased by the London Jews' Society of the Anglican Church in 1926

        (5) Today it is used as a hostel and a place of meeting for Messianic groups and Congregations

JARMUTH

1. One of the cities of the anti-Gibeonite League - Joshua 10:3, 5

2. The king was killed by Joshua - Joshua 10:23; 12:11

3. City of the Tribe of Judah - Joshua 15:35

4. Rebuilt after the return from Babylon - Nehemiah 11:29

JERICHO (TEL ES-SULTAN) (TULUL ABU EL-ALEIK)

1. Located about 825 feet below sea level

    a.   Four miles west of the Jordan River at the foot of the hills in the Wilderness of Judah

    b.   An oasis located at a major crossroads

2. It is mentioned as a reference point -
Numbers 22:1; 26:3, 63; 31:12; 33:48; 34:15; 35:1; 36:13;
Deuteronomy 32:49; 34:1; Joshua 3:16; 4:13, 19; 5:10, 13; 13:32; 20:8;
I Chronicles 6:78

3. Known as the City of the Palm Trees - Deuteronomy 34:3;
Judges 1:16; 3:13; II Chronicles 28:15

4. Part of the area that Moses saw - Deuteronomy 34:3

5. Joshua sent the two spies to spy out the city - Joshua 2:1-24

6. The fall of Jericho - Joshua 6:1-25; 8:2; 9:3; 10:1, 28, 30; 24:11; Hebrews 11:30

7. Became Joshua's base against Ai - Joshua 7:2

8. The king was killed by Joshua - Joshua 10:1, 28, 30; 12:9

9. The curse of Joshua was pronounced - Joshua 6:26

10. The curse of Joshua was fulfilled in I Kings 16:34

11. The southern border of Ephraim - Joshua 16:1, 7

12. The northern border of Benjamin - Joshua 18:12

13. Given to Benjamin - Joshua 18:21

14. At one time controlled by Moab - Judges 3:13

15. Place where David's ambassadors were to remain until their beards grew back - II Samuel 10:5; I Chronicles 19:5

16. One of the locations of the Schools of the Prophets - II Kings 2:5, 15

17. The Elijah and Elisha episode - II Kings 2:4-18

18. Elisha healed the bitter waters here - II Kings 2:19-22

19. The captives of Judah were returned to Jericho by Israel - II Chronicles 28:15

20. Area where Zedekiah was captured - II Kings 25:5; Jeremiah 39:5; 52:8

21. Rebuilt after the return from Babylon - Ezra 2:34; Nehemiah 7:36; 7:36

22. Residents helped to rebuild the wall - Nehemiah 3:2

23. During the Hellenistic Period, the city began to spread beyond the tel and became famous for dates and balsam

24. Given to Cleopatra by Mark Anthony who later sold it to Herod the Great

25. The New Testament Jericho was built by Herod the Great and here he also died

26. Mentioned in the story of the Good Samaritan - Luke 10:30

27. The healing of Bartimeus occurred here - Matthew 20:29-34; Mark 10:46-52; Luke 18:35-43

28. The story of Zaccheus - Luke 19:1-10

29. Jericho fell to the Romans in A.D. 70 after a fierce battle in which the Jews tried to destroy the valuable balsam trees and according to Pliny, "A battle raged over every tree"

30. After the Bar Cochba Revolt, the Jewish population dwindled

31. In the Byzantine Period, several churches were built and many monasteries were founded all around it

32. Modern Jericho is an Arab city and a thriving center of agriculture and tropical fruit with a total population of 16,000

    a. 10,000 live in the city itself

    b. 4,000 live in refugee camps and small villages nearby

33. Altogether there are three Jerichos

    a.   Old Testament Jericho (Tel es-Sultan)

    b.   New Testament Jericho (Tulul Abu el-Aleik)

        (1) Site of one of Herod's palaces; also where he died

        (2) It became an Episcopal See as early as the fourth century

        (3) Site of the Church of the Mother of God restored by Justinian in the sixth century

        (4) Town revived by the Crusaders who called it "New Jericho"

    c.   Modern Jericho first began during the Byzantine Period

34. In 1993, Israel agreed to withdraw from Jericho by April 13, 1994 and give it full autonomy under the Palestine Liberation Organization (PLO) as part of the "Gaza-Jericho first" agreement before granting autonomy to the West Bank

35. Things to see

    a.   The Old Testament Tel - 23 cities on top of each other

    b.   Elisha's Spring

        (1) The spring for Old Testament Jericho

        (2) Arabic Name: '*Ain es-Sultan,* Spring of the Sultan

    c.   The New Testament remains

    d.   The Hisham Palace built in 724 by the Umayyads

        (1) *Hirbet el-Mafjar*

        (2) Originally believed to be built by Caliph Hisham, the son of Abd-el-Malek, (hence the name) but now known to have been the pleasure palace of Caliph Walid II (724-743), Hisham's heir

        (3) Water was brought in from Ein Duyuk, about three miles west, by means of an aqueduct

        (4) Destroyed by an earthquake in 749

    e.   The Mount of Temptation

        (1) Peak is 1,130 feet above the Jericho plain

        (2) The place of the third temptation - Matthew 4:8-10

        (3) Possible site of the Fortress of Dok where Simon Maccabee was murdered in 134 B.C.

        (4) Today: The Quarantal Monastery

            (a) Greek Orthodox monastery half-way up the mount

            (b) Name is Arabic corruption of Latin *quarantena,* meaning "forty"

            (c) Monastery incorporates the rows of caves inhabited by hermits

        (d) With Arab conquest in the seventh century, the monks were scattered

        (e) In the 12th century, the Crusaders restore it but soon evacuated and not used for hundreds of years

        (f) Present monastery built between 1875-1905 with and provided by the Russian Orthodox Church

  f. The Jericho Synagogue

    (1) From the seventh century

    (2) Contains a mosaic floor depicting a seven branch lampstand, a ram's horn, a palm branch and the Ark of the Covenant

    (3) Contains Hebrew and Aramaic inscriptions

        (a) Hebrew - Peace be upon Israel

        (b) Aramaic - Blessed are all the holy congregation, the old and the young, who with the help of God, made this mosaic. He who knows their name and the name of their sons and of their family shall write them in the Book of Life with all the righteous people and friends of Israel Shalom. Amen.

JERICHO ROAD

1. The story of the Good Samaritan - Luke 10:30-37

2. Where Zedekiah was captured - II Kings 25:1-7; Jeremiah 52:4-8

JERUSALEM (AL QUDS)

1. Historical Periods

  a. 3500 B.C. - First settlement on the Eastern Hill

  b. 2500 B.C. - Earliest mention comes from the Ebla Tablets

  c. 19th century B.C. - Mentioned in Egyptian Execration Texts

    (1) The Early Execration Texts mention two kings of Jerusalem: Sha'an and Yeqar'am

    (2) The Later Execration Texts name only one in which only the first syllable is preserved: Ba. . .

  d. 14th century B.C. - Mentioned in the El Amarna Letters, six of which were written by Jerusalem's Canaanite king, Abdi-Hepa

  e. Israelite Period - 1400-586 B.C.

    (1) Jerusalem becomes the capital

    (2) The First Temple is built

  f. Babylonian Period - 586-536 B.C.

    (1) Foreigners move into the southern part of the Land

    (2) Jerusalem and northern Judah remain empty

g. Persian Period - 536-332 B.C.

　(1) The Jews return

　(2) The city, the walls and the Temple are rebuilt

h. Hellenistic Period - 332-63 B.C.

　(1) Alexander the Great - 332-312 B.C.

　(2) Ptolemies - 312-198 B.C.

　(3) Seleucids - 198-167 B.C. - The Maccabean Revolt

　(4) Hasmoneans - 167-63 B.C.

　　(a) Jerusalem begins to expand to the Western Hill and surrounded by the First Wall

　　(b) Development of the Pharisees and Sadducees

i. Roman Period - 63 B.C. - A.D. 324

　(1) During the Herodian Period (40 B.C. - A.D. 70), Jerusalem expands northward, surrounded first by the Second Wall and then the Third Wall

　(2) Destroyed in A.D. 70

　(3) Rebuilt as a Roman city in A.D. 135 and named: *Aelia Capitolina*

　　(a) *Aelia* - Family name of Hadrian

　　(b) *Capitolina* - Reference to the three capitoline gods: Jupiter, Juno and Minerva

　(4) Christianity begins to spread

　(5) From A.D. 70 until the end of the third century, the city remained without a wall, even during the times it was being built up

j. First Byzantine Period - A.D. 324-614

　(1) The building of many churches over Christian holy sites

　(2) Reached the peak of its Byzantine development during the reign of Emperor Justinian (527-565)

k. Persian Period - A.D. 614-629

　(1) The destruction of these churches

　(2) Jews allowed to return

l. Second Byzantine Period - A.D. 629-638 - Jews again banished

m. First Moslem Period - A.D. 638-1099

　(1) Umayyads - A.D. 638-750 (Ramlah and Damascus)

　　(a) Rebuilt Jerusalem

　　(b) Turned the Temple Mount into a Moslem holy site

　　(c) Built the Dome of the Rock

　　(d) Jews were permitted to return to Jerusalem and became caretakers of the Temple Mount

    (2) Abbisids - A.D. 750-877 (Bagdad)

        (a) The *El-Aksa* Mosque built

        (b) Jews were forbidden to enter the Temple Mount

        (c) Jerusalem suffers decline

    (3) Fatimids - A.D. 877-1071 (Cairo)

        (a) The Church of the Holy Sepulchre destroyed

        (b) Large influx of Karaite Jews until they equaled the number of other Jews in the city

    (4) Seljuk Turks - 1071-1099 (Bagdad)

        (a) Wide spread mistreatment of Christians

        (b) Desecration of churches

n. The Crusader Period - 1099-1187

    (1) Became the capital of the Latin Kingdom of Jerusalem

    (2) Rebuilding of the Churches

    (3) Jerusalem enters a period of prosperity

    (4) Jewish community destroyed and ceased to exist

    (5) Greek holy place confiscated by Latins

o. Second Moslem Period - 1187-1517

    (1) Ayyubids - 1187-1250 (Damascus and Cairo)

        (a) Walls of Jerusalem fortified but later demolished in 1219

        (b) Jews permitted to return to the city

        (c) Overall population decreases due to fear of living in unfortified city

        (d) Construction and renovation carried out on the Temple Mount

        (e) Interrupted by the short Second Crusader Period (1229-1244) during which time the Jews were again expelled

        (f) In 1243-1244, the city was invaded by the Khwarizmians who massacred the Christians and destroyed church buildings

    (2) Mamelukes - 1250-1517 (Egypt)

        (a) Development of religious institutions but it remained politically and economically insignificant

        (b) Many Pilgrimages

        (c) The Citadel of David was reinforced in 1310 but otherwise Jerusalem remained an unwalled city

        (d) Jewish community begins to grow

            i.   Initially in the area of modern Mount Zion

            ii. Later in the 14th century, it spread to the present Jewish Quarter

p. Ottoman Turkish Period - 1517-1917 (Istanbul)

  (1) Rebuilt the walls of Jerusalem during 1535-1542

  (2) Turned Jerusalem into a typical oriental town

  (3) Reached the height of its development during the rule of Suleiman the Magnificent and, thereafter, it went into constant decline with no new buildings or constructions

  (4) New Jewish neighborhoods begin outside the walls in the 19th century with the population beginning to grow again

  (5) By 1860, the Jews were the majority population of Jerusalem

  (6) Local government was centered on key families whose authority was passed down dynastically, father to son

    (a) The Nashashibis

    (b) The Husseins

    (c) The Alamis

    (d) The Khalidis

  (7) There was an interruption of Turkey's rule during 1831-1840 with the Egyptian conquest of Palestine which spurred the 19th century growth and which continued when the Turks began

    (a) New construction inside the Jewish Quarter and Jewish neighborhoods outside the wall

    (b) New buildings and churches in the Christian Quarter and along the Via Dolorosa

    (c) Christian group also began to spread outside the city wall with places like the Russian Compound, the American Colony, the Germany Colony and buildings opposite the New Gate

    (d) Moslems begin building north of the Old City opposite the Damascus and Herod Gates

  (8) Protestants begin to get a foothold starting with the Anglican Christ Church inside the Jaffa Gate

q. British Mandate Period - 1917-1948

  (1) Jerusalem grew and expanded

  (2) Establishment of garden neighborhoods such as Talpiot, Rahavia, the German Colony, the Greek Colony, the American Colony and Romema

  (3) Period of Jewish and Arab tensions

r. Israeli-Jordanian Period: Divided City - 1948-1967

  (1) New City becomes the capital of Israel

  (2) Development of the New City

    (a) The Jewish city expands westward since, on all the other sides, it was surrounded by Jordan

   (b) The Arab city expands primarily northward but also somewhat eastward

   (3) Construction of many public buildings on both sides of the border

s. Israeli Period: Unified City - 1967 - Present

   (1) Jewish Quarter rebuilt

   (2) Municipal boundaries expanded

   (3) There has been a massive increase in the building of new neighborhoods

      (a) First phase: 1968-1970 - Surrounding Arab Sheich Jarrah

         i.   Sanhedria Hamurheret

         ii. Ramot Eshkol

         iii. Maalot Dafna

         iv. Givat Hamivtar

         v.   Givat Shapira (French Hill)

      (b) Second Phase: 1970-1980 - North and South

         i.   Neve Yaakov - North

         ii. Ramot Allon - North

         iii. East Talpiot - South

         iv. Gilo - South

      (c) Third Phase: 1980 - Present

         i.   Pisgat Zeev - To close the gap between Neve Yaakov and French Hill

         ii. Har Nof - A new religious suburb

   (4) New public buildings built in East Jerusalem

      (a) The Government Office Complex

      (b) Israel Police Force Headquarters

   (5) Commercial Center Development

   (6) Cultural Centers

   (7) New neighborhoods connected with new wide roads

   (8) Since the *Intifada* began in 1987, there has been continuous tension between Jews and Arabs

   (9) There has been a gradual increase in the religious population so that the Orthodox now make up 27% of the Jewish population

2. Names for the City

   a. Salem - Genesis 14:18

   b. Jebus - Judges 19:10

   c. Jerusalem - Joshua 10:1

      d.   The City of God - Psalm 46:4

      e.   Zion - Isaiah 60:14

      f.   Holy City - Isaiah 52:1

      g.   Hephzibah - Isaiah 62:4

      h.   Ariel - Isaiah 29:1-7

      i.   *Aelia Capitolina* (Hadrian in A.D. 135)

      j.   Al-Kuds (Arab)

3.   Biblical History - Most frequently mentioned city in Scripture

      a.   First mentioned in relationship to Melchizedek - Genesis 14:18-20

      b.   Leader of the Anti-Gibeonite League - Joshua 10:1-5

      c.   King was killed by Joshua - Joshua 10:23; 12:10

      d.   Border between Judah and Benjamin - Joshua 15:8

      e.   Smitten and burned by Judah - Judges 1:8

      f.   Given to the Tribe of Benjamin - Joshua 18:28; I Chronicles 8:28

      g.   Retained by the Jebusites - Joshua 15:63; Judges 1:21

      h.   The Levite and his concubine refused to stay here because it was Jebusite - Judges 19:10-13

      i.   Goliath's head brought to Jerusalem - I Samuel 17:54

      j.   Made the capital of Israel by David - II Samuel 5:6-10; I Kings 2:11; I Chronicles 3:4; 11:4-9; 28:1; 29:27

      k.   Inhabited by various tribes - I Chronicles 9:3, 34

      l.   Several of the sons of David were born here - II Samuel 5:13-16; I Chronicles 3:5-8; 14:3-7

      m.   Ninth and last resting place of the Ark of the Covenant - II Samuel 6:1-19; I Chronicles 15:1-28; 23:25; II Chronicles 1:4

      n.   The shields of Hadadezer brought to Jerusalem - II Samuel 8:7; I Chronicles 18:7

      o.   Became the home of Mephibosheth - II Samuel 9:13

      p.   Joab returned to Jerusalem after fighting Ammon - II Samuel 10:14; I Chronicles 19:15

      q.   The Bathsheba and Uriah incident occurred here - II Samuel 11:1-12:25

      r.   David returned to Jerusalem after fighting Ammon - II Samuel 12:26-31; I Chronicles 20:1-3

      s.   The Absalom revolt included Jerusalem - II Samuel 14:23-20:3

      t.   Joab returned to Jerusalem after the defeat of Sheba - II Samuel 20:7, 22

      u.   The numbering of Israel by David involved Jerusalem - II Samuel 24:8, 16; I Chronicles 21:4, 15-16

v. Became the forced home of Shimei, a son of Saul - I Kings 2:36-46

w. Solomon built a wall around Jerusalem - I Kings 3:1; 9:15

x. Solomon sacrificed before the Ark in Jerusalem after his prayer for wisdom was answered - I Kings 3:15; II Chronicles 1:13

y. Solomon built the Temple and brought the Ark into the Temple in Jerusalem - I Kings 8:1-11; I Chronicles 6:10, 32; II Chronicles 2:1-7:22 (2:7, 16; 3:1; 5:2; 6:6)

z. Solomon built his own house in Jerusalem - I Kings 9:19; II Chronicles 8:6

aa. The Queen of Sheba came to Jerusalem - I Kings 10:1-10; II Chronicles 9:1-12

bb. Solomon made Jerusalem a strong, wealthy city - I Kings 10:26-27; II Chronicles 1:14-17; 9:22-28, 30

cc. Solomon's fall involved Jerusalem - I Kings 11:1-42 (7, 13, 29, 32, 36, 42)

dd. All the kings of Judah reigned from Jerusalem

    (1) Rehoboam - I Kings 12:18, 21; 14:21; II Chronicles 10:18-12:16 (10:18; 11:1, 5, 14, 16; 12:2, 4, 5, 7, 9, 13)

    (2) Abijam (Abijah) - I Kings 15:1-8; II Chronicles 13:1-22 (2)

    (3) Asa - I Kings 15:9-24; II Chronicles 14:1-16:14 (14:15; 15:10)

    (4) Jehoshaphat - I Kings 22:41-50; II Chronicles 17:1-21:1 (17:13; 19:1, 4, 8; 20:5, 15, 17, 18, 20, 27, 28, 31)

    (5) Jehoram - II Kings 8:16-24; II Chronicles 21:1-20 (5, 11, 13, 20)

    (6) Ahaziah - II Kings 8:25-29; 9:27-28; II Chronicles 22:1-9 (1-2)

    (7) Athaliah - II Kings 11:1-20; II Chronicles 22:10-23:21 (23:2)

    (8) Jehoash (Joash) - II Kings 11:21-12:21; II Chronicles 24:1-27 (1, 6, 9, 18, 23)

    (9) Amaziah - II Kings 14:1-22; II Chronicles 25:1-28 (1, 23, 27)

    (10) Azariah (Uzziah) - II Kings 15:1-7; II Chronicles 26:1-23 (3, 9, 15)

    (11) Jotham - II Kings 15:32-38; II Chronicles 27:1-9 (1, 8)

    (12) Ahaz - II Kings 16:1-20; II Chronicles 28:1-27 (1, 10, 24, 27)

    (13) Hezekiah - II Kings 18:1-20:21 (18:2, 17, 22, 35; 19:10, 21, 31); II Chronicles 29:1-32:33 (29:1, 5; 30:1, 2, 3, 5, 11, 13, 14, 21, 25; 31:4; 32:2, 9, 10, 12, 18, 19, 22, 23, 25, 26, 33)

    (14) Manasseh - II Kings 21:1-18 (1, 4, 7, 12, 13, 16); II Chronicles 33:1-20 (1, 4, 7, 9, 13, 15)

    (15) Amon - II Kings 21:19-26; II Chronicles 33:21-25 (21)

    (16) Josiah - II Kings 22:1-23:30 (22:1, 14; 23:1, 2, 4, 5, 6, 9, 13, 20, 23, 24, 27, 30); II Chronicles 34:1-35:27 (34:1, 3, 5, 7, 9, 22, 29, 30, 32; 35:1, 18, 24)

(17) Jehoahaz - II Kings 23:31-33; II Chronicles 36:1-4

(18) Jehoiakim - II Kings 23:34-24:6; II Chronicles 36:5-8

(19) Jehoiachin (Jechoniah, Coniah) - II Kings 24:8-17;
II Chronicles 36:9-10

(20) Zedekiah - II Kings 24:18-25:7; II Chronicles 36:11-13

ee. Jeroboam built rival worship centers to Jerusalem -
I Kings 12:26-30

ff. Taken by Shishak in the days of Rehoboam - I Kings 14:25;
II Chronicles 12:1-9

gg. Threatened by the Syrians - II Kings 12:14-18

hh. The north wall was broken by Jehoash, the king of Israel, after
defeating Amaziah, the king of Judah, and then plundered -
II Kings 14:13-14; II Chronicles 25:23-24

ii. Besieged by Israel and Syria in the days of Ahaz - II Kings 16:5;
Isaiah 7:1-2

jj. Threatened by Sennacherib in the days of Hezekiah -
II Kings 18:13-19:37

kk. Manasseh corrupted the city assuring divine judgment -
II Kings 21:10-16; 23:26-27

ll. Destroyed by Babylon in 586 B.C. - II Kings 24:1-25:17;
II Chronicles 36:5-21; Jeremiah 52:1-30

mm. Cyrus issued a decree allowing for the rebuilding of Jerusalem -
II Chronicles 36:22-23

nn. In the Return, three key men played a role for Jerusalem

(1) Zerubbabel - Rebuilt the Temple - Ezra 1-6

(2) Ezra - Rebuilt the spiritual values - Ezra 7-10

(3) Nehemiah - Rebuilt the city wall - Nehemiah 1-13

oo. Origin of Mordechai's family - Esther 2:6

pp. Major theme of the prophets and poets of Israel and mentioned
over 6,000 times

(1) In the Poetic Books - Psalm 51:18; 68:29; 79:1, 3; 102:21; 116:19;
122:2, 3, 6; 125:2; 128:5; 135:21; 137:5, 6, 7; 147:2, 12;
Ecclesiastes 1:1, 12, 16; 2:7, 9; Song of Solomon 1:5; 2:7; 3:5, 10;
5:8, 16; 6:4; 8:4; Lamentations 1:7, 8, 17; 2:10, 13, 15; 4:12

(2) In the Prophets - The only Old Testament prophets that
do not mention Jerusalem are Hosea, Jonah, Nahum,
Habakkuk and Haggai

qq. It is a major area of ministry by Jesus in all four Gospels

rr. It is the scene of early church history in the Book of Acts

ss. In the New Testament Epistles, it is mentioned in Romans 15:19, 25, 26; I Corinthians 16:3; Galatians 1:17, 18; 2:1; 4:25, 26; Hebrews 12:22

tt. In the Revelation - 3:12; 21:2, 10

uu. Rabbis: Ten measures of beauty descended from Heaven; nine were taken by Jerusalem and one by the rest of the world (*B. Kiddushin* 98b)

4. Jerusalem: The New City

   a. Ammunition Hill (*Givat Ha-Tachmoshet*) - Memorial to the heaviest fighting in the Six-Day War

   b. The Center for Conservative Judaism - Israel's headquarters for the Conservative Movement

   c. The *Davidka* - The 1948 mortar gun

   d. Ein Kerem

      (1) Former Arab village now a Jewish suburb of Jerusalem

      (2) Traditional birthplace of John the Baptist - Luke 1:39

      (3) Churches

         (a) The Russian Convent and the Church of Zechariah (1871) - The Provoslavik Russian Church

         (b) The Church of Saint John the Baptist - The home of Zecharias and Elizabeth and where John was born

            i. First built in the fourth century and then destroyed by the Samaritans in the sixth century who killed all the monks

            ii. Rebuilt by the Crusaders in 1102

            iii. After the Arab conquest, it was turned into a *khan*

            iv. Given to the Franciscans in 1485

         (c) The *Terra Sancta* Hospice

         (d) The Church of the Visitation

            i. Mary's visit to Elizabeth

            ii. Built in 1955 by the Franciscans

            iii. Contains plaques with Mary's Song in 42 languages

         (e) The Church of Saint Elizabeth the Just

         (f) The Convent of the Sisters of Zion - Built in 1860

   e. The Garden Tomb - Protestant site since 1883

      (1) So identified by General Charles Gordon

      (2) Archaeologically, it is part of a complex of tombs dating to the eighth and seventh century B.C. and could not be Joseph's new tomb

      (3) It does not match any of the characteristics of Second Temple Period tombs

f. Gordon's Calvary - Protestant site since 1883

    (1) So identified by General Charles Gordan

    (2) Often based on typology

        (a) Located north of the city and Jesus would have been killed north of the Temple altar just as the animals were killed north of the altar

        (b) "Unless the types are wrong . . . [the Church of the Holy Sepulchre] should never have been taken as the site"

            i. The sacrifices were on the north side of the altar and the site is north of the city

            ii. But the Church of the Holy Sepulchre was located north of the Second Wall - Something Gordon did not know

    (3) Wrongly assumed that the Church was inside the city walls in Jesus' day

g. The Great Synagogue (1980) and the *Hechal Shlomo* (1953 - 1958) - The seat of the two chief rabbis of Israel

h. Hadassah Hospital - Contains the Chagall Windows: Twelve stained-glass windows portraying the Twelve Tribes of Israel

i. Haneviim Street - The Street of the Prophets

    (1) The Davidka Square - Where the Davidka mortar is placed

    (2) The Anglican Compound - Founded by the London Society for Promoting Christianity Among the Jews

    (3) The Christian and Missionary Alliance Church and House

    (4) The *Bikur Holim* Hospital

    (5) The German Hospital - Now part of the *Bikur Holim*

    (6) The Messianic Assembly - One of the oldest Messianic Congregations in Israel

    (7) The Russian Women's Hospice - Now *Yad Sarah*

    (8) *Beth Tavor* - The Swedish Theological Institute

    (9) The Ethiopian Consulate

    (10) The Italian Hospital - Now part of the Department of Education and Culture

    (11) The French Compound - Saint Joseph Convent and School

    (12) Off the Street of the Prophets

        (a) Ethiopia Street

            i. The home of Eliezer Ben Yehudah - The Father of Modern Hebrew

            ii. The Ethiopian Church

                a) The compound is known as "The Hill of Paradise"

    b) The Church is called "The Bond of Mercy"

    c) Begun by Ethiopian Emperor Johannes IV in 1882 and completed by Emperor Menelik II in 1893

(b) Bnai Brith Street - The Bnai Brith House built in 1902 to house the headquarters for that organization

(c) Ticho Lane

    i. Ticho House - Building built in 1868 by a wealthy Moslem named Hajj Rashid and acquired by Abraham and Anna Ticho in 1924, an eye doctor and artist respectively and now an artist house displaying her works

    ii. Rabbi Kook's House - The residence of the Chief Rabbi of Palestine: Abraham Isaac Hacohen Kook (1865-1936) and his *Yeshivah*

(d) Shivtei Yisrael Street

    i. The Church of Saint Paul

        a) Built in 1874 as an Anglican Church

        b) After 1948 it became part of the Finnish Messianic Center

    ii. The Finnish Compound - Site of Finnish school and a Messianic Congregation

j. Hebrew Union College - Built in 1963 to house the center of Reform Judaism in Israel

k. The Hebrew University

    (1) *Givat Ram* campus built in 1958 to replace the Mount Scopus campus during the period of 1948-1967

    (2) The Jewish National and University Library is the largest library in the Middle East and contains two million volumes

    (3) Contains the Jerusalem Botanical Gardens

l. Herod's Family Tomb

    (1) Burial place of Mariamne and their two sons

    (2) Discovered in 1892

m. The Israel Museum - The largest museum of Israel built in 1965 with three main wings: Archaeology, Judaica and Art

n. Jeremiah's Grotto - The supposed site of the writing of the Book of Lamentations

o. The Knesset - The Seat of Government built in 1966

p. *Mahaneh Yisrael* - The Second Quarter built outside the wall in 1864-1918

q. *Mahaneh Yehudah* - The largest open market in Jerusalem established in 1928

r. *Mea Shearim*

    (1) Meaning: One Hundred Gates

    (2) The fifth Jewish Quarter built outside the Old City walls in 1874–1882

    (3) Now inhabited by the Hasidim (Ultra-Orthodox) Community

    (4) Originally built as a rectangle with long blocks providing protection and at night it was closed by six gates

s. The *Menorah* - Seven branched bronze lampstand made by Beno Elkin and given as a gift by Great Britain to Israel depicting scenes from Jewish history

    (1) The First Branch

        (a) Isaiah and the Messianic Kingdom as prophesied in Isaiah 2:2-4

        (b) Rabban Yochanan Ben Zakkai and Yavneh (A.D. 70)

        (c) The Golden Age of Spanish Jewry (10th-11th century)

        (d) The Babylonian Captivity - Weeping by the waters of Babylon

    (2) The Second Branch

        (a) Ezra the Scribe - Reading the Law

        (b) Job and his three friends

        (c) The Talmud - Building a fence around the Law

        (d) The Aggadah - King Solomon going out to listen to the poetry of birds

    (3) The Third Branch

        (a) David and Goliath

        (b) Illegal immigration - Of Jews during the British Mandate (1917-1948)

        (c) Abraham the Patriarch - Purchasing the Cave of Machpelah

    (4) The Fourth (Central) Branch

        (a) Moses with Joshua and Hur against Amalek

        (b) The Tablets of the Ten Commandments

        (c) Rachel weeping for her children and Ruth, the Moabitess

        (d) Ezekiel and the Vision of the Dry Bones

        (e) The Warsaw Ghetto Revolt

        (f) "Hear O Israel" - Deuteronomy 6:4

        (g) Struggle and revival - The Jewish resettlement of the Land of Israel

    (5) The Fifth Branch

        (a) Simon Bar Cochba

    (b) The Messianic Hope - The Sun of Righteousness

    (c) Jacob wrestling with the Angel

(6) The Sixth Branch

    (a) Hillel the Elder - Teaching the Gentile while standing on one foot: "What is hateful to you do not to others. All the rest is commentary. Now go and study."

    (b) Rabbi Hanina ben Teradion - Burned to death while wrapped in a Torah scroll for teaching it in violation of Roman law

    (c) The Kabbalah - Jewish mysticism

    (d) The Halachah - Jewish religious law

(7) The Seventh Branch

    (a) Jeremiah and the Book of Lamentations

    (b) The Maccabees - Warring against the Syrian Greeks

    (c) The Hasidic Movement

    (d) Nehemiah rebuilding the walls of Jerusalem

(8) The verse crossing the first and seven branches is a quotation from Zechariah 4:6 - *Not by might, nor by power but by My spirit says Jehovah*

t. The Model of Ancient Jerusalem - At the Holy Land Hotel

(1) Replica of Jerusalem at the eve of its destruction - A.D. 66-70

(2) Completed in 1969

(3) Scale - 1:50

u. The Monastery of the Holy Cross

(1) By tradition, built where the tree grew out of which the cross of Jesus was made, which in turn was an off-shoot of the Tree of Life

(2) Built in the sixth century by King Tatian of Georgia

(3) Destroyed in A.D. 614 by the Persian invasion

(4) Rebuilt by Emperor Heraculus after the Byzantine reconquest

(5) Destroyed by the Fatimids under Caliph El Hakim in 1009

(6) Rebuilt in the 11th century by a Georgian monk

(7) Rebuilt by the Crusaders

(8) In the 13th century, Shota Rustareli, Georgia's most famous poet, wrote his epic, *Panther Skin*, here

(9) Destroyed by Sultan Baybars and turned into a mosque

(10) Returned to the Georgians in 14th century

(11) In 1643, it was reconstructed and renovated under Abbot Nikephorus

(12) Sold to the Greek Orthodox Church in 1858

(13) Housed a Greek Orthodox Seminary during 1885-1908 and was considered the best seminary in the Middle East

v. Mount Herzle - The Tomb of Theodore Herzle, the founder of the Zionist Movement, whose body was re-interred here in 1949

w. *Nahalat Shiva* - The third neighborhood built outside the wall in the 1870's

x. *Notre Dame* Hospice - Built in 1884-1904 by the French Assumptionist Fathers and was both a monastery and a hospice for pilgrims

y. The Pontifical Biblical Institute - Built in 1927, it is the only Jesuit Monastery in Israel

z. The Rockefeller Museum

(1) The Archaeological Museum of the Holy Land

(2) The first museum of archaeology in Israel built in 1930 - 1938 by the British Mandatory Government

aa. The Russian Compound

(1) The Third Wall extended to this point

(2) Served as the camp of the Second Roman Legion during the siege of Jerusalem under Titus

(3) At the First Crusade, Tancred attacked Jerusalem from this point

(4) During the Ottoman Turkish Period, it served as a parade ground and military race horse course

(5) Acquired by the Russian Orthodox Church in 1853 and buildings constructed between 1859-1889

(a) The Northern and Southern Gates - Built in 1890

(b) The Holy Trinity Cathedral - Dedicated in 1872 in the presence of then Prince (and later Czar) Nicholas and one of the first churches in Jerusalem to be built with bells

(c) The Duhoynia Russian Mission Building - Office and residence of the Muscovite Patriarchate built in 1863, now used as a courthouse

(d) The Sergei Imperial Hospice - Named after Prince Sergei Romanov, the son of Czar Alexander II, built in 1890 to house Russian pilgrims who were members of the nobility and had rooms for seventy guests

(e) The Elizabeth Hospice

i. Built in 1864 to house male pilgrims for as many as three hundred at a time

ii. Today it serves as a place of detention by the Israeli Police Department

(f) The Elizabeth Women's Hospice

   i. Built in 1864 to house women pilgrims and could accommodate 671 women at once

   ii. During the British Mandate it was turned into the Jerusalem Central Prison for Jewish underground prisoners and as many as 550 Jewish prisoners were incarcerated here

   iii. Now the Hall of Heroism and the Museum of the Underground Prisoners commemorating the heroes of the underground movement

(g) The Nicholas Hospice - Built in 1903 to house 1200 pilgrims

(h) The Russian Hospital and Pharmacy

   i. Built during 1863-1865

   ii. Used as a hospital by the Israeli Army during the War of Independence

   iii. Today it houses the Ministry of Health

(i) Russian Consulate Building

   i. Built in 1863 and used by the British as a maternity ward

   ii. 1949-1987 - Used as laboratory of the medical school of Hebrew University

   iii. Now the office of the Jerusalem Development Company

(6) During the British Mandate, the area was rented by the British Government

(7) In 1948, it was taken over by the Israeli Government to house the police department, law offices and courts and continues to function in this way till the present date

(8) In 1958, all of the buildings were purchased by the Israeli Government except for the Cathedral and the South Long Building of the mission

(9) The Finger of Og - Remains of a cracked pillar intended for the Herodian Temple

bb. The Saint George Cathedral

(1) The center of the Anglican Church in Israel

(2) Has a squared bell tower with four small towers imitating a Church in Oxford, England and named after King Edward VII

cc. The Sanhedrin Tombs - Second Temple burial caves with 71 burial niches

dd. The Shrine of the Book - Home of the Dead Sea Scrolls

ee. The Third Wall - The wall built by a Agrippa II in A.D. 44 to enclose the new Bethesda Suburb ff. The Tomb of the Kings

    (1) Located 2,625 feet north of the present wall

    (2) Misnamed since it was once thought to be the tombs of the Judean Kings

    (3) Another Jewish tradition made this the tomb of Kalba Sava, the father-in-law of Rabbi Akiba

    (4) Actually, the Tomb of Queen Helena of Adiabene who converted to Judaism in the first century and was buried here in A.D. 50

    (5) One of the sarcophagi found inside had the inscription, "Queen Saddan"

gg. The Tomb of Simon the Just

    (1) By tradition from the 14th century, it was believed to be the tomb of a Jewish High Priest from the third century B.C.

    (2) An inscription shows it to be the tomb of a Roman matron named Julia Sabina

hh. The Tourjeman Post - Site of the Mandelbaum Gate, the only crossing between East and West Jerusalem during 1948-1967 and now turned into a museum

ii. *Yad Vashem* - The memorial to the six millon Jews killed in the Holocaust

    (1) Name based on Isaiah 56:5 - *I will give in my house and within my walls a memorial* (yad) *and a name* (vashem)

    (2) The Historical Museum - The story of the Holocaust as told through photographs, documents and various artifacts arranged chronologically

    (3) The Hall of Names - The listing of names of those who perished as given by surviving friends and relatives. A total of three million names have been compiled

    (4) The Hall of Remembrance - Contains the Eternal Light and the names of 22 Nazi concentration and/or extermination camps

    (5) The Wall of Remembrance Plaza

        (a) The Warsaw Ghetto Revolt

        (b) The Last March

        (c) Hebrew: *In your blood live* - From Ezekiel 16:6

    (6) The Children's Memorial - In remembrance of the 1,500,000 children killed

    (7) The Avenue of the Righteous Gentiles

        (a) Carob trees (Saint John's Bread Trees) planted, when they came to visit Israel, by Gentiles who helped Jews during the Holocaust

        (b) Includes that of Corrie Ten Boom and Oscar Schindler

        (8) The Danish Boat - Responsible for saving 600 of the 8,000 Jews rescued by the Danish Underground Reserve

        (9) The Valley of the Destroyed Communities - Memorial of 5,000 destroyed communities with their names engraved on stone

  jj. *Yemin Moshe* and *Mishkenot Shaananim*

        (1) The first suburb to be built outside the wall in 1860 and 1892 respectively and thus the beginnings of the New City

        (2) The windmill was built by Moses Montefiore in 1857 to provide work for the residents of the New Quarter and it operated for 25 years

5. The Mountains Around Jerusalem - Psalm 125:2

  a. *Nabi Samwil*

        (1) 2,942 feet above sea level

        (2) Moslem Tomb of Samuel

           (a) This tradition began with the Byzantines

           (b) In A.D. 530, Emperor Justinian had a Church built here called Saint Samuel

           (c) The Crusaders built the *Saint Samuel de Shiloh* Church

           (d) In the 11th century, the Karaites built a synagogue here

           (e) In the 12th century, the Jews of Jerusalem built a synagogue here

           (f) In the 16th century, the Moslems took the site and built the present mosque on it

           (g) Today it is used as a synagogue

        (3) Possibly "the high place of Gibeon" where the Tabernacle of Jehovah stood - I Chronicles 16:39; 21:29

        (4) If so, this is the place where Solomon prayed - I Kings 3:4-14

  b. Mount Scopus

        (1) 2,720 feet above sea level

        (2) Site of the city of Nob

           (a) David ate the holy bread - I Samuel 21:1-9

           (b) It was the city of priests - I Samuel 22:19

           (c) The priests of this city were all killed by Saul - I Samuel 22:6-19

           (d) Taken by Sennacherib - Isaiah 10:32

           (e) Rebuilt after the return from Babylon - Nehemiah 11:32

           (f) In the Prophets: Isaiah 10:32

        (3) The camp of the Greeks during the Hellenistic Period and it was they who gave it this name - The place of the legendary meeting between the Jewish High Priest and Alexander the Great in 332 B.C.

(4) The military camp of Titus during the First Jewish Revolt was here

(5) Military camp of the Crusaders was here

(6) The Jerusalem War Cemetery (British Military Cemetery) - For those who fell in Palestine during World War I

(7) Original site of the Hebrew University founded in 1918 and inaugurated in 1925

(8) Original site of the Hadassah Hospital built in 1939

(9) After the War of Independence, the top of the mountain area was given to Israel but the entire bottom of the mountain was given to Jordan; hence there was no more access to the Hebrew University and Hadassah Hospital, necessitating the building of a new hospital and new campus elsewhere

(10) After the Six-Day War, the place came back under Jewish control and now serves as a second campus for the Hebrew University and a second Hadassah Hospital

(11) Jerusalem *Talmud*: He who sees Jerusalem from Scopus must tear his clothing [in grief]

c. Mount of Olives

(1) 2,680 feet above sea level

(2) 240 feet above the city of Jerusalem

(3) David came over this mountain when he fled from Absalom - II Samuel 15:30

(4) Hushai the Archite was sent back from the Mount of Olives to counteract the counsel of Ahitophel - II Samuel 15:30-37

(5) Ziba lied about Mephibosheth - II Samuel 16:1-5

(6) Fourth and final position of the Shechinah Glory in its departure from Israel - Ezekiel 11:23

(7) Jesus often resorted to it as a place of retreat - Matthew 26:30; Mark 14:26; Luke 21:37; 22:39

(8) The Olivet Discourse - Matthew 24:3-25:46; Mark 13:3-37; Luke 21:5-36

(9) He wept over Jerusalem from here - Luke 19:37-44

(10) The Ascension occurred from here - Acts 1:6-12

(11) At the time of the Second Coming and the Campaign of Armageddon, Jesus will return to this mountain and it will split - Zechariah 14:1-5

(12) It was once heavily wooded with olive trees providing oil for the Temple but these trees were cut down by the Romans to use for besieging Jerusalem in A.D. 68-70

(13) At the time of the Second Temple, it was the place of the Red Heifer Sacrifice

(14) During the Second Temple period, fires were kindled here to announce the New Moon

(15) On the Mount of Olives, the following things are to be found

    (a) Bethany and Bethphage - Matthew 21:1; Mark 11:1; Luke 19:29

    (b) The traditional tombs of Zechariah and Haggai - A tradition originating in the Middle Ages

    (c) The oldest Jewish graves and their desecrations by the Jordanian army

        i.   Jewish burials since the 15th century

        ii.   Contains about 70,000 Jewish graves

        iii. By Jewish tradition, the final resurrection will occur here

    (d) Augusta Victoria Hospital

        i.   Built in 1898 as a hospice for German pilgrims and named after the wife of Kaiser Wilhelm II

        ii.   During World War I, it served as the headquarters of General Pasha - The Ottoman Turkish military leader

        iii. During the British Mandate, it served as the residence of the British High Commissioner - 1920-1925

        iv. During World War II, it served as a British Military Hospital

        v.   The Church and bell tower were badly damaged in 1927 and only recently renovated and in use once again

        vi. In 1949, it was an UNRWA Hospital

        vii. Today, it is an Arab Hospital supported by the World Lutheran Organization

    (e) Gethsemane - Matthew 26:30-56; Mark 14:26-52; Luke 22:39-53; John 18:1-11

    (f) Modern Jewish graves including that of Menachem Begin and the 48 people killed in the Jewish Quarter in 1948

    (g) The Bethpage Chapel

    (h) The Church of the Ascension (Russian Orthodox)

        i.   The Church was built during 1870-1887 by the White Russians over earlier Crusader remains

        ii.   Now a monastery since 1907

    (i) The Dome of the Ascension

        i.   Originally a Byzantine and a Crusader Church

        ii.   Converted into a Moslem Mosque in 1187

(j) The *Pater Noster* Carmelite Sisters Convent

    i.   Contains the Lord's Prayer in eighty-two languages

    ii. Destroyed in the Persian Invasion but rebuilt by the Crusaders

    iii. Destroyed again by Saladin

    iv. Present Church built in 1875

(k) The Church of the *Eleona* - Where Jesus taught the Lord's Prayer to His disciples

(l) The Basilica of *Dominus Flevit* (Franciscan)

    i.   Where Jesus wept over Jerusalem - Luke 19: 41-44

    ii. The Church built in 1955 over Byzantine remains

    iii. Contains tombs and ossuaries of Jewish believers in the Messiah

(m) The Church of Mary Magdalene (Russian Orthodox)

    i.   Built in 1885-1888 by Czar Alexander III in memory of his mother

    ii. Marks the place where Jesus prayed in Gethsemane

    iii. By tradition, dating to the 14th century, Mary, the mother of Jesus, appeared to Thomas at this spot because he refused to believe that she had ascended into Heaven and dropped her girdle into his hands

(n) The Church of All Nations

    i.   Also known as The Church of the Agony

    ii. The present church built in 1919

    iii. Marks the spot where the disciples were left to pray in Gethsemane

(o) Mary's Tomb - The Church of the Assumption

    i.   The original was Byzantine built in the fourth-fifth century where Christian traditions claimed Mary was buried

    ii. The upper floor was added in the sixth century

    iii. It was destroyed by the Persian Invasion in A.D. 618

    iv. The present church was built by the Crusaders and given to the Benedictine Order

    v. Destroyed by Saladin in 1187 but rebuilt in the 18th century

    vi. It now belongs to the Greek Orthodox and the Armenians who share it with the Syrian and Coptic Church

(p) The Church of *Vivi Galilaei* (Greek Orthodox)

    i.   Meaning: "Men of Galilee"

    ii. Site of the Ascension

    iii. Site where Gabriel told Mary that she was about to die

    iv. Present building built in 1894

(q) Pelagia Cave

    i.   Jewish tradition - The Tomb of Huldah the Prophetess (II Kings 22:14-20)

    ii. Christian tradition - The Tomb of Pelagia, the fifth century ascetic of Antioch

    iii. Moslem tradition - Tomb of Rabia al-Addawyya of the eighth century

(r) The Grotto of Gethsemane

    i.   A burial cave hewn out in the Byzantine Period and also used during the Crusader Period and now turned into a chapel

    ii. Marks the betrayal of Judas

    iii. Controlled by the Franciscans since 1392

d. The Mount of Offense or Corruption or Scandal

   (1) It is 2,450 feet above sea level

   (2) Arabic names

      (a) *Ras el-Amud* - The Head of the Pillar

      (b) *Beten el-Hawa* - The Belly of the Winds

   (3) Solomon built three pagan temples to the gods of Ammon, Moab and Edom on this mount - I Kings 11:7-8

   (4) These temples were destroyed by Josiah - II Kings 23:13-14

   (5) Site of the town of Silwan - Arabic name derived from the nearby Pool of Siloam

   (6) Site of the Franciscan Custody of the Holy Land

e. The Mount of Evil Counsel (*Abu Tor*)

   (1) Arabic names

      (a) *Abu Tor*

      (b) *Gebel el-Mukabber* - Telescope Mountain

   (2) Served as the encampment for the Maccabees

   (3) It served as a Roman encampment during the First Jewish Revolt

   (4) Today it is occupied by Government House - The United Nations headquarters building in the Middle East

   (5) During the Six-Day War, the first decisive battle over East Jerusalem was fought here

   (6) Site of the Haas Promenade

    f.   Mount Zion

      (1) It is 2,510 feet above sea level

      (2) This was first settled at the end of the First Temple Period about the seventh century B.C.

      (3) The Upper City of New Testament times

      (4) The birthplace of the Messianic Jewish Movement

          (a) Here the Church was born

          (b) Here they met regularly and here the Jerusalem Council took place

          (c) After A.D. 70 the Church of Zion was built by Jewish believers and used by them until A.D. 135

      (5) The Byzantine Period

          (a) One of the first four churches built in the Holy Land, erected here by Constantine and called the Church of Mount Zion

          (b) Destroyed by the Persians in A.D. 614; the remains of which were found under the Dormition Abbey and the Cenacle

      (6) The Pilgrim of Bordeaux who visited Jerusalem in A.D. 333 reported the existence of seven synagogues on Mount Zion

      (7) The Crusader Period - The Church of Our Lady of Mount Zion was built over the ruins of the Byzantine Church

      (8) In 1267, Nahmanides (Ramban) built a synagogue here

      (9) The House of Caiaphas was here

          (a) The Church was built in 1145

          (b) The Armenian tradition puts the house of Caiaphas here

      (10) The Tomb of David

          (a) A tradition dating back to the 12th century put the Tomb of David here

          (b) The Crusaders built a church on this site

          (c) It was turned into a mosque after the Moslem reconquest

          (d) The Franciscans received it back during 1438-1453

          (e) In 1524, the Moslems turned the building into a mosque again and Jews were forbidden to enter until 1948

          (f) The tomb is marked by a large stone sarcophagus covered with a large red drape with the Star of David and topped by 22 solid silver Torah Crowns for the 22 kings who followed David

          (g) The niche behind the tomb is part of a wall of the ancient Messianic Congregation

(11) The Coenaculum (Cenacle)

  (a) Site of the traditional Upper Room where the Last Supper took place and where the descent of the Holy Spirit took place

  (b) Part of the 12th century Crusader Church of Our Lady of Mount Zion

  (c) In 1335, was given to the Franciscans who made repairs

  (d) In 1551, the Franciscans were expelled and it was turned into a mosque until 1948

  (e) Now marked by the Cenacle

(12) The Church of Peter of Galicantu (Roman Catholic - Assumptionist Fathers)

  (a) By Catholic tradition, the home of Caiaphas

  (b) Where Peter denied Christ

  (c) Site of a Byzantine Church destroyed by the Persians in A.D. 614

  (d) The Crusaders rebuilt the Church and first named it "Cock-Crowing"

  (e) The present Church was built in 1931

(13) The Chamber of Martyrs - A memorial to the victims of Nazi Germany

(14) The Dormitian Abbey

  (a) Benedictine Monastery marking where Mary went into her eternal sleep

  (b) Given as a gift to Kaiser Wilhelm II in 1898

  (c) The present building was built in 1906 - 1910 on the site where The Church of Mount Zion stood

(15) The Church of Saint Annas (Armenian)

  (a) Armenian site of the home of Annas, the father-in-law of Caiaphas

  (b) The Church was built in 1300 and called The Church of the Angels

  (c) It was renamed in 1350

(16) The Franciscan Convent - The Franciscans were only allowed to return to Mount Zion during the British Mandate and built this Monastery in 1936

(17) The Greek Orthodox Monastery

(18) The Bishop Gobat School and Protestant Cemetery

  (a) Was originally built in 1853 and named after the second Protestant Bishop in Jerusalem - Samuel Gobat

  (b) It was originally an Arab vocational school

        (c) Today it houses the Institute of Holy Land Studies

        (d) Buried in the Protestant Cemetery

           i.   The first two Protestant Bishops of Jerusalem

           ii. Flanders Petrie

           iii. Conrad Schick

           iv. The Spaffords - The founders of the American Colony

6. The Valleys of Jerusalem

   a. The Valley of Hinnom

      (1) Hebrew: *Gei Hinnom*, The Ravine of Hinnom

        (a) The valley of depravity and sin

        (b) The Greek term, *Gehenna,* arises from the Hebrew name of this valley

      (2) Arabic: *Wadi er-Rababeh* - Because here the shepherds played a one-stringed instrument called a *rababeh* while watching their flocks

      (3) The valley is about two miles long beginning at *Mahaneh Yehudah* Quarter until it runs into the Kidron Valley at Ein Rogel

      (4) Biblical History

        (a) Northern border of Judah - Joshua 15:8

        (b) Southern border of Benjamin - Joshua 18:16

        (c) Ahaz burned his children here - II Chronicles 28:3

        (d) Manasseh burned his children here - II Chronicles 33:6

        (e) Known as Topheth and was destroyed by Josiah - II Kings 23:10

        (f) Topheth was condemned by Jeremiah - Jeremiah 7:31-33; 19:1-15; 32:35

        (g) Northern point of the Judean return from Babylon - Nehemiah 11:30

        (h) Akeldama: The Field of Blood is located here - Matthew 27:5-10; Acts 1:18-19

           i.   The Byzantine Christian community used the area as a cemetery

           ii. The Crusader Order known as the Knights of Saint John used it for the same purpose and buried poor pilgrims here - The Hospitalers of Saint John built the Crusader Church of Saint Mary in A.D. 1143

           iii. The caves were used by hermits throughout history

           iv. The Monastery of Saint Onuphrius (Greek Orthodox) was built here in 1874 and named after an Egyptian hermit of the fourth century - Built on the remains of the Church of Saint Mary

     v.   Area contains about eighty burial caves from the Herodian Period including the likely tomb of Annas the High Priest

(5) The site of the Serpent's Pool of the first century

    (a) Josephus called it the Pool of the Eye of the Crocodile

    (b) Arabic: *Birkat es-Sultan* - The Sultan's Pool of Suleiman who renovated the pool and built a fountain on the dam

    (c) The Crusader Period: Called *Lacus Germanicus,* The Lake of Germain

    (d) Later, Christian pilgrims called it the Pool of Bathsheba thinking that this was where David saw her

    (e) The present pool was built by Mameluke Sultan Barkuk at the end of the 14th century

    (f) Measurements: 585 long by 220 feet wide by 39 feet deep

    (g) Today it is an amphitheater for outdoor performances

(6) The Mamilla Pool

    (a) Remains of an aqueduct from the Herodian Period that brought water from the Mamilla Pool to the Pool of the Towers in the Christian Quarter of the Old City now known as Hezekiah's Pool

    (b) The park contains an old Moslem cemetery

    (c) The pool measurements: 318 feet long by 213 feet wide by 21½ feet deep

    (d) This is soon to become a pedestrian mall

    (e) The Convent of *Saint Vincent de Paul* - First building to be built on this street in 1886

(7) *Hutzot Hayozer*: The Artist Quarter

    (a) Part of the neighborhood built by Jews from the Old City in 1892

    (b) Destroyed in 1948 and became part of no-man's land until 1967

(8) The Hinnom Cable - Manually operated cable car used during the War of Independence in 1948 to bring military supplies to Mount Zion and the wounded soldiers back over the valley

(9) The valley contains First and Second Temple Period, Byzantine and Crusader Tombs

(10) The Karaite Cemetery - Here since the 19th century

(11) Served as the eastern and southern end of the city until the building of *Mishkenot Shaananim*

    b. The Tyrophean (or Tyropoeon) Valley (The Central Valley)

       (1) Only reference to this name is in Josephus

       (2) It begins at the Morasha Quarter north of the city, running south through the Damascus Gate along Haggai Street (*el-Wad*), coming out the Dung Gate and runs into the Kidron Valley north of the Pool of Siloam and where Kidron and Hinnon Valleys join

       (3) At one time this valley lay between the Upper City on the west, the Temple Mount and the City of David on the east; running north-south and divides the Old City between east and west

       (4) Over the centuries it has been filled in and no longer appears as a valley within the city but does appear as a valley as it exits the Dung Gate

       (5) The present day street within the city called, in Arabic, *el-Wad*, Valley Street, follows the line of this valley which continues along the Western Wall and out the Dung Gate down to the City of David and the Pool of Siloam

    c. The Kidron Valley

       (1) Divides Jerusalem from Mount Scopus and the Mount of Olives

          (a) Begins at Simon the Just Valley (*Wadi el-Joz*) north of the city near Mea Shearim, running west to east

          (b) As it turns south, it becomes the Kidron

          (c) The deepest and longest valley in Jerusalem

          (d) The valley winds for 21 miles to the Dead Sea

          (e) Arabic: *Wadi en-Nar*, The Valley of Fire

       (2) Biblical History

          (a) David fled from Absalom via the Kidron - II Samuel 15:23

          (b) The two priests of Zadok and Abiather were sent back to Jerusalem from this valley - II Samuel 15:24-29

          (c) Marked Solomon's limitations to Shimei's travels - I Kings 2:36-38

          (d) Asa destroyed his mother's idol in the Kidron - I Kings 15:13; II Chronicles 15:16

          (e) Josiah destroyed the idols at Kidron - II Kings 23:4-7, 12

          (f) Hezekiah destroyed uncleanness of the Temple in the Kidron Brook - II Chronicles 29:16; 30:14

          (g) Jesus crossed it to get to Gethsemane - John 18:1

          (h) In the future, it will be characterized by holiness - Jeremiah 31:40

(i) The section of the valley that parallels the wall and the Mount of Olives, also known as the Valley of Jehoshaphat where the Gentiles will be judged - Joel 3:1-3, 12, 14; Matthew 25:31-46

(3) The Church of Saint Stephen - A Greek Orthodox Church dedicated to Stephen, the first martyr

(4) The Jebusite Wall - The remains of the Davidic Period of the city

(5) The Waters of the Kidron Valley

  (a) The Spring of Gihon (*Umm al-Daraj*)

    i. From a word meaning "to cough" since the spring "coughs" up its water six to eight times a day

    ii. Also known as the Dragon's Well - Nehemiah 2:13

    iii. Arabic: *Ein Sitti Miryam*, Saint Mary's Spring, based on the Crusader tradition that here Mary came to fetch water and where she washed the swaddling clothes

    iv. Arabic: *Ein Umm ed-Daraj*, The Spring of the Mother of Steps, because of the bedrock steps leading down to the spring

    v. Solomon was crowned by this spring - I Kings 1:32-48

    vi. Shaft through which David took the city - II Samuel 5:8

    vii. Hezekiah's Tunnel was begun and continued for 1,758 feet to the Pool of Siloam - II Kings 20:20; II Chronicles 32:30

    viii. Manasseh built a wall in this area - II Chronicles 33:14

  (b) The Pool of Siloam

    i. Marked the end of Hezekiah's Tunnel - II Kings 20:20; II Chronicles 32:30

    ii. Zedekiah escaped through this tunnel - II Kings 25:4

    iii. Rebuilt in the days of Nehemiah - Nehemiah 2:14; 3:15

    iv. Mentioned in Isaiah's prophecies in 8:5 and 22:9-11

    v. Jesus' healing of the man born blind occurred here - John 9:1-41

    vi. The Tower of Siloam fell - Luke 13:4-5

    vii. In the Second Temple Period, this was where the ceremony of the Drawing of the Water on the Feast of Tabernacles took place and so it became the background to Messiah's statement in John 7:37

    viii. In the fifth century, Empress Eudocia (A.D. 444-460) built a church over the pool called Our Savior the Illuminator - Destroyed by the Persians in A.D. 614 and never rebuilt but turned into a mosque

    (c) Ein Rogel

        i.   At the point of the juncture of the Hinnom and Kidron Valleys located 340 feet below the Temple Compound and about 120 feet deep

        ii. Northern border of Judah - Joshua 15:7

        iii. Southern border of Benjamin - Joshua 18:16

        iv. The loyal spies for David hid here and learned the news to report to David - II Samuel 17:17-21

        v.   Adonijah's attempt to gain the throne from here - I Kings 1:9, 41-53

        vi. Arabic: *Bir-Ayyub*, The Well of Job, because of an Arab tradition that Job was healed after washing here

  (6) The Tombs

    (a) The Tomb (or Pillar) of Absalom (Traditional)

        i.   Carved out of bedrock and is 26 feet high

        ii. Jewish name based on II Samuel 18:18

        iii. Arabic: *Tantur Firaon*, Pharaoh's Crown

        iv. The structure dates only to the Hasmonean Period

    (b) The Tomb of Jehoshaphat (Traditional) - Behind the Pillar of Absalom

    (c) The Tomb of Saint James (Traditional)

        i.   From the first century B.C.

        ii. Arabic: *Diwan Firaon*, Pharaoh's Divan

        iii. Jewish Tradition - The house "set apart" for King Uzziah after he was stricken with leprosy and expelled from Jerusalem in II Chronicles 26:21

        iv. In A.D. 352, it was converted by monks into a church named after James; hence, its traditional name

        v.   Inscription shows that this is actually the family tomb of the priestly line of Hezir mentioned in I Chronicles 24:15 and Nehemiah 10:20-21: "This is the tomb and monument of Alexander, Hannioch, Yoezer, Judah, Simon, Johanan, the sons of Joseph, the son of Ored, Joseph and Eliezer, sons of Hanniah, priests of the Hezir family."

    (d) The Tomb or Pyramid of Zechariah (Traditional)

        i.   Built in the first century with a roof shaped like a pyramid

        ii. Jewish Tradition - The Tomb of the Zechariah of II Chronicles 24:20

        iii. Christian Tradition - The Zechariah who was the father of John the Baptist

        iv. Arabic: *Qabar Jose Firaon* - The Tomb of
            Pharaoh's Wife

   (7) The Church of Saint Stephen (Greek Orthodox) - Built in
       1960 over the traditional place of the stoning of Stephen

7. The City of David - The Jerusalem of David's Day

  a. Jebusite remains

  b. Remains of David's Jerusalem

  c. Warren's Shaft: The Jebusite water shaft - Shaft through which
      David took the city - II Samuel 5:8

8. The Walls and Gates of Jerusalem - Psalm 48:12-14

  a. The History of Jerusalem's Walls

   (1) Solomon built a wall around Jerusalem - I Kings 3:1; 9:15

   (2) Broken by Joash, king of Israel - II Kings 14:13;
       II Chronicles 25:23

   (3) Fortified by Uzziah - II Chronicles 26:9

   (4) The wall by Ophel was strengthened by Jotham -
       II Chronicles 27:3

   (5) It was further strengthened by Hezekiah - II Chronicles 32:5

   (6) Manasseh built the outer wall to the City of David -
       II Chronicles 33:14

   (7) Destroyed by Babylon - II Kings 25:10; II Chronicles 36:19;
       Jeremiah 39:8; 53:14

   (8) Built up by Zerubbabel - Ezra 4:13; 5:9

   (9) Further greatly rebuilt by Nehemiah - Nehemiah 2:13-4:23

  (10) More of the wall was built throughout the Hasmonean
       Period and further strengthened by Herod the Great

  (11) Third wall was built by Agrippa II in A.D. 44 on the crest
       overlooking the Simon the Just Valley (*Wadi el-Joz*)

  (12) Destroyed by the Romans in A.D. 70

  (13) From A.D. 70 until the end of the third century, the city
       was not surrounded by a wall

  (14) The city was rebuilt as *Aelia Capitolina* under Hadrian in
       A.D. 135 but the wall was built at the end of the third
       century with four main gates, one on each side and though
       their Roman names are not known, they correspond to the
       modern gates

     (a) North - Damascus Gate

     (b) West - Jaffa Gate

     (c) East - Lion's Gate

     (d) South - Zion Gate

(15) By the end of the Byzantine Period, the city wall had six gates

    (a) David's Gate - Now the Jaffa Gate

    (b) Saint Stephen's Gate - Now the Damascus Gate

    (c) The Dung Gate

    (d) The Jericho Gate - Now the Lion's Gate

    (e) Two additional gates around Mount Zion

(16) The Arab invasion further strengthened the wall and later the Crusader Kingdom built segments of the wall

(17) The present wall was built by Suleiman II the Magnificent in 1535-1542, often on foundations of earlier walls

    (a) It is 2½ miles in circumference

    (b) It averages between 34-38 feet high (from a low of 16 feet to a high of 50 feet)

    (c) It averages 10-15 feet thick at the base

    (d) The top of the wall has a paved path that can be reached by steps

    (e) It has 35 square towers - Six on the southern and eastern walls, eight on the western wall and 15 on the northern wall, which was the weakest

(18) Throughout Jerusalem's history, there have been angelic messengers standing on the wall - Isaiah 62:6-7

b. The Western Wall

(1) The Jaffa Gate

    (a) Hebrew: Jaffa Gate - For the road to Jaffa goes from here

    (b) Early Arabic name: *Bab Mihrab David*, The Gate of David's Prayer Niche, because of the mosque located in the citadel

    (c) Modern Arabic: *Bab el Khalil*, The Gate of the Friend, for it leads to Hebron

    (d) Byzantine and Crusader name: *Porte David*, The Gate of David, because of its proximity to the Tower of David in the Citadel

    (e) At various times it was also known as the Bethlehem Gate, for it also leads to Bethlehem

    (f) Omar took the city at this gate in A.D. 637

    (g) The present Turkish Gate was built in 1538 on the remains of the previous Crusader Gate

    (h) The hole in the wall by the Jaffa Gate was made in 1898 so that Wilhelm II of Germany could enter in his royal carriage

    (i) Through this gate, General Allenby walked on foot; marking the British conquest of Jerusalem in 1917

    (j) Closed - 1948-1967 during the division of the city

(k) It opens on the *Omar Ibn Khattab Square*

    i.   In the 19th century, it was the central business district of the Old City

    ii. The Grand New Hotel - Built in 1889 by the Greek Orthodox Church

    iii. The Petra Hotel - Built in the 19th century by a wealthy Jew and originally named after him: The Amdursky Hotel

    iv. The Austrian Post Office - The first of several foreign post offices and which now houses the Christian Information Center

    v. The two tombs are of Suleiman's architects who built the wall and were then executed by him - the only tombs to be found within the wall

    vi. Now also called the Jaffa Gate Square

(2) The Citadel of David

  (a) Originally surrounded by a wall

  (b) Site of David's Tower

    i.   In the Byzantine, early Moslem and Crusader Periods, the name was applied to the Tower of Phasael of the Herodian Palace

    ii. In the 19th century, it was applied to the minaret

  (c) Area of the three-towered guard compound of Herod the Great's palace

  (d) The present walls and towers were mostly built in the Middle Ages with additions during the Ottoman-Turkish period

  (e) During the Mameluke Period, it was fortified and served as the home of the governor

  (f) The modern citadel gate was built by Suleiman the Magnificent in 1531-1532

  (g) From the steps of the Citadel, General Allenby officially took control of the city for the British on December 11, 1917

  (h) The historical periods discovered

    i.   The First Temple Period

    ii. The Herodian Period

    iii. The Byzantine Period

    iv. The Early Moslem Period

    v. The Crusader Period

    vi. The Mameluke Period

    vii. The Ottoman Turkish Period

c. The North Wall

   (1) The New Gate

     (a) Arabic: *Bab es-Sultan Abdul Hamid*, The Gate of the Sultan after Abdul Hamid II

     (b) It was built in 1899 to give an outlet from the Christian Quarter of the city towards the new Christian settlements outside the city

     (c) Closed - 1948-1967

   (2) The Shechem Gate

     (a) The largest of the city gates

     (b) Built at the upper reaches of the Tyrophean Valley

     (c) Hebrew: Shechem Gate - Because the road leads to Shechem

     (d) The Byzantine Period: Saint Stephen's Gate - Due to one tradition that he was stoned here

     (e) Middle Ages: Jews called it Abraham's Gate

     (f) Arabic: Damascus Gate - Because it leads to Damascus

     (g) Arabic: *Bab el-Ammud*, The Gate of the Pillar (column)

       i. The Madaba Map shows a pillar just inside the gate of *Aelia Capitolina*

       ii. This was a 72 foot high column and the start of the Roman milage distances to other places

     (h) The present gate is on top of two others, which would be those of Herod the Great and Hadrian

     (i) The Roman Plaza: The Gate of *Aelia Capitolina* built by Hadrian and marked the beginning of the Cardo at the Hadrianic Damascus Gate

   (3) King Solomon's Quarries - The Cave of Zedekiah

     (a) The name was given to it by freemasons because of their belief that this was the place where Solomon quarried stones for the Temple (I Kings 5:15-17; 6:7) and the freemasons began holding ceremonies in this cave

     (b) Also known as the Cave of Zedekiah, for tradition says he escaped through this cave - II Kings 25:4-5; Jeremiah 52:7-8

     (c) Moslem Tradition: Here Korah and his followers were swallowed up by the earth - Numbers 16:32

     (d) It goes about 700 feet under the Moslem Quarter with a width of about 300 feet and a height of 45 feet

     (e) It extends from the wall until almost to the Via Dolorosa

(f) Here was discovered an etching of a winged cherub which helped date the original quarrying to the First Temple Period

(g) Used as a quarry throughout the centuries until it was blocked and forgotten

(h) It was re-discovered by an American, James Turner Barclay in 1854

(i) Sealed shut during the Jordanian Period - 1948-1967

(j) It was re-opened by Israel in 1968 and renovated in 1985

(4) Herod's Gate

    (a) The main gate for the market area of the Old City

    (b) Given this name because a tradition from the Middle Ages places this as the area of the palace of Herod Antipas

    (c) Arabic: *Bab Es-Zahira*, The Gate of Flowers

d. The East Wall

(1) The Lion's Gate

    (a) Known as the Lion's Gate because of four lions engraved into the upper segment of the gate

        i. According to legend, Suleiman the Magnificent put the lions there due to a dream that he had - If he did not build the walls of Jerusalem, he would be devoured by lions

        ii. It is believed by some that these are panthers put in by Sultan Baybars during the Mameluke Period in the 13th century

    (b) Also known as Saint Stephen's Gate, for it is believed that Stephen was stoned outside this gate

    (c) Arabic: *Bab Sitti Miriam*, The Gate of Our Lady Mary, because it leads to the Church of Mary's Tomb

    (d) Arabic: *Bab el-Asbat*, The Gate of the Tribes

    (e) The Gate of Jehoshaphat - A medieval Christian name since it led to the Valley of Jehoshaphet

    (f) Modern Arabic name: *Bab er-Riha*, The Jericho Road, a medieval Arabic name

    (g) In the Six-Day War this was the gate that the Israelis penetrated in the battle for the city

(2) The Golden Gate

    (a) Arabic: *Bab el-Daheriyeh*, The Eternal Gate

        i. On the site of the Susa Gate of the Herodian City

        ii. The Arabic name is probably a corruption of *horaia*, the Greek word meaning "beautiful" (Acts 3:1-2)

      (b) Jewish Tradition - The Shushan Gate of the Temple Compound

         i.   Because of this belief, here the Jews came to pray

         ii. When the area became a Moslem cemetery in the Ayyubid Period, Jews could no longer pray there and so began to pray at the Western Wall

      (c) Christian Tradition - The Beautiful Gate

         i.   Where Jesus entered on Palm Sunday - John 12:13

         ii. Where Peter healed the cripple - Acts 3:1-6

      (d) The gate is composed of two arches

         i.   The North Arch: *Bab el-Tobeh,* The Gate of Repentance

         ii. The South Arch: *Bab el-Rahmeh*, The Gate of Mercy

      (e) Built in the fifth or sixth century by the Byzantines

      (f) By 629, it was in ruins and rebuilt by Heraclius

      (g) 810 - Closed by Arabs

      (h) 1102 - Reopened by Crusaders but only for the yearly occasions

      (i) 1187 - Walled up by the Ayyubids

      (j) It was closed in 1546 - Re-walled by Suleiman

   (3) The Pinnacle of the Temple

      (a) The Southeast corner of the city wall and the Temple Compound

      (b) Highest point from the top of the wall to the ground measuring 216 feet

      (c) It is the site of the second temptation of Jesus - Matthew 4:5-7

  e. The South Wall

   (1) The Single Gate

      (a) Crusader-built gate

      (b) Led to Solomon's Stables

      (c) Sealed by the Ayyubids

   (2) The Triple Gate

      (a) The Eastern Huldah Gates

      (b) The present gate is of Umayyad origin in the seventh century but it is in the same place as the Herodian Gates

      (c) Now sealed

   (3) The Double Gate

      (a) The Western Huldah Gates

      (b) Now sealed

(4) The Dung Gate

    (a) The lowest of all the gates

    (b) Arabic: *Bab el-Magharibeh*, The Gate of the Moors, because it once led to the Moors neighborhood of the Old City

    (c) Arabic: *Bab Silwan*, The Gate of Silwan, because it faces the Village of Silwan

    (d) Since the second century, it was the gate from which waste was dumped

    (e) Leads out into the Tyrophean Valley

    (f) Renovated in 1985

    (g) Nearby to the west is an ancient blocked gate reopened in 1995

        i. Original builders of this gate are unknown

            a) Many believe this to be the "Tanner's Gate" built in the 12th century by the Crusaders

            b) Others believe this to be part of an Ayyubite watch tower built in the 13th century

        ii. It is located at the southern end of the Cardo that bisected Byzantine Jerusalem from north to south

        iii. It was blocked up when the Turks rebuilt the wall in the 16th century and had remained blocked until 1995

(5) The Zion Gate

    (a) Built in 1541

    (b) Called by this name because it was the gate for the Jewish Quarter leading out to Mount Zion

    (c) Arabic: *Bab Harat al-Yahud*, The Gate of the Jewish Quarter

    (d) Arabic: *Bab el-Nabi Daoud*, The Gate of David the Prophet, because it leads out into the area where David's Tomb is located

    (e) Today, it faces the area of the Upper City of New Testament times

f. Biblical and Ancient Gates

(1) The Gate of Ephraim - Along the North Wall

    (a) II Kings 14:13

    (b) II Chronicles 25:23

    (c) Nehemiah 8:16

    (d) Nehemiah 12:39

(2) The Fish Gate - Along the north wall and possibly same as the Gate of Ephraim

    (a) II Chronicles 33:14

    (b) Nehemiah 12:39

(3) The Sheep Gate - In the northeastern part of Jerusalem near the Antonia Fortress

    (a) Place where sheep were bought and sold

    (b) Especially sheep used for sacrifice

    (c) Nehemiah 3:1, 32

    (d) Nehemiah 12:39

    (e) John 5:2

(4) The Gate of Benjamin - In the Northeast part of the city and possibly the same as the Sheep Gate

    (a) Jeremiah 20:2

    (b) Jeremiah 37:13-18

    (c) Jeremiah 38:7

    (d) Zechariah 14:10

(5) The Fountain Gate or the Gate of the Spring - Along the eastern wall of the City of David which led to the Gihon Spring

    (a) Nehemiah 2:14

    (b) Nehemiah 3:15

    (c) Nehemiah 12:37

(6) The Casemate Wall Gate or the Gate Between the Two Walls - Located at the Southeastern part of the city

    (a) II Kings 25:4

    (b) Jeremiah 39:4

    (c) Jeremiah 52:7

(7) The Gate of the Waters (The Water Gate) - At the far southeastern part of Jerusalem where there was much water since that is where the Kidron, Hinnom and Tyrophean Valleys came together

    (a) Perhaps the same as the Casemate Wall Gate

    (b) Nehemiah 3:26

    (c) Nehemiah 12:37

    (d) Nehemiah 8:1, 16

(8) The Potsherd Gate - Located on the southern wall toward the southeastern corner

    (a) Led to Ein Rogel and Topheth

    (b) Jeremiah 19:2

(9) The Dung Gate - On the south wall and may be the same as the Potsherd Gate

  (a) Nehemiah 2:13

  (b) Nehemiah 3:13-14

  (c) Nehemiah 12:31

(10) The Gate of the Essenes - On the south wall toward the west

  (a) Mentioned by Josephus

  (b) Open to a road that went to the Kidron and the Dead Sea near Qumran

(11) The Garden Gate - On the northwestern side of the city

  (a) Mentioned by Josephus

  (b) May be the Gate of Hebrews 13:12

(12) The Corner Gate - On the northwest side and may be the same as the Garden Gate

  (a) II Kings 14:13

  (b) II Chronicles 25:23

  (c) II Chronicles 26:9

  (d) Zechariah 14:10

(13) The Valley Gate

  (a) II Chronicles 26:9

  (b) Nehemiah 2:13

  (c) Nehemiah 3:13

(14) The Old Gate

  (a) Nehemiah 3:6

  (b) Nehemiah 12:39

(15) The Gate of the Guard

  (a) Nehemiah 3:25

  (b) Nehemiah 12:39

(16) The Horse Gate

  (a) II Kings 11:16

  (b) II Chronicles 23:15

  (c) Nehemiah 3:28

  (d) Jeremiah 31:40

(17) The East Gate - Nehemiah 3:29

(18) The Gate of Hammiphkad - Nehemiah 3:31

9. Jerusalem: The Old City Interior

   a. Circumference: Two and one-half miles around

   b. Divided into four quarters: Jewish, Christian, Armenian and Moslem quarters with a total population of 27,000

     (1) The Jewish Quarter - The southeast section of the city

       (a) History

         i. First settled by the Kings of Judah in the eighth century B.C.

         ii. Resettled during the Hasmonean Period until destroyed in A.D. 70

         iii. Rebuilt as a Jewish Quarter in the seventh century following the Arab Conquest but driven out by the Crusaders in the 12th century

         iv. Rebuilt again in 1400 in its present location

         v. Population increased with the Spanish Expulsion in 1492 and the Turkish Conquest in 1517

         vi. By 1850, the Jewish Quarter had 23 synagogues

         vii. In 1875, the Jewish population was 15,000

         viii. With the building of Jewish neighborhoods outside the wall, the Jewish population began to decrease

         ix. By the time of the War of Independence, the Jewish Quarter only had 1,700 Jews

         x. Destroyed in 1948 by the Jordanian Legion but rebuilt after 1967

         xi. Now houses about 5,000 residents

       (b) The Main Street: The Jewish Quarter Road

       (c) Borders

         i. South - The Wall between the Zion and Dung Gates

         ii. East - The Western Wall

         iii. North - The Street of the Chain

         iv. West - The Armenian Quarter

       (d) The Cardo

         i. The remains of the main north-south street of *Aelia Capitolina* built in the second century

         ii. Extends from the Damascus Gate to the Zion Gate

         iii. Contained the Crusader Market

         iv. Contains the City Wall (the First Wall) from the First and Second Temple Periods

    (e) Hezekiah's Wall - The Broad Wall

        i.   Built by Hezekiah - II Chronicles 32:5

        ii. Mentioned in Nehemiah 3:8 and 12:38

        iii. Part of the northern fortifications

            a) Seven yards wide

            b) About 215 feet long

    (f) The Burnt House - Remains of the A.D. 70 destruction of the house belonging to the priestly family known as Bar Kathros

    (g) The *Hurbah* Synagogue

        i.   Originally a courtyard for Ashkenazi Jews built in 1700 by the followers of a Polish Kabbalist, Rabbi Yehudah He-Chasid, who died five days after arriving into Jerusalem

        ii. Destroyed by Arabs in 1721 and, therefore, named *Hurbah*, meaning "ruin," and remained so for 90 years

        iii. The synagogue was built in 1856-1864 - It became the tallest synagogue in the Jewish Quarter and the center of the Ashkenazi community and was called Beit Yaakov Synagogue but still referred to as "*Hurbah*"

        iv. The synagogue was destroyed on May 27, 1948 by the Jordanians who blew it up by placing explosives on the dome and therefore again appropriately named as "*Hurbah*"

        v.   The full name: The *Hurbah* of Rabbi Yehudah He-Chasid

    (h) The Ramban Synagogue

        i.   Named after Rabbi Moishe Ben Nahman (Nahmanides) who came to Jerusalem in 1267 and established a synagogue on Mount Zion

        ii. The synagogue was moved within the walls and within the Jewish Quarter in 1400 and named after him and became the only synagogue in the Jewish Quarter

        iii. The mosque overshadowing the synagogue was built by a Jew who converted to Islam; laying the seeds of conflict

        iv. Destroyed by Moslems in 1474 but rebuilt

        v.   The Jews were forbidden to worship in the synagogue in 1588

        vi. For 380 years, it was used as a workshop

(i) The Four Sephardic Synagogues

   i. The center of the Sephardic community from the 16th century until 1948

   ii. Built below ground level contrary to Jewish custom in order to be inconspicuous and avoid Moslem wrath

   iii. Last position held by Jewish defenders of the Jewish Quarter before its fall in 1948

   iv. The Synagogues

      a) The Prophet Elijah Synagogue

         i) Built in 1588 when it became forbidden for Jews to use the Ramban Synagogue

         ii) Original name was "The Holy Congregation of the Talmud Torah" because a *yeshivah* was here

         iii) Renamed in 1874 when the *yeshivah* was moved to another location

         iv) The new name was based on a legend that Elijah appeared as the 10th male to form a *minyan* and then disappeared

         v) Today it is being used as an Ashkenazi synagogue

      b) The Yochanan Ben Zakkai Synagogue

         i) Built in 1615 and named "The Great Holy Congregation"

         ii) The present name given after 1850

         iii) The place where the Sephardic Chief Rabbi assumes his office

      c) The Central Synagogue

         i) This was originally the women's courtyard for the second synagogue

         ii) It was built as a separate synagogue in 1750

      d) The Istanbul Synagogue

         i) Built by Turkish Jews in 1764

         ii) Used by Ashkenazi Jews when they could no longer worship in the *Hurbah*

(j) Saint Mary's German Hospice

   i. From the 12th century built for German pilgrims

   ii. To provide for German pilgrims who could not speak the official language: French

(k) The Archaeological Garden

(l) The Anan Ben David Synagogue: Karaite Synagogue - Built after 1400 and became the center of the Karaite community

(m) The *Nea* Church

    i. Full original name: The New Church of Mary - Called by the local population as simply, "The Nea"

    ii. Built by Emperor Justinian in A.D. 543 just off the Cardo

    iii. Measures 245 x 373 feet - The largest church of Jerusalem at that time

    iv. Destroyed in A.D. 614 by the Persians

    v. Destroyed again by an earthquake in the eighth century

(n) The Herodian Quarter

    i. Part of the Upper City of the first century

    ii. The wealthy class of the Herodian Period

    iii. Completely destroyed in A.D. 70

(o) The *Batei Mahsei*, The Shelter Houses

    i. Also known as the *Deutschplatz*, The German Square

    ii. Large square built by German and Dutch Jews between 1860-1890 to provide houses for one hundred poor immigrants

    iii. Residents called it *Harechavah Hayeshanah*, The Old Square

    iv. The place of the surrender of the Jewish Quarter to the Jordanians on May 28, 1945

    v. Contains the Rothschild House

        a) Used as the Jordanian military headquarters - 1948-1969

        b) Now houses the Jewish Quarter Development Company

    vi. The ruins in the courtyard date from the first century but were brought here from other parts of the city

(p) The *Galed* - The Memorial to the Forty-Eight

    i. Commemorates 48 residents of the Jewish Quarter who fell in the fighting for the Jewish Quarter in 1948

    ii. The bodies were buried here contrary to Jewish law since it was dangerous to take the bodies outside the wall

    iii. After the Six-Day War, they were reburied on the Mount of Olives on August 4, 1967

(q) The Israelite Tower

    i.   A gate tower of the First Temple Period - Destroyed by the Babylonians in 586 B.C.

    ii. Remains of the Hasmonian fortifications

(r) The *Tiferet Yisrael* Synagogue

    i.   Built in 1862-1872 for the Chassidim by Nissan Bak

    ii. In November 1869, Emperor Franz Josef of Austria donated the money to finish the roof

    iii. At the time, it was part of the unique skyline for the Old City

    iv. Destroyed by the Jordanians in 1948

(s) The Bazaar - From the Crusader Period but the exact purpose is unknown

(t) The Temple Institute - Run by The Faithful of the Temple Mount, a group making objects for the Third Temple

(u) The Western Wall (Wailing Wall)

    i.   Remains of the Western Temple Compound Wall - The lower seven Herodian stone layers

    ii. The Turkish Sultan, Suleiman the Magnificent, gave a seventy foot section of the wall in a narrow alley as a place for Jewish prayer

    iii. After the Six-Day War in 1967, a large space in front of the Wall was made and widened from the original seven foot wide alley-lane

    iv. There are 19 more courses or layers of Herodian stone below ground level for 68 feet

    v. Total length: 1,552 feet

    vi. The plaza section is 280 feet

(v) Wilson's Arch - The remains of an arch that supported a bridge across the Tyrophean Valley

(w) Robinson's Arch - An arch which supported a staircase from the Tyrophean Valley into the Temple Compound

(x) The Western Wall Tunnel

    i.   A tunnel underneath the Moslem Quarter and runs for 400 yards along the continuation of the Western Wall

    ii. An archway (now blocked) leads to another tunnel that in turn may lead to where the Holy of Holies stood

    iii. Uncovered was the largest stone used for a building block measuring about 40 feet long, 12 feet wide, 13½ feet high and weighing 570 tons

(2) The Christian Quarter - The northwest section of the city

  (a) Development

     i. In the 11th century, the Fatimids obligated the Christians to fortify the city wall in this section

     ii. The Byzantine Emperor assisted them by providing the necessary funds

     iii. In a treaty between the Fatimids and the Byzantine Emperor, this section was given to Christians as a dwelling place and the Moslem inhabitants moved to other areas of the city

  (b) The Main Roads

     i. The Christian Quarter Road

     ii. The Greek Orthodox Patriarchate Road

     iii. The Greek Catholic Patriarchate Road

     iv. The Latin Patriarchate Road

  (c) The Monastery of Savior

     i. Franciscan Monastery which headquarters the Custody of the Holy Land entrusted to the Franciscans by Pope Clement IV in 1342

     ii. Originally founded on Mount Zion in 1335, they were expelled in 1552

     iii. In 1560, they purchased the site from Georgian Christians who had a small nunnery called in Arabic *Deir el-Ammun*

     iv. Sits on 2½ acres of land near the New Gate

  (d) The Latin Patriarchate - Established by the First Crusade in 1099

     i. The Seat of the Latin Patriarch - The highest Catholic position in Israel in charge of Catholic sites in Israel, Jordan and Cyprus

     ii. The Roman Catholic Church in Israel has 170 churches and 180 religious institutions

     iii. Jerusalem has 17 Catholic Orders: Nine for monks and eight for nuns

     iv. Israel has 21 monasteries and convents, two located in the Old City

  (e) *Casa Nova* Hospice - A Catholic hospice built by the Franciscans in 1866

(f) The Greek Catholic Patriarchate - Established in 1772

    i. Originally established in Antioch, Turkey, when it broke away from the Greek Orthodox Church

    ii. In 1846, the Pope appointed a patriarch for Jerusalem

    iii. The headquarters was built in 1848

(g) The Greek Orthodox Patriarchate - Established in 451 by the Council of Chalcedon and appointed the Custodian of the Holy Sites of the Holy Land

    i. By tradition, it sits on the site of the mother of churches - The Church of James, the first bishop of Jerusalem

    ii. The earliest buildings date from the fourth century but most of the present structure dates from the 17th century with renovations in the 20th century

    iii. After the Arab Conquest in 638, the Greek Patriarchate continued to function as custodian

    iv. With the establishment of the Crusader Kingdom in 1099, the Patriarchate moved to Constantinople and returned to Jerusalem in 1187 with Saladin's conquest and the eviction of the Roman Catholics

    v. The Catholics were allowed to return in the 14th century and hostility has continued until this day

    vi. The Patriarchate sits on 3½ acres of ground making it the largest block in the Christian Quarters

    vii. Greek Orthodox Churches in the Quarter

        a) Saint Theodorus

        b) Saint Basiliceus

        c) Saint Michael

        d) Saint Catherine

        e) Saint Eptimius

        f) Saint Nicholas

(h) The Greek Orthodox Patriarchate Museum - Opened in 1980

(i) The Ethiopian Patriarchate - Located in a two-story church and convent built in 1891

(j) The Coptic Patriarchate

    i. They have a church and hospice behind the Church of the Holy Sepulchre

    ii. The Coptics are a very early Christian sect originating in Egypt and the name is a corruption of the Greek word for Egypt: *Aegyptios*

    iii. First settled in Jerusalem in the Byzantine Period

iv. Many fought against the Crusaders as soldiers in Saladin's Army

v. The Patriarchate is located in the Church of Saint Antony, who was born in Egypt and built the first Coptic Church in the fourth century

(k) The Church of the Redeemer

i. German Lutheran Church built on the foundation of the Crusader Church of *Sainte Marie la Latine* established in the 11th century

ii. The present church was built in 1898 by Kaiser Wilhelm II

iii. The bell tower provides a grand view of the Old City

(l) The *Muristan*

i. Large square in the Christian Quarter with a fountain in the center surrounded by straight streets paved since Roman times and continue to exist to this day

    a) South - David Street

    b) West - Christian Street

    c) North - Dyers' Market Street

    d) East - Butchers' Market Street

ii. In Roman times, this was a forum of *Aelia Capitolina*

iii. Present name originates from the Ayyubid Period and comes from a Persian word for "hospital" - The Crusader hospital of the Knights of Saint John of the Hospital was located here until it disappeared in the 16th century

iv. In 1903, the Greek Orthodox Patriachate built a market place in the area with seventy shops

v. The fountain was built to mark the 25th anniversary of the rule of Sultan Abdul Hamid

(m) The Mosque of Omar - The actual mosque named after Omar ibn el-Khattab who was the one that conquered Jerusalem for the Moslems in 638 and the mosque was built by Saladin

(n) Church of Saint John the Baptist

i. A Greek Orthodox Monastery built in 1842 on the remains of the Crusader Church of *Sainte Marie la Latine*

ii. The basement of the church has Byzantine remains of the fifth-sixth century

    (o) Coptic Khan

        i.   A hospice built in 1838 for Egyptian pilgrims

        ii. Now a Coptic monastery named after Saint George, the patron saint of the Copts

    (p) Hezekiah's Pool

        i.   Second century B.C. pool misnamed after Hezekiah because of the belief that this was the upper pool of Hezekiah

        ii. Josephus calls it the Amigdalon Pool - Corruption of the Hebrew: The Pool of the Pillars

        iii. Arabic: *Birkat Hamman el-Batrak*, The Pool of the Patriarch's Bath, because of its proximity to the Greek Catholic Patriarchate

        iv. Once a reservoir filled by rain water, it is now used by the locals as a garbage dump

        v. Measurements: 250 feet long by 148 feet wide by 10 feet below street level

    (q) The Roman Column

        i.   A lamp post imbedded into a stone column with a Latin inscription honoring the Tenth Roman Legion

        ii. The Tenth Roman Legion destroyed Jerusalem in A.D. 70 and occupied the area now known as the Armenian Quarter for 250 years

    (r) The Church of Holy Sepulchre (to be described under Via Dolorosa)

    (s) Alexander Nievsily Church

        i.   Russian Orthodox Church

        ii. Contains the remains of the eastern most parts of The Church of the Holy Sepulchre and a gate that once led to the Cardo

    (t) Christ Church

        i.   Anglican Church - The first Protestant church in the Old City

        ii. The land was purchased in 1830 and the church built in 1841-1848 and consecrated on January 21, 1849

        iii. Built by the London Society for Promoting Christianity Among the Jews (Now known as CMJ - Church's Ministry Among the Jews) - to do Jewish missionary work in the Holy Land and for this reason the church was built much like a synagogue

      iv. Here, the first Protestant Bishopric was established in 1840 and the first Bishop of Jerusalem was a Jewish believer named Michael Solomon Alexander, a former rabbi - The first Jewish bishop of Jerusalem since A.D. 135

      v. The Seat of the Bishopric remained in Christ Church until 1898

(u) Saint Mark's Church and Convent

      i. The headquarters of the Syrian Orthodox Church also known as the Jacobites, after the sixth century founder of the sect: Jacobus Baradaeus

      ii. It is a monophysite sect which also owns parts of Mary's Tomb and the Church of the Ascension

      iii. In Jerusalem, the sect only numbers about eighty people

      iv. The present convent and church was built in the 12th century on Byzantine remains and built on the site believed to be the home of Mark and the Upper Room in the Syrian tradition

(v) Wilson House

      i. The Lutheran Hostel built in 1856 and named for explorer Charles Wilson after whom Wilson's Arch was named

      ii. It was once a home for British Missionaries

      iii. It is now owned by the German Lutheran Church

(w) The Maronite Church

      i. A fifth century sect based in Lebanon

      ii. It has had a Patriarchal Vicar in Jerusalem since 1895

(3) The Armenian Quarter - The southwest section of the city

(a) Occupies one-sixth of the Old City

(b) Main road - The Armenian Patriarchate Road

(c) Population: 2,000

(d) History

      i. This is the oldest Christian community - The first country to adopt Christianity in the third century under Saint Gregory and, hence, sometimes called The Gregorian Church

      ii. The first pilgrims began to arrive shortly thereafter and established a quarter

      iii. Also established Armenian Centers on Mount Zion and the Mount of Olives

    iv. In A.D. 426 - They built a convent on the site of the Inn of the Good Samitarian

    v. By the seventh century - There were seventy Armenian establishments in the country

    vi. In A.D. 614, the Persian-Zoroastrian invasion destroyed all the Armenian monuments and many Armenian monks were killed

    vii. In the Byzantine reconquest, Armenians were forbidden to rebuild their centers and suffered persecution at the hands of the Byzantines

    viii. In A.D. 638, the Arab invasion was welcomed by the Armenians

    ix. The Crusaders - Initially treated the Armenians with contempt but due to intermarriage by royal families in Europe, the Armenians regained much of their property in the 12th century

    x. The present main gate was built in 1646

    xi. During the years of 1915-1916 - The Armenian Genocide took place by the Turks who killed 1.5 million Armenians

    xii. Today: There are 5,000 Armenians in the Land and 2,000 Armenians in the Quarter

    xiii. The Armenian Patriarchate was established in the 12th century after the expulsion of the Crusaders

(e) Things to see

    i. The Saint James Cathedral

        a) Named after James, the brother of John, The Patron Saint of Armenia

        b) Original church was built in the fifth century, destroyed by the Persians in 614 and later rebuilt

        c) The present church was built in the 11th century on the remains of a sixth century foundation

        d) By tradition, the head of James is buried under the church and his body is buried in Spain and so is James, the half-brother of Jesus

        e) The walls of the courtyard contain the tombs of the Patriarchs

        f) The walls of the church have many old paintings depicting Armenian martyrs, saints and the Last Judgment

        g) The last queen and princess of Armenia were buried by the church in 1382

    ii. The Armenian Museum

(f) The Quarter has its own enclosed walls - Two walled-in segments within a walled city

(g) The Gates are shut from 10 p.m. until 6 a.m.

(h) The residents mostly work in other parts of the Old City as doctors, teachers and artisans

(i) They have their own school system in which they learn Armenian, Hebrew, Arabic, English and French

(4) The Moslem Quarter - The northeast section of the city

   (a) The most heavily populated quarter with a population of 16,000. Most are descendants of Moslem families who settled here after the expulsion of the Crusaders and were then joined by Moslems from Egypt, North Africa and Turkey

   (b) The main north-south street: The *Suk* (*Shuk*) or Cardo

   (c) The main east-west streets

      i. David Street

      ii. The Street of the Chain

   (d) The Street of the Chain - Contains several large Mameluke structures and serves as the southern border of the Quarter

      i. *Khan es-Sultan* - Mameluke Khan

      ii. *Tashtimuryya* - A Mameluke *Madrassa* or School

      iii. The Khalidi Library - A Crusader building that became a Moslem library which housed 12,000 books and manuscripts until 1947

      iv. *Turba Turkan Khatun*

         a) Tomb of *Turkan Khatun*, daughter of Emir Tuqtay Ibn Saljutay el-Uzbaki

         b) She was a Mongol princess from Central Asia

      v. *El-Madrassa et-Tankiziyya* (*Mahkama*)

         a) Located in a square near the Gate of the Chain

         b) Built during the Mameluke Period by *Emir Seif ed-Din Tankiz en-Nasiri* in 1328-1329

         c) Had a fountain that was fed by an aqueduct that brought water from the Pools of Solomon

         d) It was a walled courthouse in the Turkish Period

         e) Home of the Mufti under British Mandate

         f) A school under the Jordanians

         g) Jewish Tradition: This was the Chamber of Hewn Stones - The place where the Sanhedrin met

(e) Beth Habad Street along with the three market streets mark the western border of the Quarter

(f) Contains many Christian institutions, primarily along the Via Dolorosa

(g) In the 19th century, many Jews moved into the Moslem Quarter and became the majority until 1929 when they moved out due to the Arab riots

(h) After 1967, a number of Jews returned to the Moslem Quarter but remain a minority there

(i) Things to see

    i. The Three Markets - Dating from the Crusader or earlier periods and along the Cardo at the end of David Street

        a) The Butcher's Market

        b) The Spice Market

        c) The Goldsmith Market

    ii. The Gate of the Chain Square - At the end of the Street of the Chain and one of the gates entering the Temple Compound

    iii. The Cotton Merchants Market (*Suk el-Qattanim*)

        a) Covered market built in 1336-1337 running from Haggai Street to the Temple Mount

        b) The largest structure built during the Mameluke Period - 312 feet

        c) Began to deteriorate during the Turkish Period and remains desolate to this day

    iv. The Iron Gate Street and the Small Wall - A smaller version of the Western Wall

    v. *Torat Chaim Yeshivah*

        a) Contains a whole library of thousands of books, as well as furniture

        b) Protected by an Arab family during the Jordanian occupation of the Old City, 1948-1967

        c) Returned to the Jewish community by the Arab family where the keeper said, "More than me protecting the library, the library protected me"

        d) Arab family honored by Israel and given a stipend for the rest of their lives

c. The Pools of Bethesda - John 5:2-9

    (1) Now located in the compound of the Church of Saint Anne - The best preserved Crusader Church in Jerusalem. Built in 1140 near the remains of the Byzantine Church built in the fifth century (on the wall separating the two pools)

(2) The Church sits on the site believed to be the birthplace of Mary and the home of her parents: Anne and Joachim

(3) The northern pool may be the Upper Pool built by Ahaz in the eighth century B.C. (II Kings 18:17; Isaiah 7:3; 36:2)

(4) In the third century B.C., a second pool was built which may correspond with the present southern pool

(5) 150 B.C.-A.D. 70, baths were dug out for medicinal and ritual purposes where the miracle took place - Located outside the Sheep Gate

(6) The building of the third wall put this pool out of commission since it kept water from being channeled into the pools

(7) During the period of *Aelia Capitolina* (second-fourth century), it was used as a pagan cult to the Greek-Roman god of healing named Euscalapius - Same as Eshmunanu and Shedraphaus of the Semites and Serapis of the Egyptians

(8) While Juvenal was Patriarch of Jerusalem (422-458), a large Byzantine basilica was built to commemorate the miracle and the birthplace of Mary

(9) Destroyed by the Persians in 614

(10) Rebuilt by Modestus, a monk and prospered during the seventh and ninth century

(11) Destroyed by Caliph Hakim in 1010

(12) Taken by the Crusaders in 1099, who built a small monastery

(13) Around 1130, a large Romanesque Church was built

(14) In 1187, the compound was converted into a Moslem theological school called *Salahiyeh* by Sultan Saladin

(15) Period of neglect during the Turkish Period

(16) After the Crimean War in 1856, it was presented to the French Government which restored the Church

(17) In 1878, it was entrusted to the White Fathers and continues to this day

(18) The measurements: 300-330 long by 180-240 wide by 21-24 feet deep

d. The South Wall Excavations

(1) The Mount Ophel of the Bible

(2) Discovered 25 layers of civilization beginning with the Solomonic Period

(3) Main Periods discovered

(a) First Temple Period

(b) The Hasmonian Period

(c) The Herodian Period

      (d) The Byzantine Period

      (e) The Umayyad Period

      (f) The Crusader Period

   (4) Things to see

      (a) The southwest corner of the Temple Mount

         i.   About 1,450 feet exposed

         ii. Herodian stones measuring 30 feet long and weighing over 50 tons

      (b) Robinson's Arch and its Pier - Remains of a staircase from the Tyrophean Valley to the Royal Portico of the Temple Compound

      (c) Quotation of Isaiah 66:14 - *And when you see this, your heart shall rejoice and their* [instead of "your"] *bones shall flourish like an herb*

      (d) The paved Herodian Street - Served as the Cardo of the Herodian city

      (e) The Courtyard of the Umayyad Palace

      (f) The Byzantine Ruins - Typical private homes of this period

      (g) Herodian Building

      (h) Cisterns

      (i) Ritual Immersion Pools

      (j) The Enclosed Pool of the Acra Fortress - From the Hellenistic Period

      (k) Umayyad Buildings

      (l) Israelite Building from the First Temple Period

      (m) The Byzantine Residential Quarter

      (n) The Double Gate - The Western Huldah Gate used as the exit gates

      (o) The Triple Gate - Umayyad gates built on the side of the Eastern Huldah Gates which were used as the entry gates

      (p) The Single Gate

  e. The Via Dolorosa

   (1) The Development

      (a) The concept began during the Crusader Period when, on Palm Sunday, a procession began by entering the Golden Gate onto the Temple Mount, exiting the Mount through the "Gates of Sorrow" on the west and continuing to the Church of the Holy Sepulchre

      (b) The modern practice began in the 14th century and developed during the Ottoman-Turkish Period in the mid-16th century

(c) Throughout the centuries, the places varied

(d) Only nine of the 14 stations are in the Gospels and the other five were added by tradition

(e) The present 14 stages were finally fixed in the 19th century

(2) The 14 stations of the cross

    (a) The First Station: The Judgment in the Praetorium - John 18:28-19:16

        i.   In the area where the Antonia Fortress stood

        ii.   Now inside the Courtyard of the Umariyah School - A Moslem school for boys

    (b) The Second Station: The Flagellation - Where He received the cross

        i.   The Chapel of Condemnation (Franciscan) - Built in 1903-1904

        ii.   The Church of the Flagellation - Franciscan Church

        iii. The *Ecco Homo* (Behold the Man) Arch

    (c) The Third Station: The First Fall (tradition) - Marked by a Polish Catholic Church

    (d) The Fourth Station: Jesus Meets His Mother (tradition)

        i.   In the Armenian Catholic Church of Our Lady of the Spasms

        ii.   Built in 1881-1886 over the Byzantine remains of the Church of Saint Sophia and renovated in 1947-1948

    (e) The Fifth Station: Simon Takes the Cross (Franciscan)

    (f) The Sixth Station: Veronica Wipes His Face (tradition) (Greek-Catholic)

        i.   The Church of Saint Veronica built in 1882 over the remains of a sixth century monastery and rebuilt in 1953

        ii.   From the Latin *Vera Icone* - "Two likenesses"

    (g) The Seventh Station: The Second Fall (tradition)

        i.   Believed to be the site of the Gate of Judgment where Jesus was led out of the city wall

        ii.   Originally a Coptic Church acquired by the Franciscans in 1875

    (h) The Eighth Station: The Weeping over the Daughters of Jerusalem

        i.   Located in the Chapel of Saint Charalampos (Greek-Orthodox)

        ii.   Marked by a small cross carved into the wall of the Convent

(i) The Ninth Station: The Third Fall (tradition)

    i.   At the Ethiopian Coptic Church

    ii. Marked by a pillar in the wall

    iii. Extends across the roof of the Church of the Holy Sepulchre and disputed over by the Copts and the Ethiopians

(j) The Tenth Station: Garments Stripped

    i.   The Altar of the Nails of the Cross (Catholic)

    ii. Marked by a mosaic floor

    iii. Requires an assent of 14½ feet

(k) The Eleventh Station: Crucified

    i.   The nailing of Jesus on the cross

    ii. The Altar of *Stabat Mater* (Catholic)

(l) The Twelfth Station: The Setting of the Cross in place in Christ's Death

    i.   The Altar of the Crucifixion (Greek-Orthodox)

    ii. Marked by life size icons of Jesus, Mary and John

(m) The Thirteenth Station: The Body Removed

    i.   Marked by a slab called The Stone of Unction

    ii. The present pink slab is actually a marble cover protecting the real rock below because of the tendency of pilgrims to break off parts of that rock

(n) The Fourteenth Station: Jesus Laid in the Sepulchre

    i.   Covered today by a large two part structure

    ii. The First Room: The Chapel of the Angels - Where the angel sat

    iii. The Second Room: The actual tomb with a two yard wide marble slab that covers the tomb measuring 6½ feet square

    iv. Above the tomb are 43 hanging lamps: 13 for the Catholics; 13 for the Greek-Orthodox; 13 for the Armenians and four for the Coptics

    v. The chapel behind the tomb is the only part of church that is actually owned by the Coptics

(3) The last five stations are in the Church of the Holy Sepulchre

(a) Historical Background

    i.   In A.D. 135, Hadrian constructed a temple to Venus (Aphrodite) over this site holy to Messianic Jews since Christianity was considered a Jewish sect

       a) An image of Jupiter stood over the place of Calvary

   b) An image of Venus stood over the tomb

  ii. Saint Helena built The Church of the Holy Sepulchre in A.D. 336 on the site of this pagan temple

  iii. The succession of bishops was never interrupted in these early centuries

   a) The first fifteen bishops were all Jewish believers

   b) They were replaced by Gentiles after Hadrian expelled all Jews from Jerusalem in A.D.

   c) Thus the memory of such a sacred place would not have been forgotten

(b) Archeological Evidence

  i. Site stood outside the city wall of that day

  ii. Originally, a large limestone quarry from the seventh century B.C.

  iii. It was later filled and became a garden in the first century

  iv. Contains at least four tombs from the first century

(c) The Church is claimed by six different groups

  i. Roman Catholic (Franciscans)

  ii. Greek Orthodox

  iii. Armenians

  iv. Ethiopians

  v. Coptics

  vi. Syrians

(d) The present church is the fourth church since Helena built the first

  i. The First Church - Built by Helena and destroyed by the Persians in 614

  ii. The Second Church - Built in 628 by Patriarch Modestus with few changes and destroyed on September 28, 1009 by Fatimid Caliph el-Hakim Alla B'Amr

  iii. The Third Church - Built in 1042-1048 by Byzantine Emperor Constantine Monomachus

  iv. The Fourth Church - The previous church was incorporated into this one built by the Crusaders in 1099-1149

   a) Suffered a major fire in 1808 requiring major repairs but no structural changes

   b) There have been major renovations since 1960

(e) The present church is largely the Crusader Church

    i.   Originally, it had a double doorway but one was permanently sealed during the Moslem reconquest

    ii.   The Square Crusader Belfry is lower than the original

    iii.   The courtyard belongs to the Greek Orthodox Church

(f) Elements of the Church today

    i.   The Latin Chapel of Golgotha

    ii.   The Greek Chapel of Golgotha - Over the rock itself

    iii.   The Chapel of Adam - Underneath where Adam was buried and Christ's blood dripped on his skull

    iv.   The Stone of Annointings - Where the body was prepared for burial

    v.   The Armenian Sacristy

    vi.   The Tomb of Jesus

    vii.   The Chapel of the Angel - Where the angel sat

    viii.   The Chapel of the Copts

    ix.   The Chapel of the Syrians

    x.   The Burial Cave

    xi.   The Chapel of the Apparition - Where Jesus appeared to Mary Magdalene

    xii.   The Crypt of Helena

    xiii.   The Chapel of the Finding of the Cross - Where Helena found the true cross

f. The Temple Compound

(1) The History

(a) Sacrifice of Isaac - Genesis 22:1-18

(b) Acquired by payment by David - II Samuel 24:15-25; I Chronicles 21:18-22:1

(c) Temple was built by Solomon - II Chronicles 3:1

(d) The First Temple was destroyed in 536 B.C. - II Kings 25:9; II Chronicles 36:19; Jeremiah 52:13

(e) The Second Temple was built by Zerubbabel - Ezra 3:8-6:22

(f) Expanded by Herod the Great who doubled its size and renovated the Temple - 20-10 B.C.

(g) The purification of Mary and the redemption of Jesus as the firstborn at the Temple at the age of 40 days - Luke 2:22-24

(h) The encounter with Simeon and Anna - Luke 2:25-38

(i) Jesus visited the Temple at the age of 12 - Luke 2:41-51

(j)   The second temptation of Jesus took place at the Pinnacle of the Temple - Matthew 4:5-7

(k)   The money changers were driven out at the beginning of His ministry - John 2:13-22

(l)   He visited it at the Feast of Tabernacles - John 7:10

(m) The woman taken in adultery was confronted by Jesus here - John 8:1-11

(n)   Sermon on the Light of the World - John 8:12-32

(o)   Discourse on the Good Shepherd - John 10:1-18

(p)   Observance of the Feast of Chanukkah - John 10:22-39

(q)   The second cleansing of the Temple - Matthew 21:12-17; Mark 11:15-18

(r)   Jesus was tested by the Jewish leaders - Matthew 21:23-22:45

(s)   Denunciation of the Jewish leadership - Matthew 23:1-24:2

(t)   Third stage of the religious trial of Jesus - Luke 22:66-71

(u)   Activities of the Apostles in the Book of Acts, including sermons and healings - Acts 2:46-47; 3:1-4:22; 5:12-16

(v)   Paul was arrested here, which eventually led to his arrival in Rome - Acts 21:26-22:30

(w) The Second Temple was destroyed in A.D. 70

(x)   Bar Cochba reinstated the sacrificial system in A.D. 132

(y)   It was plowed by Hadrian after the Bar Cochba Revolt in A.D. 135

(z)   Hadrian built a temple to Jupiter here

(aa) During the Byzantine Period (325-638), the Temple of Jupiter was destroyed and the Temple Mount was left in ruins

(bb) In A.D. 361-362, Julian the Apostate attempted to rebuild the Jewish Temple

(cc) In 638, with the Moslem Conquest, Omar cleared the Temple Mount of all rubbish and built a Mosque of wood on the southern part of the Mount

(dd) In 691, the Dome of the Rock was built by Abdul-Malik Ibn Merwan of the Umayyads

(ee) In 1099, the Crusaders turned it into a shrine: *Templum Domini* - The Temple of the Lord

(ff)   In October 2, 1187, it was retaken by Saladin

(gg) During the Mameluke Period (1260-1517), many structures were renovated and new ones were built

(hh) During the Ottoman Turkish Period (1517-1917), more structures were built and ceramic tiles were added to the Dome of the Rock

(2) Arab name: *Haram esh-Sharif*, The Venerable Sanctuary

(3) The wall encloses about 135 acres and it is one-sixth of the Old City

(4) The Dome of the Rock

    (a) The third holiest site in Islam after Mecca and Medina

        i.   An octagon with each side measuring 63 feet

        ii. The diameter is 180 feet

        iii. It is 108 feet high

    (b) Sometimes known as the Mosque of Omar

    (c) Built in 691 as an octagon supporting a huge domed roof

        i.   Because of the sanctity of the rock in Moslem tradition

        ii. Islam recognizes its biblical sanctity

        iii. Abd el-Malik wanted it to counter-balance the Church of the Holy Sepulchre

        iv. Originally covered by mosaics until the 16th century when it was covered with marble and tile

    (d) The North Gate is known as *Bab el-Jenna*, The Gate of Paradise

    (e) The East Gate

        i.   Known as *Bab Daud*, The Gate of David

        ii. Also called *Bab Mahkamet Daud*, The Gate of the Judgment of David

    (f) The South Gate

        i.   Called *Bab Israfil*, The Gate of the Angel Raphael

        ii. Also called *Bab el-Qulbleh*, The Mecca Gate

    (g) The West Gate - *Bab el-Gharbs*, The Women's Gate

    (h) The Rock

        i.   Arabic name: *Kubbet es-Sakhra*

        ii. The Rock of the Sacrifice of Isaac/Ishmael

        iii. The Rock from which Mohammed ascended into Heaven on his horse *el-Walid*

        iv. The cave in the rock is called *Bir el-Arwah*, The Well of the Spirits. Here, four prayed: Abraham, David, Solomon, Gabriel

    (i) The Crusaders turned it into a church named *Templum Domini*, The Temple of the Lord

(j) The gold plates on the Dome were added in 1966

(k) The interior designs were made in the 17th century

(l) The exterior plates were made by Armenian craftsmen using Turkish designs

(5) The *El Aksa* Mosque

(a) It was built between 709-715 by Caliph el-Walid, the son of Malik - The oldest mosque in the borders of the Land

(b) It was built on the site of the original Judean palace

(c) Measurements: 280 square feet

(d) It was damaged or destroyed in the past by four earthquakes (747, 1033, 1927 and 1936)

(e) Used by the Crusaders as a palace for the Crusader kings and later given over to the Knights Templars who turned it into a church called *Templum Solomonis*, The Temple of Solomon

(f) Reconverted into a mosque by Saladin in 1187

(g) Today - It is a large hall measuring 180 feet by 269 feet

(h) The silver colored dome was replaced by a black dome in 1986

(6) *Istabil Suleiman*, The Stables of Solomon

(a) This is actually the original entry way into the Second Temple Compound

(b) May have been the Treasury area of the Temple Compound

(c) Used as stables by the Crusaders

(d) Also called the "Cradle of Jesus" because in Moslem tradition, Jesus was born here

(e) Measurements: 182 feet by 328 feet

(7) *Qubbat es-Silsilah*, The Dome of the Chain

(a) Located 13 feet east of the Dome of the Rock - An 11-sided, open structure

(b) By Moslem tradition, King David sat in judgement here and a chain hung from the ceiling at the time of the judgment

(c) Also known as the Chapel of Saint James the Less, for that was its function during the Crusader Period

(d) By Jewish tradition, this is where the Tablets and Aaron's Rod were kept along with the altar of Jacob and Melchizedek

(8) *Kursi Suleiman*, Solomon's Throne

(a) Near the Golden Gate, it is a squared structure with two domes

    (b) Built during the Umayyad Period (638-750)

    (c) According to Moslem tradition, this is where Solomon sat during the building of the Temple

(9) *Qubbat el-Arwah*, The Dome of the Spirits

    (a) Built as an octagon over flat bedrock where Moslem tradition states that the spirits of the dead gather

    (b) Also known as The Dome of the Tablets

    (c) Viewed by a minority to be the site of the Holy of Holies

(10) *El-Kas*, The Cup - The place of the washing of feet

    (a) Built in 1320 by the Mameluke Emir Tankiz

    (b) In Moslem tradition, the scales here are to be used as the place of the final judgment

(11) The Summer Pulpit - The marble platform on top of the stairs from the *el-Kas* containing a domed roof on pillars and the preacher's seat

(12) *Qubbat Yussuf*, Yussuf's Dome

    (a) A small cube-shaped structure open on three sides located near the Summer Pulpit

    (b) Named after Saladin Yussuf who built it in 1191 and after Yussuf Agha who restored it in 1681

(13) *Qubbat Nahawyya*, The Dome of Learning

    (a) Located next to the Yussuf Dome, it is a long building built in 1207

    (b) Contains three rooms and an underground chamber built for a more intense study of the Arabic language

(14) *Qubbat en-Nabi*, The Dome of the Prophet

    (a) The closest dome to the Dome of the Rock

    (b) It is lead-covered and supported by eight marble columns built by a Turkish Sultan: Mohammed Bek

(15) *Qubbat el-Miraj*, The Dome of the Ascension

    (a) Located west of The Dome of the Rock; it is built as an octagon

    (b) By Moslem tradition, here Mohammed prayed before his ascent into Heaven

    (c) It was used as a baptistry by the Crusaders

(16) *Qubbat el-Khadr*, The Dome of Elijah

    (a) Built as a hexagon

    (b) By Moslem tradition, here Solomon confined the spirits

(17) *El Burak* Steps

    (a) The 23 feet long steps in front of the Dome of the Chain facing the Mount of Olives

(b) Named after Mohammed's miraculous horse on which he rode from Mecca to Jerusalem

(18) *Qubbat Suleiman*, The Dome of Solomon

   (a) Located near the Dark Gate

   (b) It is an octagon from the Umayyad Period (638-750)

   (c) By Moslem tradition, Solomon prayed here when the Temple was finished

(19) *Qubbat Yussuf Agha*, The Dome of Yussuf Agha

   (a) A domed structure built in the 17th century

   (b) It is now used as the ticket booth

(20) *Qubbat Musa*, The Dome of Moses - Located by the Chain Gate, it is an octagon built in 1249 by the Ayyubid Sultan Saladin

(21) *Madrassa el-Jawilyya* - The Umariyah College built on the rock where the Antonia Fortress stood

(22) *Madrassa el-Uthmanyya*: College - Near the Gate of the Bath, it is named after the wealthy woman who built it in 1436-1437 during the Mameluke Period and who was buried next to the college

(23) *Madrassa el-Fakhryya* College

   (a) Built about 1300 against the southern part of the Western Wall by the Moghrabi Gate

   (b) Built with six domes and named after the Coptic judge who converted to Islam

(24) *Ala el-Din el-Basir* Fountain

   (a) A square drinking fountain built in the 12th century and renovated in the 15th

   (b) Gathered water from the Pools of Solomon through the Chain Gate

(25) The Fountain of *Qayt Bey*

   (a) Stands in front of the College of *el-Uthmanyya*

   (b) It is a drinking fountain from the Mameluke Period

   (c) Built as an octagon with a dome which was fed with the water from the Pools of Solomon through the Chain Gate

   (d) It was named after the Sultan who renovated it in 1482

(26) The Fountain of *Qasem Pasha* - An octagonal fountain south of *Qayt Bey* named after the person who built it in 1527

(27) *Matzatabat et-Tein*, The Fig Tree Alcove

   (a) A square prayer area south of *Qasem Pasha* measuring 29.5 feet square

   (b) So named because of a fig tree that grew here when it was built in 1760

(28) The Woman's Mosque

    (a) It was built west of the *El-Aksa* mosque by the Knights Templars to store arms and living quarters

    (b) Also called the White Mosque

    (c) Measurements: 40 feet by 240 feet

(29) The Gates of the Compound

    (a) *Bab el Rahmeh*, The Gate of Mercy, The Golden Gate

        i. Served as both a city gate and a Temple Compound Gate

        ii. It is a double gate with each part having its own name: The Gate of Mercy and The Gate of Repentance

        iii. In 631, the Byzantine Emperor entered through these gates returning the true cross previously captured by the Persians

        iv. During the Crusader Period, the gate was opened twice a year: Palm Sunday and the Exaltation of the Cross

        v. With the Moslem reconquest, it was blocked and served as a Moslem prayer house until the 15th century

        vi. In the Middle Ages, Jewish people came here to mourn the destruction of the Temple. When the area was turned into a Moslem cemetary, the Jews moved to the Western (Wailing) Wall

        vii. The present gate dates to the Umayyad Period with changes made in subsequent periods

        viii. The Turks converted it into a watch tower and sealed the gates

        ix. Jewish tradition: Gate will be opened when the Messiah comes

        x. Moslem tradition: The Day of Judgment will take place here

        xi. Christian tradition: These are the gates through which Jesus entered on Palm Sunday

        xii. Today it is used as a storehouse

    (b) *Bab el-Asbat*, The Gate of the Tribes

        i. The northeast gate of the Temple Compound

        ii. Moslem tradition: Named after the Tribes of Israel who passed through it after visiting the Temple

        iii. The gate dates from the Ottoman Turkish Period

   (c) *Bab Hitta*, The Gate of Atonement

      i.   A gate on the north wall in the center

      ii. Built in the 10th century and renovated in 1220 by the Ayyubid Sultan El-Muazzam

      iii. Name was based on a Moslem tradition that here the Israelites were required to say *hitta* (atonement) before they could enter Jerusalem

   (d) *Bab el-Atim*, The Dark Gate

      i.   The most western gate on the north wall

      ii. Named after the dark passage leading to it

      iii. Built in the Mameluke Period

      iv. Also called The Gate of the Glory of the Prophets

      v.   Moslem legend: Through this gate Caliph Omar came to pray when he first came to Jerusalem

   (e) *Bab el-Ghawanima*, The Ghawanima Gate - The most northern gate on the western wall

   (f) *Bab en-Natir*, The Gate of the Inspector

      i.   The next northern gate on the western wall

      ii. Named after the Inspector of the Sanctuaries of both Jerusalem and Hebron

      iii. He also built a house nearby which later became a jail and so this gate is also called *Bab el-Habs*: The Jail Gate

      iv. Built in the Ayyubid Period by Sultan El-Muazzam in 1203 on the foundation of an older Crusader gate called Michael's Gate

      v.   Because the Supreme Moslem Council is close to this gate, it is also known as *Bab el-Majlis*: The Gate of the Council

   (g) *Bab el-Hadid*, The Iron Gate

      i.   A gate built in 1357 on the western wall

      ii. Marked by a horseshoe arch

   (h) *Bab el-Qattanin*, The Gate of the Cotton Merchants

      i.   A gate on the western wall built in the Mameluke Period by the Tankiz in 1336-1337

      ii. The gate opened to the Cotton Market on Ha-Gai Street

   (i) *Bab el-Matharn*, The Gate of Purification

      i.   On the western wall, connected to the previous gate by a passageway

ii. Built in the Mameluke Period by Emir Ala ed-Din Aidugdai about 1270

iii. Also called the Gate of the Bath - Because, until the end of the Ottoman Turkish Period, there was a Turkish bathhouse nearby

(j) *Bab es-Silsileh,* The Gate of the Chain

    i. The main gate of the western wall

    ii. Actually has two gates

        a) North - *Bab es-Sakina*, The Divine Gate - Now sealed

        b) South - The Gate of the Chain, which is open

    iii. Opens on the Street of the Chain - The continuation of David Street and at times known as David's Gate

(k) The Moghrabi Gate: The Gate of the Moors

    i. The most southern gate on the western wall

    ii. The main entry for most tourist at the ascent from the Western (Wailing) Wall

    iii. The name was based on the fact that outside this gate was the quarters of the Maghrabi Moslems until 1967

(30) The Islamic Museum

    (a) Rectangular building measuring 32 feet by 100 feet

    (b) Built in the Umayyad Period

    (c) In the Ayyubid Period it was given to the North African Moslem Community in Jerusalem

    (d) Renovated by the Turkish Sultan: Abdul Aziz in 1871

    (e) It was turned into a Moslem museum in 1923

10. Jerusalem: Other Basic Facts

    a. This is now Israel's largest city with a total population of 560,000 with the Jewish population being 400,000

    b. The main Jewish downtown shopping center comprises a triangle of streets: Jaffa Road, King George Street and Ben Yehudah Street, which is also a pedestrian mall

11. Maps

    a. Old Testament Jerusalem - 1000 - 586 B.C.

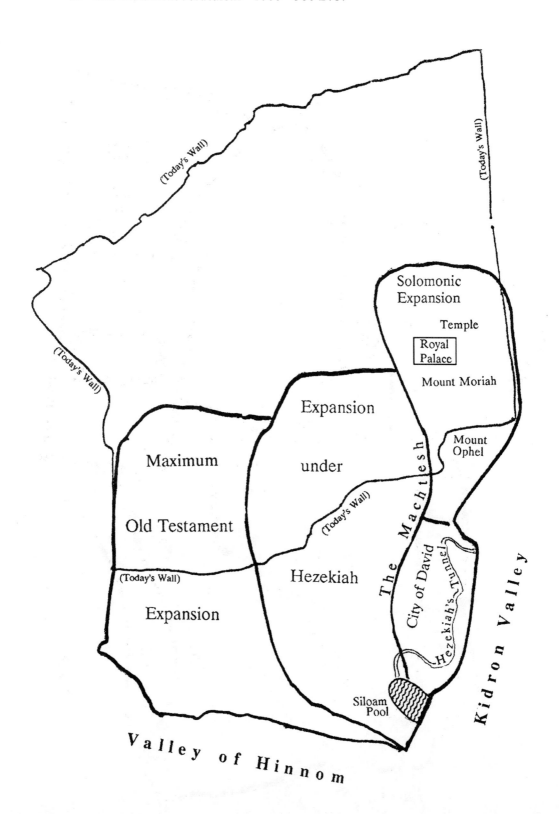

11. Maps

    b. New Testament Jerusalem - Second Temple Period

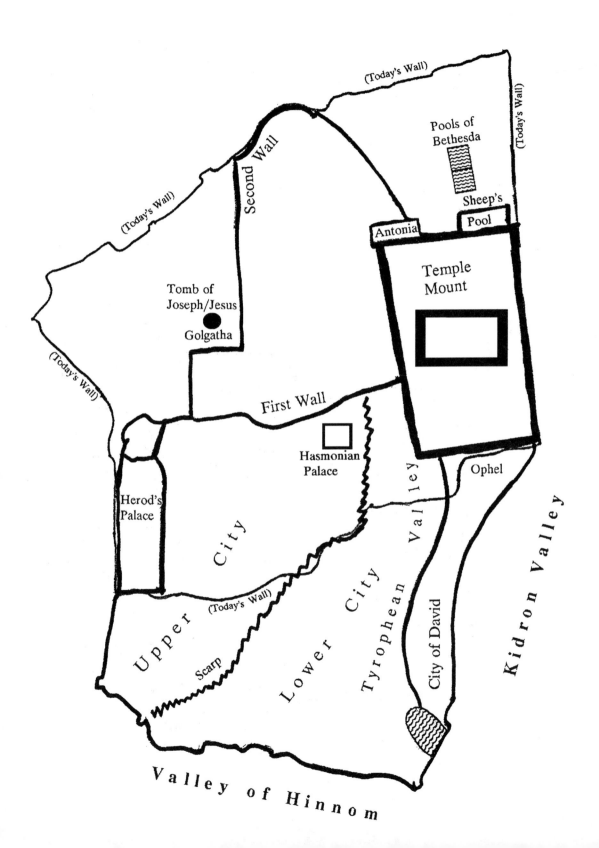

11. Maps

c. Messiah's Last Week - A.D. 30

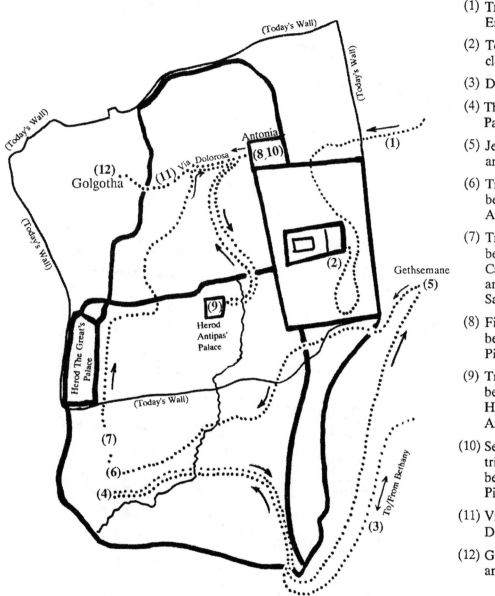

(1) Triumphal Entry

(2) Temple cleansed

(3) Daily trips

(4) The Last Passover

(5) Jesus arrested

(6) Trial before Annas

(7) Trial before Caiaphas and the Sanhedrin

(8) First trial before Pilate

(9) Trial before Herod Antipas

(10) Second trial before Pilate

(11) Via Dolorosa

(12) Golgotha and tomb

11. Maps

d. Jerusalem - A.D. 70

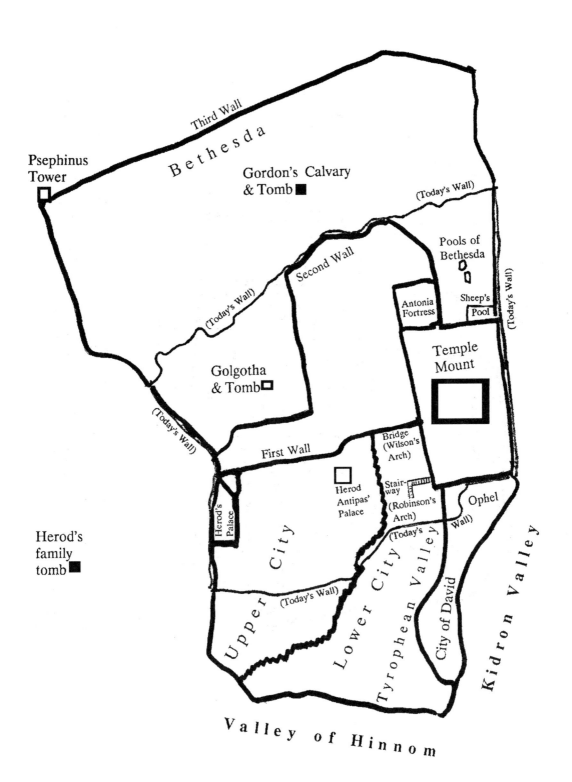

11. Maps

    e. Jerusalem: Aelia Captolina - A.D. 135 - 326

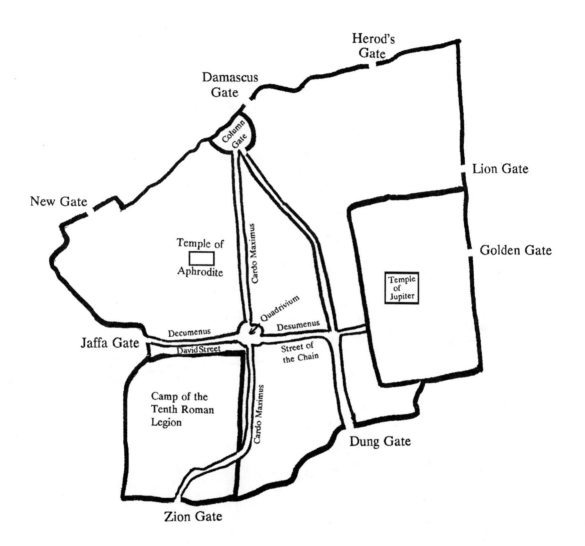

11. Maps

    f.   Jerusalem: Byzantine Period - A.D. 326 - 638

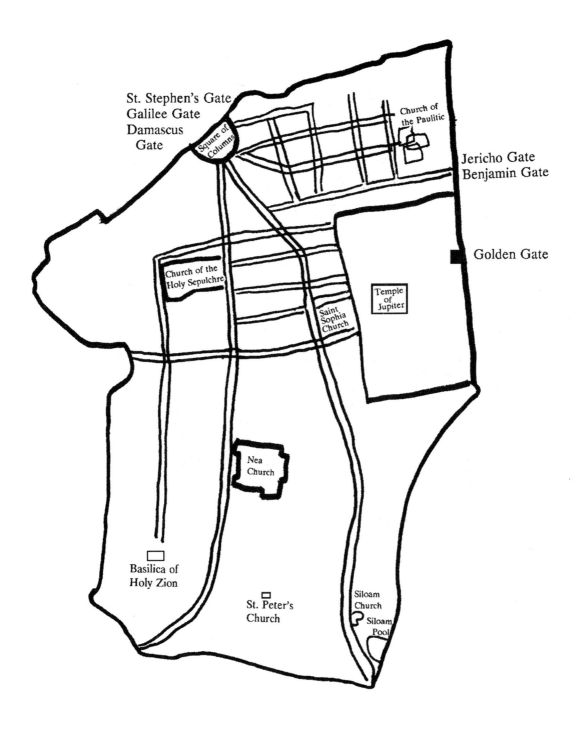

11. Maps

   g. Jerusalem: Early Arab - A.D. 638 - 1099

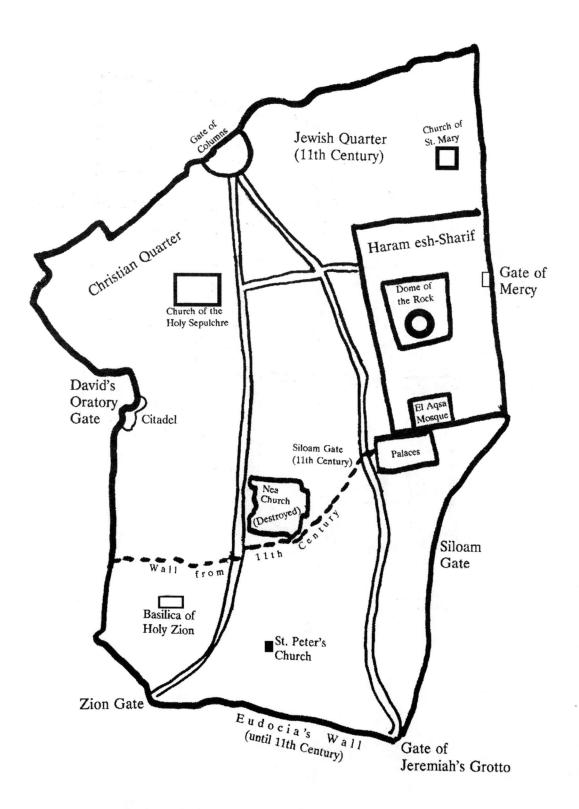

11. Maps

h. Jerusalem: Crusader Period - A.D. 1099 - 1187

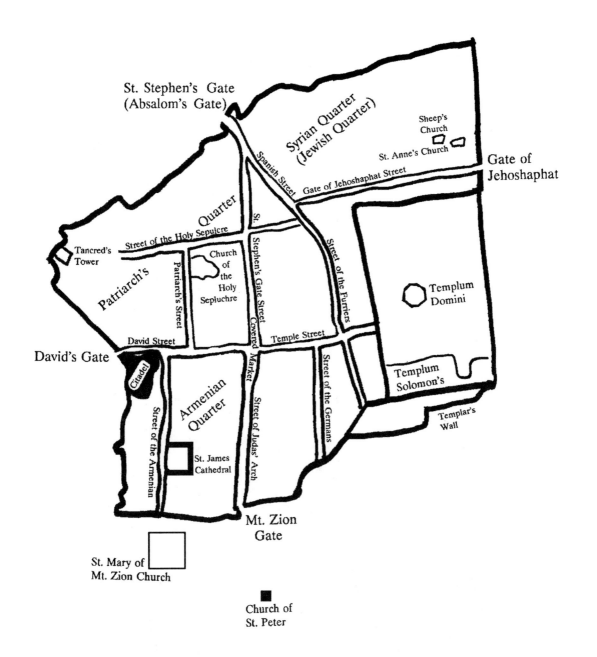

St. Stephen's Gate
(Absalom's Gate)

Syrian Quarter
(Jewish Quarter)

Sheep's
Church

St. Anne's Church

Gate of
Jehoshaphat

Spanish Street

Gate of Jehoshaphat Street

Quarter

Street of the Holy Sepulcre

Tancred's
Tower

Church
of
the
Holy
Sepluchre

St. Stephen's Gate Street

Street of the Furriers

Patriarch's

Patriarch's Street

Templum
Domini

David Street

David's Gate

Citadel

Covered Market

Temple Street

Street of the Germans

Templum
Solomon's

Armenian
Quarter

Street of the Armenian

Street of Judas' Arch

St. James
Cathedral

Templar's
Wall

Mt. Zion
Gate

St. Mary of
Mt. Zion Church

Church of
St. Peter

11. Maps

    i.   Jerusalem: Ayyubid Period - A.D. 1187 - 1250

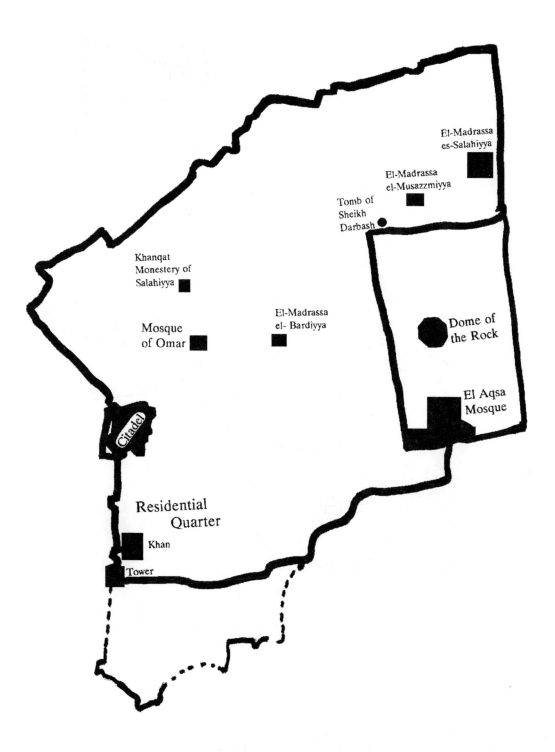

11. Maps

j. Jerusalem: Mameluke Period - A.D. 1250 - 1517

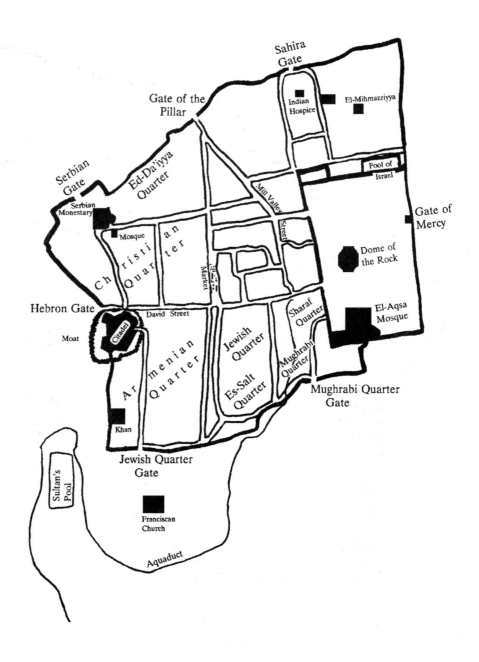

11. Maps

    k.   Jerusalem: Ottoman Turkish Period - A.D. 1517 - 1917

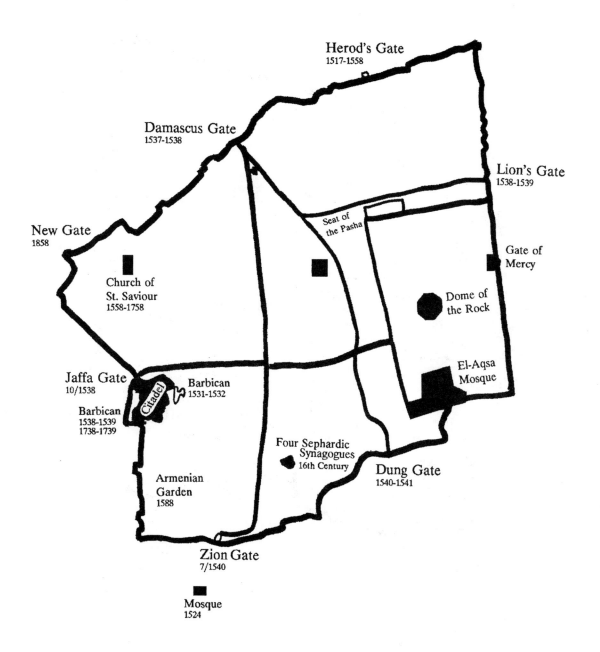

11. Maps

1. Jerusalem: The Old City Today

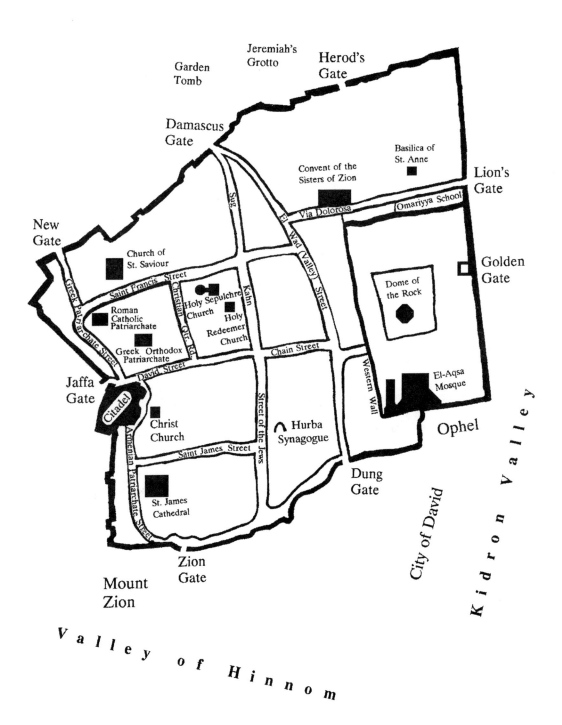

11. Maps

m. Jerusalem: The Old City and Surrounding Area Today

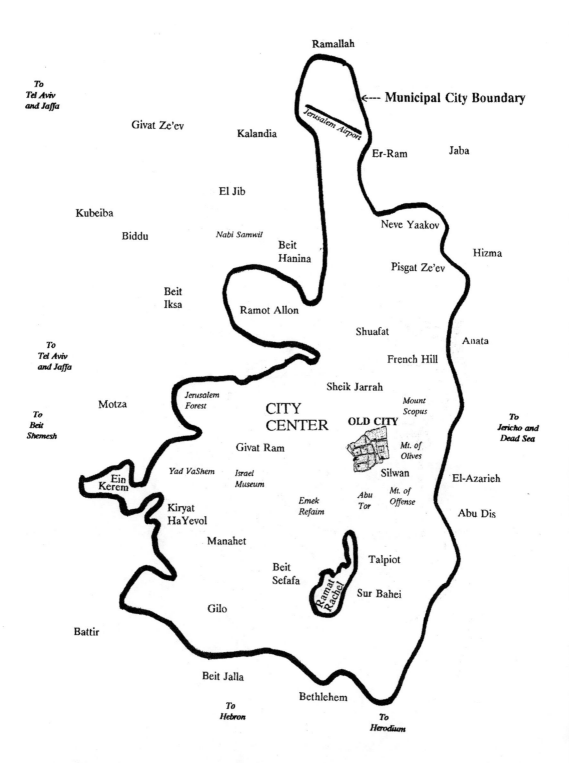

11. Maps

n. Jerusalem: The New City

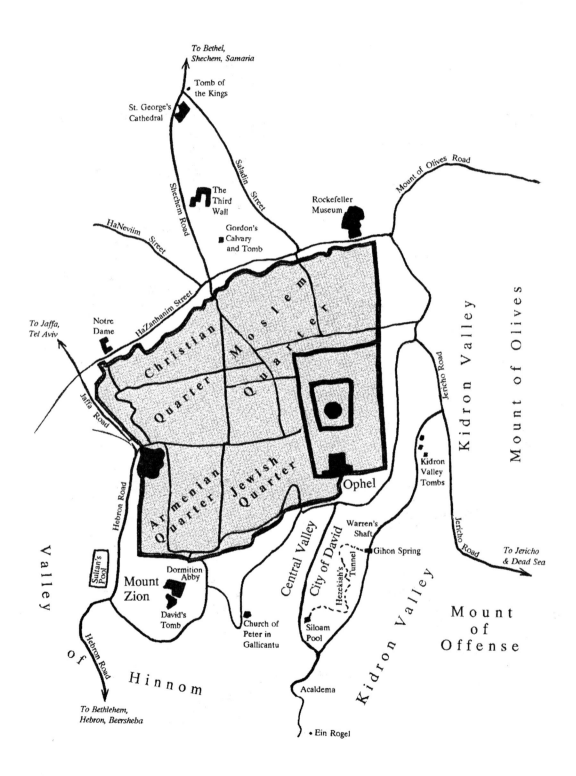

JERUSALEM - THE JORDAN RIVER

JESHANA (EIN SINYA)

One of the cities taken by Abijah from Jereboam - II Chronicles 13:19

JEZREEL

1. A city of the Tribe of Issachar - Joshua 19:18

2. Part of the area of the Israelite camp of Saul against the Philistines - I Samuel 29:1

3. The Philistine armies moved into this area from Aphek - I Samuel 29:1

4. Home of Ahinoam, one of David's wives - I Samuel 25:43; 27:3; 30:5; II Samuel 2:2; 3:2; I Chronicles 3:1

5. Within the Fifth Solomonic District - I Kings 4:12

6. The winter home of Ahab - I Kings 21:1

7. Ahab and Elijah arrived there after the contest at Carmel - I Kings 18:45-46

8. Elijah fled towards the Sinai from here - I Kings 19:1-3

9. The story of Naboth's vineyard - I Kings 21:1-29

10. Joram went to be healed of his wound and was visited by Ahaziah - II Kings 8:29; II Chronicles 22:6

11. Involved in the revolt of Jehu and Jezebel killed - II Kings 10:14-36

12. Heads of Ahab's sons were delivered - II Kings 10:1-11

13. In the Prophets: This blood of Jezreel was to be avenged - Hosea 1:3-5, 11

14. It guarded the descent from Samaria to the Jezreel Valley

THE JORDAN RIVER

1. From Mount Hermon to the Dead Sea

    a. 150 miles by air and 310 miles in actual flow

    b. Descending from 3000 feet above sea level to 1300 feet below

    c. The longest river in the Promised Land

2. The river has four sources

    a. Banyas (Hermon)

    b. Dan

    c. Baragit (Iyon Valley - Tanur)

    d. Hatzbani (Senir)

3. Served as the Canaan border and a general border throughout history - Numbers 22:1; 26:3, 63; 31:12; 35:10, 14; Deuteronomy 1:5; 2:29; Joshua 2:10; 9:10; 12:1, 7; 20:8; 23:4; I Chronicles 26:30

4. Marked the eastern border of the Land - Numbers 34:12

5. Jacob crossed this border into the Land of Canaan - Genesis 32:10

6. Included in what the twelve spies spied out - Numbers 13:29

7. Area of Israelite encampment before crossing it - Numbers 33:48-50; 35:1; 36:13; Deuteronomy 1:1

8. It marked the tribal border between the Cisjordanian and Transjordanian Tribes - Numbers 32:5, 19, 21, 29, 32; 34:15; Deuteronomy 3:22; 4:41-49; Joshua 1:14-15; 13:8, 23, 27, 32; 14:3; 17:5; 18:7; 22:4, 7, 25; 24:8; Judges 11:13, 22; I Chronicles 6:78; 12:15, 37

9. Moses was forbidden to cross the Jordan - Deuteronomy 3:27; 4:21-22; 31:2

10. Israel was told to cross the river - Numbers 33:51; 35:10; Deuteronomy 12:10; 4:26; 9:1; 11:30-31; 27:2, 4, 12; 30:18; 31:13

11. Joshua ordered to cross the river - Joshua 1:2, 11

12. The men of Jericho searched to this limit for the two spies - Joshua 2:7

13. The Jordan River parted when Joshua crossed - Joshua 3:1-17 (1, 8, 11, 13, 14, 15, 17); 7:7; 24:11; Psalm 114:3, 5

14. Twelve stones were taken out of the Jordan after the crossing to commemorate the event - Joshua 4:1-24 (1, 3, 5, 7, 8, 9, 10, 16, 17, 18, 19, 20, 22, 23)

15. News of the crossing of the Jordan River spread throughout the Land - Joshua 5:1; 9:1-2

16. It marked the border for seven tribes

    a. Western border of Reuben - Joshua 13:23

    b. Western border of Gad - Joshua 13:27

    c. Eastern border of Judah - Joshua 15:5

    d. Eastern border of Ephraim - Joshua 16:1, 7

    e. Eastern border of Benjamin - Joshua 18:12; 19-20

    f. Eastern border of Issachar - Joshua 19:22

    g. Eastern border of Naphtali - Joshua 19:33-34

17. After the taking of the Land, an altar was set up by the river by the 2½ Transjordanian tribes - Joshua 22:10-11

18. Ehud the Judge guarded the fords of the Jordan - Judges 3:28

19. Mentioned in Deborah's song - Judges 5:17

20. Gideon the Judge also guarded the fords of the Jordan - Judges 7:24

21. Gideon crossed the Jordan in pursuit of the Midianites - Judges 7:25; 8:4

22. The Ammonites crossed the river to oppress Israel - Judges 10:8-9

23. Jephthah guarded the fords of the river against Ephraimites using the test of Shibboleth - Judges 12:5-6

24. Some Jews of the Cisjordan crossed the river during the Philistine oppression - I Samuel 13:7; 31:7

25. Crossed by Abner in his flight from Joab - II Samuel 2:29

26. David crossed the river in pursuit of the Syrians - II Samuel 10:17; I Chronicles 19:17

27. David crossed the river in flight from Absalom - II Samuel 17:16, 22; I Kings 2:8

28. Absalom crossed this river - II Samuel 17:24

29. David crossed the Jordan River again when he returned from the war against Absalom - II Samuel 19:15-43 (15, 17, 18, 31, 36, 39, 41); I Kings 2:8

30. Border of those loyal to David after Sheba's revolt - II Samuel 20:2

31. Joab crossed the river for the census - II Samuel 24:5

32. Elijah was fed by the ravens by the river - I Kings 17:3-5

33. Elijah parted the Jordan - II Kings 2:6-8

34. Elisha parted the Jordan - II Kings 2:13-14

35. Naaman healed after dipping seven times in the Jordan - II Kings 5:8-14

36. The limit to where the Syrians were pursued - II Kings 7:15

37. The border of Hazael's conquests - II Kings 10:33

38. In the Poetic Books - Job 40:23; Psalms 42:6; 114:3, 5

39. In the Prophets - Isaiah 9:1; Jeremiah 12:5; 49:19; 50:44; Ezekiel 47:18; Zechariah 11:3

40. The ministry of John the Baptist - Matthew 3:1-6; Mark 1:4-5; Luke 3:2-3; John 1:28; 3:26

41. Jesus baptized - Matthew 3:13-17; Mark 1:9-11; Luke 3:21-22

    a. Marked by a two mile stretch of the western shore line where, by tradition, John baptized Jesus

    b. Marked by Five Churches

       (1) *Deir el-Habagh* - Monastery of the Ethiopians built in the 19th century

       (2) Enclosure of the Franciscans - Catholic built in 1935

       (3) Monastery of John the Baptist - Greek Orthodox

          (a) Built 1954 over remains of a fifth century Byzantine Church destroyed in 614 by the Persians and rebuilt in 1128 by the Crusaders

          (b) Arabic Name: *Qasr-el-Yahud*, The Citadel of the Jews, since, by tradition, this is where Israel crossed the Jordan River

       (4) Monastery of John the Baptist - Syrian Orthodox built in the beginning of the 20th century

       (5) *El-Qasair*, The Citadel

          (a) Earth mounds containing ruins of a Byzantine Church

          (b) By tradition, this is where Elijah went up

    c. *Deir Hajla* - Saint Germasimus

        (1) Arabic name means "Monastery of the Partridge" which preserves the Hebrew name, Beth Hoglah

        (2) One of the traditional sites of the baptism of Jesus though it is not on the river

        (3) Monastery founded by Saint Jerome (Hieranimus) at the end of fourth century

        (4) Originally called Laura of Calamon but renamed after the head monk of another monastery

        (5) Present monastery built in 1882

42. In the ministry of Jesus - Matthew 4:15, 25; 19:1; Mark 3:8; 10:1; Luke 4:1; John 10:40

43. The eastern border of the Millennial Israel - Ezekiel 47:18

KADESH BARNEA

1. It was part of the route of the invasion of the five kings against the four - Genesis 14:7

2. Border of the sojournings of Abraham - Genesis 16:14; 20:1

3. Israelite encampment - Numbers 13:26; 33:36-37; Deuteronomy 1:1-46 (2, 19, 46); 32:51; Judges 11:16-17

4. The twelve spies were sent out from here - Numbers 32:8; Deuteronomy 9:23; Joshua 14:6-7

5. The twelve spies returned here - Numbers 13:26

6. Miriam, the sister of Moses, died here - Numbers 20:1

7. Moses struck the rock here - Numbers 20:2-13; Deuteronomy 2:14

8. Moses sent the message to the king of Edom about requesting passage through - Numbers 20:14-22

9. Location of the Waters of Meribah - Numbers 27:14; Deuteronomy 32:51; Ezekiel 47:19; 48:28

10. Marked the southern boundary of the Land - Numbers 34:4

11. Marked the southern boundary of the conquest - Joshua 10:41

12. Marked the southern boundary of Judah -Joshua 15:3

13. It will mark the southern boundary of the Millennial Israel - Ezekiel 47:19; 48:28

KATZRIN

1. A large Jewish city during the Byzantine Period and into the Arab Period - One of 27 such Jewish sites

2. It was destroyed in an earthquake in 746 and never fully recovered

3. Today the ancient town has been partly reconstructed including the House of Rabbi Abun and the synagogue

4. Today, the only Jewish city on the Golan and its capital containing a total 4,000 residents

KEDESH NAPHTALI (QADIS)

1. The King was killed by Joshua - Joshua 12:22

2. City of the Tribe of Naphtali - Joshua 19:37; I Chronicles 6:76

3. One of the six Cities of Refuge - Joshua 20:7

4. Levitical City - Joshua 21:32; I Chronicles 6:72

5. Home of Barak - Judges 4:6

6. It was possibly the area where Barak gathered the armies of Israel - Judges 4:6-19 (6, 9, 10, 11)

7. If so, this is the area where Sisera was killed - Judges 4:11, 21

8. Fell under Tiglath Pileser III - II Kings 15:29

9. During the Second Temple Period, it had a mixed population of Jews, Syrians and Greeks

10. Flourished during the Middle Ages and repopulated with Jews

11. Discovered here were the largest burial caskets in Israel

12. Also found was the largest and best preserved Roman temple

13. Traditional tombs of Deborah, Barak, Heber the Kenite and Yael

KINNERETH (KHIRBET EL-UREIMA)

1. First settled in the third millennium B.C. by Canaanites

2. Conquered by Egypt in 1468 B.C.

3. Fortified city of Naphtali - Joshua 19:35

4. Smitten by Ben Hadad at Asa's request - I Kings 15:20; II Chronicles 16:4

5. Destroyed by Tiglath Pileser III in 732 B.C.

6. Sometimes the city gave its name to the Sea of Galilee - Numbers 34:11; Deuteronomy 3:17; Joshua 11:2; 12:3

KIRYAT YEARIM (ABU GHOSH) (KIRYAT EL-ANAB)

1. The origin is given in I Chronicles 2:50, 52

2. Other names

   a. Kiryath Baal - Joshua 15:60; 18:14

   b. Baalah - Joshua 15:9, 11

   c. Baale Judah - II Samuel 6:2; I Chronicles 13:6

3. One of the cities of the Gibeonite League - Joshua 9:17

4. Marked the northern border of Judah - Joshua 15:9-10

5. City of the Tribe of Judah - Joshua 15:60

6. Occupied by Judah - Joshua 15:60; Judges 18:12

7. Marked the southern border of Benjamin - Joshua 18:14-15

8. Here the Camp of Dan rested on the way north to their new settlement - Judges 18:11-12

9. It became the eighth stop of the Ark of the Covenant which stayed here for twenty years - I Samuel 6:21-7:2; II Samuel 6:1-12; I Chronicles 13:5-6; II Chronicles 1:4

10. Home of Urijah the Prophet killed by Jehoiakim - Jeremiah 26:20-23

11. Rebuilt after the return from Babylon - Ezra 2:25; Nehemiah 7:29

12. Home of the Tenth Roman Legion after it destroyed Jerusalem

13. Church originally built by Crusaders on the foundations of a Byzantine church - The present church was built in 1924

14. Original Arab name: *Kiryat el-Anab*

   a. Hebrew name - The Town of the Groves

   b. Arabic name - Translation of the Hebrew

   c. Renamed *Abu Ghosh* in the early 19th century after the town's most powerful chief

15. The Arabic name of the tel on which stands the modern church is *Deir el-Azar*, after Eleazar, the son of Abinadab, in whose home the Ark of the Covenant remained for twenty years

KISHON RIVER

1. It marked the border of the Tribe of Zebulun - Joshua 19:11

2. The camp of Sisera - Judges 4:7, 13; Psalm 83:9

3. The flooding of the Kishon helped defeat Sisera - Judges 5:20-21

4. The prophets of Baal were killed here by Elijah - I Kings 18:40

KUNEITRA

1. Formally largest city on the Golan Heights

2. Primarily a Circassian City

3. Up until the Six-Day War, it was the headquarters of the Syrian Army

4. After the *Yom Kippur* War in 1973, it was returned to Syria

5. Now a ghost town

LACHISH

1. In Egyptian records, it is mentioned in the Amarna Letters

2. Originally a Hyksos city

3. One of the cities of the Anti-Gibeonite League - Joshua 10:3, 5

4. Taken by Joshua - Joshua 10:31-35

5. The king was killed by Joshua - Joshua 10:23; 12:11

6. Given to the Tribe of Judah - Joshua 15:39

7. Fortified by Rehoboam - II Chronicles 11:9

8. Amaziah the king was killed here - II Kings 14:17-19; II Chronicles 25:27

9. Besieged and destroyed by Sennacherib - II Kings 18:13-17; 19:8; II Chronicles 32:9; Isaiah 36:2-3; 37:8

10. Destroyed by Babylon - Jeremiah 34:7

11. Rebuilt in the return from Babylon - Nehemiah 11:30

12. In the Prophets: Micah 1:13

13. One of the more famous archaeological finds are the 21 Lachish Letters

    a. One of the letters talks about subversiveness led by a prophet who may have been Jeremiah

    b. One of the letters reads: "We are watching for the signal fires of Lachish which my Lord is giving for we cannot see Azekah."

    c. It is clear that this Lachish letter was written after the statement of Jeremiah 34:7

LATRUN

1. Site on the important intersection where the road from the coast divides into two separate ways to Jerusalem: the Beth Horon Road and the Shaar HaGai Pass

2. The Latrun Castle - Located above the monastery

    a. Built by the Crusaders in 1089 and entrusted to the Knight Templars

    b. Named *Le Toron des Chevaliers*, The Tower of the Knights

    c. Arabic Name

       (1) First - *el-Atrun*

       (2) Later - *Latrun*

       (3) In the 15th century, the pilgrims understood the Arabic Latrun to mean *latro*, Latin for "robber" and took it to mean the birthplace of the good robber and called it *Castallum boni latroni*, The Castle of the Good Robber

    d. Here Richard the Lionhearted held Saladin at bay until the Crusader defeat at the Horns of Hattin and then he withdrew to Ashkelon

3. The Latrun Monastery - The Latrun Abbey

    a. Built in 1890 by monks of the Trappist Order who follow a strict vow of silence

    b. Monastery of vineyards and winery

4. The Latrun Fort

    a. Built by the British as a police station who turned it over to the Arabs on the eve of The War of Independence

    b. On Black Saturday in 1946, most of the Jewish leaders were arrested and interned here

    c. One of the three blockades of the Tel Aviv - Jerusalem Highway in the War of Independence

    d. Jewish forces tried to take it three times (May 12, May 19 and June 9, 1948) but failed with the loss of 200 fighters

    e. A fourth attempt was made July 17th but failed and the second cease-fire took effect July 18th

    f.   As a result, Jordan retained the Latrun Fort and the Valley of Ayalon became a no man's land for nineteen years

    g.   In the Six-Day War, it was taken without a fight on June 6, 1967 since it was already abandoned by the Arab Legion

    h.   Now a museum for the Armored Corps

LEBONAH (LUBAN)

It is a city mentioned in location with Shiloh - Judges 21:19

LIBNAH

1. Taken by Joshua - Joshua 10:29-32

2. The king was killed by Joshua - Joshua 10:39; 12:15

3. City of the Tribe of Judah - Joshua 15:42

4. Levitical City - Joshua 21:13; I Chronicles 6:57

5. Revolted against Joram - II Kings 8:22; II Chronicles 21:10

6. Besieged and taken by Sennacherib - II Kings 19:8; Isaiah 37:8

7. Home of Hamutal, Josiah's wife and the mother of Jehoahaz - II Kings 23:31

8. She was also the mother of Zedekiah - II Kings 24:18; Jeremiah 52:1

LOD - LYDDA - DIOSPOLIS

1. City of the Tribe of Benjamin - I Chronicles 8:12

2. Rebuilt in the return from Babylon - Ezra 2:33; Nehemiah 7:37; 11:35

3. Here Peter healed Aeneas - Acts 9:32-35, 38

4. In the post-New Testament period, it was known as Diospolis

5. The base of many important rabbis between the First and Second Jewish Revolt and famous for its textiles and pottery

    a.   Rabbi Eliezer ben Hyrcanus

    b.   Rabbi Tarpon

    c.   Rabbi Akiba

    d.   Rabbi Yehudah

6. The Sanhedrin moved here from Yavne

7. After the Bar Cochba Revolt, it was settled by pagans

8. Septimus Severus (153-211) renamed the city Diospolis. In the fifth century it was the Synod of Diospolis that tried and acquitted Pelagius

9. During the Byzantine Period, it was called Georgiopolis after Saint George

10. After the Arab Conquest, it was the capital of the Province of Filastin until Ramle was built

11. It became an important Crusader city until it was taken by the Mamelukes in 1260

12. By legend, it is the birthplace and burial place of Saint George who slew the dragon

13. Today it is a mixed Arab-Jewish town

MAALEH ADDUMIM (TALAT ED-DAMM)

1. Meaning: The Bloody Ascent - From exposed red limestone tinted with iron oxide

2. Marked the northern border of Judah - Joshua 15:7

3. Marked the southern border of Benjamin - Joshua 18:17

4. Traditional site of the Inn of the Good Samaritan

    a. The present one built in 1903 on the site of a previous Byzantine Monastery

    b. Arabic Name: *Khan el-Ahmar*, The Red Inn

5. Above the Khan are the remains of a castle called *Qala'at ed-Dum*, The Castle of Blood

MAALEH AKRABBIM (NAKEB A-TZAFI)

1. Marked the southern border of the Land - Numbers 34:4; Judges 1:36

2. Marked the southern border of Judah - Joshua 15:3

3. The present road was made by the British alongside the Roman road

4. In the War of Independence, the Golani Brigade used this road to capture Eilat

5. On July 7, 1949, the road was improved as part of Operation Aravah and the monument commemorates the event in April 1950

6. On March 18, 1954, terrorists from Jordan attacked a bus on this road, killing 11 of 13 people

7. In 1993, the road was improved for all vehicles

MADON

1. Located on what is now the Horns of Hattin

2. Part of the northern confederacy against Joshua - Joshua 11:1

3. The king was killed by Joshua - Joshua 12:19

MAMRE (RAMAT EL KHALIL)

1. One of the dwelling places of Abraham - Genesis 13:18; 14:13; 18:1

2. Close to and thus associated with Hebron and the Cave of Machpelah - Genesis 13:18; 23:17, 19; 25:9; 35:27; 49:30; 50:13

3. God reaffirmed His covenant with Abraham - Genesis 15:1-21

4. God appeared to Abraham - Genesis 18:1

5. The home of Isaac - Genesis 35:27

Mamshit - Kurnub (Mampsis)

1. One of the three Nabatean/Byzantine cities in the Negev; first built in the third century B.C. and flourished until the second century A.D.

2. On the caravan route leading to the Aravah and Petra

3. Mentioned in the Nitzana Papyrus

4. One of only two cities shown in the Negev section of the Madaba map

5. The city had no natural water source and so the Nabateans constructed three dams to gather water from the meager rainfall in Wadi Mamshit which in turn channeled the water into the city resevoirs and cisterns

6. For economic purposes, the Nabateans raised pigs and began raising race horses and bred what became known as Arabian Horses

7. The Byzantines made the city part of its south-east border defense system and built the wall around the city

8. During the Byzantine Period, it had a population of 1,500

9. Found here was a bronze jug containing over 10,000 silver drachmas and tetradrachmas dating from the first and second century

10. History of the city came to an end at about the time of the Arab Invasion in A.D. 636

11. Things to see

    a. Remains of two Byzantine Churches

       (1) One of which is named The Nilus Church

       (2) The Eastern Church - The crosses on the mosaic floor show the church was built before 427 when putting crosses on floors was banned due to the possibility of stepping on them

    b. Caravanasarai

    c. City Wall

    d. Nabatean Palace

    e. Tower

    f. The Dams

    g. The Bathhouse and Public Pool

    h. Nabatean and Byzantine Houses

    i. Three Cemeteries: Nabatean, Roman and Byzantine

Maon

1. The origin is given in I Chronicles 2:45

2. City of the Tribe of Judah - Joshua 15:55

3. Home of Nabal and Abigail who later became the wife of David - I Samuel 5:2

4. One of the refuge places for David's flight from Saul - I Samuel 23:24-28

5. Here Saul searched for David - I Samuel 23:24-28

MARESHAH (TEL SANTAHANNAH) - MARISSA

1. City of the Tribe of Judah - Joshua 15:44; I Chronicles 4:21

2. Fortified by Rehoboam - II Chronicles 11:8

3. Ethiopians defeated by Asa - II Chronicles 14:9-14

4. Home of Eliezer the Prophet - II Chronicles 20:37

5. In the Prophets: Micah 1:15

6. After 586 B.C., it was occupied by the Idumeans and became their capital

7. Joined by the Sidonians in the fourth century B.C.

8. Became an administrative center during the Greek Period

9. Conquered by John Hyrcanus in 113 B.C. who forced inhabitants to convert to Judaism

10. Destroyed by the Parthians in 40 B.C. and replaced by Beth Guvrin (For additional information, see "Beth Guvrin")

11. Things to see

    a. The Northern Burial Site - From the third-second century B.C.

    b. Cisterns - Under a house destroyed in 113 B.C. by John Hyrcanus

    c. The Olive Oil Press Cave - Over 20 underground oil presses from the third century B.C. producing about nine tons a year, meeting local demands and exported to the Coastal Plain and to Egypt

    d. The Columbarium Cave - Containing 2,000 niches used to raise pigeons and doves or for cremated remains

    e. The Polish Cave - Fourth to third century B.C. cave used for collecting water. In 1943, Polish soldiers carved the names of "Poland" and "Warsaw" and the Polish Eagle giving it its name

    f. The Bath Cave - Over 20 hewn stones used as bathtubs in third and second century B.C. with water flowing through conduits

    g. The Corner Tower of the Acropolis - Northwest corner of the upper city, dating from third and second century B.C. with a wall dating from the First Temple Period containing inscriptions and drawings

       (1) Burial caves from the third to second century B.C.

           (a) The Apollophanes Cave

           (b) The Musicians Cave

       (2) Population consisted of Edomites, Sidonians, Greeks, Egyptians and a very few Jews

       (3) A total of 34 Greek inscriptions have been found with the most important reading: "Apollophanes, son of Sesmaios, 33 years chief of the Sidonians at Marise, reputed the best and most kin-loving of all those of his time; he died, having lived 74 years"

(4) Contains wall painting of animals (lion, rhinoceros, porcupine, lynx, fish, hippopotamus, wolf, onyx, elephant, horse, bull, griffin, rooster, eagle), man (herald, musicians, hunter) and *Kerberos*, the guard-dog of the underworld

h. The Sidonian Burial Caves from the third to second century B.C.

MASADA

1. Possibly it was the stronghold of David - I Samuel 22:4-5; 23:14; 24:22

2. Jonathan Maccabee originally built a fortress here

3. Herod the Great rebuilt this stronghold in 36 B.C. and it became one of his three fortresses

 a. 1,432 feet above the shore of the Dead Sea

 b. 132 feet above sea level

 c. 1,950 feet long

 d. 650 feet wide

 e. 4,250 feet in circumference

4. Here he left his family for refuge after the Parthian Invasion while he proceeded to Rome to seek help and receive an army

5. In A.D. 66, as the First Jewish Revolt began, Masada was captured by Menachem ben Yehudah, the leader of the Sicarii (named after the short dagger, *sica*, that they carried in their robes), the most extreme of the Zealots, who was later killed in Jerusalem by his opponents

6. After the fall of Jerusalem in A.D. 70, 967 men, women and children sought refuge here under Eliezer Ben Yair, the nephew of Menachem ben Yehudah

 a. The Romans, under Flavius Silva, with the 15,600 strong Tenth Legion, came and built a solid seige wall about six feet thick and about seven miles in circumference around this mountain to keep any Jews from successfully fleeing

 b. Along the wall the Romans built eight separate army camps

 c. Masada finally fell on the 15th of *Nisan* (the first day of Passover) in A.D. 73 after the ramp was built all the way to the top of the wall and the breech in the wall was made by the use of a battering ram

 d. Fell by mass suicide - Only two old women and five children survived

 e. Ostraca were found having eleven names, one of which had the name ben Yair, the leader

7. Only other time it has been inhabited is by Byzantine monks in the fifth-sixth century A.D.

8. Rediscovered in 1838 by the American, Edward Robinson, who found it by the use of a telescope viewed from Ein Gedi and in 1842 by the English painter Tipping who was illustrating for an English edition of the writings of Josephus

9. Things to see
   a. Snake Path
   b. Casemate Wall
   c. Roman Ramp
   d. The Herodian three-level palace (the Northern Palace)
      (1) The Upper Terrace - A complex of four rooms with a semi-circular balcony that served as the living quarters
      (2) The Middle Terrace - A circular pavilion with a wing containing additional rooms and a path along the western slopes that led to two reservoirs
      (3) The Lower Terrace - Containing a large square building and a private bath house containing a cold room (frigidarium), a warm room (tepidarium) and a hot room (caldarium); skeletons were found of the Jewish defenders
   e. Storehouses - Where food and weapons were stored
   f. The Bathhouse
   g. The Synagogue - Here, a fragment of the last two chapters of Deuteronomy and Ezekiel 37 were found
   h. The Scroll Room - Writings of the Zealots
   i. The Breach Point - Where the Romans breached the wall
   j. The Western Palace - Remains of beautiful mosaic floors
   k. Byzantine Church
   l. The Great Pool
   m. The Columbarium for raising pigeons
   n. The Great Cistern
   o. The Southern Citadel

MEDITERRANEAN SEA

1. Names
   a. The Great Sea - Numbers 34:6
   b. The Sea of the Philistines - Exodus 23:31
   c. The Utmost or Uttermost Sea - Deuteronomy 11:24; 34:2; Joel 2:20
   d. The Hinder Sea - Zechariah 14:8
   e. The Sea of Joppa - Ezra 3:7
2. Marked the western border of the Promised Land - Numbers 34:6-7; Joshua 1:4; 9:1
3. Part of the Land that Moses saw - Deuteronomy 34:2
4. Marked the western border of Judah - Joshua 15:12, 47
5. Marked the western border of Ephraim - Joshua 16:3, 8
6. Marked the western border of Manasseh - Joshua 16:9

7. Marked the western border of Asher - Joshua 19:29

8. It will mark the western border of Millennial Israel - Ezekiel 47:15, 19-20; 48:28; Zechariah 14:8

9. Simon the Tanner had his home by this sea - Acts 10:6, 32

10. Paul sailed this sea - Acts 27:30, 38, 40; 28:4

MEGIDDO (TEL EL-MUTASALLIM)

1. Arabic name - "Governor's Hill"

2. Guarded the Megiddo Pass

3. Place of the dividing line of the Via Maris

    a. The break to the north went to Tyre, Sidon, Baalbek and Ugarit

    b. The road east went to Damascus

4. The tel has 22 cities on top of each other

5. In Egyptian records, it is mentioned in the campaigns of Thutmose III, Amenhotep II and in the Amarna Letters

6. The king was killed by Joshua - Joshua 12:21

7. Given to the Tribe of Manasseh - Joshua 17:11; I Chronicles 7:29

8. The Canaanites retained control - Joshua 17:12; Judges 1:27

9. Part of the area involved in the defeat of Sisera - Judges 5:19

10. In the Fifth Solomonic District - I Kings 4:12

11. One of the three fortified cities of Solomon - I Kings 9:15

12. Here Ahaziah died after being smitten by Jehu - II Kings 9:27

13. Josiah killed - II Kings 23:29-30; II Chronicles 35:22-24; Zechariah 12:11

14. Conquered by Tiglath Pileser III

15. During the Persian Conquest, it was rebuilt and became the capital of the Persian Province

16. Abandoned during the Hellenistic Period

17. In 1918, General Allenby decisively defeated the Turks at Megiddo and thus received the title, Lord of Megiddo

18. It will serve as the main area for the gathering grounds of the allies of the Antichrist in the Campaign of Armageddon - Revelation 16:12-16

19. Things to see - Built in the ninth century B.C.

    a. Bronze Age Gates - The Canaanite Gates

    b. The Solomonic Gates - The Iron Age Gates

    c. The Canaanite Sacred Compound

    d. The Massebot Shrine - Local shrine from the Israelite Period

    e. The public grain silo

    f. "The Solomonic Stables" - Debated whether these are stables or public buildings or store houses

    g. The Solomonic Palace

h. The Assyrian Palace - The most complete Assyrian Palace found in the land

i. Israelite houses

j. The water tunnel is 210 feet long

MEI NEPHTOAH (LIFTA)

1. Marked the northern border of Judah - Joshua 15:9

2. Marked the southern border of Benjamin - Joshua 18:15

3. Home of Maharia, one of David's mighty men - II Samuel 23:28

4. Home of Heleb, one of David's mighty men - II Samuel 23:29

5. Home of one of the conspirators against Gedaliah - Jeremiah 40:8

6. Rebuilt after the return from Babylon - Ezra 2:22; Nehemiah 7:26

7. One of the homes of the Temple Singers - Nehemiah 12:28-29

MEROM

1. In Egyptian records, it is mentioned by Ramses II

2. In Assyrian records, it is mentioned by Tiglath Pileser III

3. The northern confederacy against Joshua was defeated - Joshua 11:5-8

4. The king was killed by Joshua - Joshua 12:20

MERON

1. The tomb of Rabbi Shimon Bar Yohai and his son Eliezer is located here

    a. He is believed to be the author of the *Zohar*, the key book of Cabalism

    b. If so, it dates back to the second century

2. Here a second century synagogue is to be found

    a. A Jewish legend says that when the lintel falls, the Messiah will come

    b. The lintel finally fell shortly after the Six-Day War but no Messiah arrived

3. On Lag ba-Omer, young Jewish boys receive their first haircut in accordance with Deuteronomy 18:4; considered to be the first fruit

METULAH

1. The most northern Jewish town in Israel founded by 59 Eastern European Jewish settlers in 1896 on lands purchased by a representative of Edmond de Rothschild for the purpose of establishing a community of Jewish farmers with each family working its own land

2. It was harassed in the early days by Druze, Turks and Arabs

3. At the fall of Tel Hai in 1920, it was evacuated

4. The fields of Metulah, located in the Iyon Valley, were given to Lebanon after the War of Independence

5. The town then became a summer resort town

6. A result of the Lebanon Civil War was the formation of "The Good Fence" located here

7. Present population - 1,500

METZUDAT YESHA (NABI YUSHA)

1. Moslem tomb of Joshua

2. One of eight Galilee fortresses built by the British to guard the northern roads of the British Mandate in the late 1930's

3. The British turned the fort over to Arab forces on April 15, 1948

4. A Jewish attack by the Palmach on the same day to capture the fortress failed with the loss of four men

5. A second attack on April 20, 1948 also failed with the loss of 22 men

6. A third attack on May 16, 1948 finally succeeded with the loss of two men; the Arabs surrendered when Piper Cubs flew over, dropping primitive bombs

7. Because a total of 28 lives were lost, it is now also called *Metzudat Koah* (*Koah*, meaning "strength," has a numerical value of 28)

MICHMASH (MUKHMAS)

1. Area of the Saul and Jonathan Philistine War - I Samuel 13:1-14:46 (13:2, 5, 11, 16, 23; 14:5, 31)

2. Part of the military camp of Saul - I Samuel 13:2

3. Served as the camp of the Philistines - I Samuel 13:5, 11, 16, 23

4. Philistine garrison smitten - I Samuel 14:5-15

5. Philistines smitten - I Samuel 14:31

6. Taken by Sennacherib - Isaiah 10:28

7. Rebuilt after the return from Babylon - Ezra 2:27; Nehemiah 7:31; 11:31

8. Between the years 156-152 B.C., after the death of Judah Maccabee, it served as Jonathan Maccabee's headquarters where he united the rebels and where he began his reign over Judea

MIGDAL APHEK - MIRABEL CASTLE

1. Other names

   a. Arabic

      (1) *Majdal Tzadek* - After Sheikh Tzadek el-Jamain who revolted against the Turks

      (2) *Majdal Yabah*

   b. Crusaders: *Mirabel*, Beautiful Surprise

2. Crusader structure built at the beginning of the 12th century on earlier Roman remains

3. Inscription on the lintel from the Byzantine Period reads - "Place of Death of Saint Kyrikos"

4. Guarded the main north-south road which was also the Via Maris

5. Captured in 1187 by el-Adel, the brother of Saladin and made it his headquarters for a while

6. Sheikh Tzadek moved into it at the beginning of the 19th century and set up his own local government until it was recaptured by the Turks who exiled him in 1852

MIGDOL - MAGDALA - TARICHEA

1. City on the Via Maris

2. Full name: *Magdal Nunya*, meaning "fish tower" and its Greek equivalent was *Tarichea*, meaning "day fish"

3. An important Jewish city which specialized in fishing and fish processing

4. Same as Dalmanutha of Mark 8:10

5. City of the Tribe of Naphtali - Joshua 19:38

6. In the New Testament Period, the city had 40,000 residents

7. Home of Mary Magdalene - Matthew 27:56, 61; 28:1; Mark 15:40, 41; 16:1, 9; Luke 8:2; 24:10; John 19:25; 20:1, 18

8. Here Jesus came after the feeding of the 4,000 - Matthew 15:39; Mark 8:10

9. Pharisees and Sadducees asked for a sign - Matthew 15:39-16:4

10. Fortified by Josephus and for a while it was his headquarters - But it was destroyed by Romans in the First Jewish Revolt

11. Port base for the Zealot Navy and where a navel battle was fought

12. Site of the discovery of the first century boat known as the Kinneret Boat, the Galilee Boat, the Magdala Boat or the Jesus Boat - Oldest boat ever found in Israel so far

MIZPAH (TEL ES-NASBE)

1. City of the Tribe of Benjamin - Joshua 18:26

2. Tribes of Israel took their oath against Benjamin and so began the anti-Benjaminite War - Judges 20:1, 3; 21:1, 5, 8

3. Gathering ground of Samuel against the Philistines - I Samuel 7:5-12

4. The Stone of Ebenezer erected - I Samuel 7:12

5. It was part of Samuel's circuit - I Samuel 7:16

6. Saul was announced as Israel's king - I Samuel 10:17-24

7. Fortified by Asa from the stones used by Baasha to fortify Rama - I Kings 15:22; II Chronicles 16:6

8. Home of Jeremiah after the fall of Jerusalem - Jeremiah 40:6

9. Home of Gedaliah - II Kings 25:23; Jeremiah 40:8-12

10. It was against Mizpah that Ishmael attacked and killed Gedaliah - II Kings 25:23, 25; Jeremiah 40:7-41:17 (40:6, 8, 10, 12, 13, 15; 41:1, 3, 6, 10, 14, 16)

11. Rebuilt after the return from Babylon - Nehemiah 3:15, 19

12. Members of this city helped to rebuild the wall - Nehemiah 3:7-19

13. In the Prophets: Hosea 5:1

14. Judah Maccabee gathered his forces for the battle against Gorgias

MODIIN (MIDYAH) (TEL ERAS)

1. Home of the Maccabees

2. In 167 B.C., the Maccabean Revolt began here

3. The Maccabean Tombs

    a. Arabic: *Kubur el-Yahud*, Graves of the Jews

    b. May only date back to Roman times

MONASTERY OF SAINT GEORGE

1. Greek Orthodox Monastery built in the fifth century in Wadi Qelt

2. Founded by John of Thebes who became a hermit and moved here from Egypt in 480 in honor to the Holy Virgin

3. When John died in 525, the monastery was renamed after him

4. The most famous monk to live and die here was Gorgias of Cosiba and the monastery was renamed Saint George in his honor

5. Active from the fifth to the ninth century

6. Rebuilt during Crusader Period but fell into disuse and ruins after the Crusaders were expelled

7. In 1878, a Greek monk named Kalinikos settled in Wadi Qelt and began restoring the monastery completing it in 1901

8. In 1952, the belfry was donated by the Greek Patriarch of Jerusalem

9. The cave above is dedicated to Elijah since, by a medieval tradition, he was fed by the ravens here

MONTFORT (KALAT EL-QUREIN)

1. Built about 1150 on earlier Roman remains for the protection of Acre by the Frankish Crusaders and called *Montfort*, Strong Mountain

2. In 1229, it was sold to the Teutonic Knights, who called it *Starkenburg*, meaning "strong mountain"

3. In 1271, it fell to the Moslems under Mameluke Sultan Baybars who allowed the knights to leave in peace

4. The castle was not inhabited again

5. Arabic Name - The Castle on the Horn

MORESHETH GATH

1. Fortified by Rehoboam - II Chronicles 11:8

2. Home of Micah the Prophet - Micah 1:1

3. In the Prophets: Micah 1:14

MOUNT OF BEATITUDES

1. In ancient times, known as Mount Eremos

2. Catholic site of the Sermon on the Mount - Matthew 5-7

3. The present church was built over an earlier Byzantine Church by Italians in 1936 and the symbols on the pavement symbolize the following:

   a. Justice

   b. Prudence

   c. Fortitude

   d. Charity

   e. Faith

   f. Temperance

4. The church is run by Franciscan nuns of the Immaculate Heart of Mary Order

5. The Italian Hospice was first built in 1926

MOUNT CARMEL

1. It comes from two Hebrew words: *Kerem El* meaning the "Vineyard of God"

2. Unlike Israel's other mountain ranges, the Carmel runs from the northwest to the southeast

   a. It is a mountain range that has steep cliffs on both sides

   b. It juts into the Mediterranean Sea

   c. Receives a great deal of rainfall

   d. The narrow strip of shoreline at its foot is composed of fossilized sand dunes

3. Measurements

   a. 1,810 feet above sea level

   b. 1,470 feet high; Average 500 feet

   c. 15 miles long

   d. 3-8 miles wide

4. Divides the Plain of Asher from the Plain of Sharon

5. Venis, a general of Pharaoh Cheops I, (23rd century B.C.) called it "The Gazelle's Nose"

6. Thutmose III called it "The Holy Head"

7. Taken by Joshua - Joshua 12:22

8. It marked the border of four tribes

   a. Asher

   b. Zebulun

   c. Issachar

   d. Manasseh

9. The mount itself belonged to Asher - Joshua 19:26

10. The contest on Carmel between Elijah and the prophets of Baal - I Kings 18:18-46 (19, 20, 42)

    a. By tradition, the event took place at *Muhraqah* - Arabic for "scorching"

        (1) Mentioned by Rabbi Benjamin of Tudela (1165)

        (2) Mentioned by Rabbi Jacob of Paris (1228)

        (3) Nearby is *Bir el-Muhraqa* which may have provided the water for the sacrifice

    b. Today it is the site of the Carmelite Monastery

        (1) Built by them in 1848

        (2) Front chapel built in 1867

        (3) The present monastery was completed in 1883

11. Here Elisha stayed - II Kings 2:25; 4:25

12. Mentioned in Song of Solomon 7:5

13. In the Prophets: Isaiah 33:9; 35:2; Jeremiah 46:18; 50:19; Amos 1:2; 9:3; Micah 7:14; Nahum 1:4

14. In 107 B.C., it was taken by the sons of John Hyrcanus

15. The Carmel Caves - Remains of both Neanderthal Man and Homo Sapiens found here showing the two co-existed at the same time

16. Home of two large Druze Villages

    a. Usfiya

    b. Daliyat el-Carmel

MOUNT EBAL (JEBEL ASKAR)

1. 3,077 feet above sea level

2. The mountain of cursing - Deuteronomy 11:29; 27:13-26; Joshua 8:33-35

3. Joshua commanded to build an altar here - Deuteronomy 27:4

4. Joshua fulfilled the order - Joshua 8:30-31

5. The Arabic name reflects the name Sychar and the foot of the mountain

MOUNT GERIZIM (JEBEL ET-TUR)

1. 2,848 feet above sea level

2. The mountain of blessing - Deuteronomy 11:29; 27:11-12; Joshua 8:33-35

    a. The Arabic name reflects the Aramaic *tura bricha*

    b. Meaning: "Mountain of Blessing"

3. Jotham's speech - Judges 9:7-21

4. The Samaritans built their temple here which was destroyed by John Hyrcanus in 125 B.C.

   a. Rebuilt and later renovated by Hadrian and functioned for 200 years

   b. Destroyed in the fourth century

   c. Byzantines built a church here which was destroyed in the Arab Invasion

5. The Samaritan Woman's statement, "on this mountain" refers to this mount - John 4:20

6. The tomb is that of Sheikh Anim

MOUNT GILBOA

1. 1,648 feet above sea level

2. The camp of Saul - I Samuel 28:4

3. Saul and his three sons were killed here - I Samuel 31:1-8; II Samuel 1:6-10; 21:12; I Chronicles 10:1-8

4. Part of the lament of David - II Samuel 1:21-23

MOUNT HERMON (JEBEL ESH-SHEIKH)

1. 5 x 20 miles culminating in three peaks

   a. Each 1/4 mile from the other

   b. Its highest peak is 9,230 feet above sea level

   c. Highest mountain in Israel with the Israeli side (*Mitzpe Shelagim*) measuring 7,200 feet above sea level

   d. Highest mountain in all of the Promised Land

2. Other names

   a. Sirion - Deuteronomy 3:8; Psalm 29:6

   b. Senir - Deuteronomy 3:9; Ezekiel 27:5

   c. Sion - Deuteronomy 4:48

   d. Baal-Hermon - Judges 3:3; I Chronicles 5:23

   e. Baal-Gad - Joshua 11:17; 12:7; 13:5

   f. Aramaic Talmudic name: *Tur Talga*, Snow Mountain

   g. Arabic names

      (1) *Jabel A-Talg*, Snow Mountain

      (2) *Jabel A-Sheikh*, Old Man Mountain

3. Marked the northern boundary of Bashan - Deuteronomy 3:8-9; 4:48; Joshua 12:1; 13:5, 11

4. Conquered under Moses - Deuteronomy 3:8

5. Part of the northern confederacy against Joshua - Joshua 11:3

6. Joshua controlled it - Joshua 11:17; 12:1, 5

7. Marked the northern boundary of the Transjordanian Tribes - Joshua 12:1-13:11

8. Given to the Tribe of Manasseh - Deuteronomy 3:13; I Chronicles 5:23

9. The land beyond Mount Hermon was considered part of the Land that remained to be taken - Judges 3:3

10. Noted for its majesty - Psalm 42:6; 89:12; Song of Solomon 4:8

11. Noted for its dew - Psalm 133:3

12. Most likely the Mount of Transfiguration - Matthew 17:1, 9; Mark 9:2, 9; Luke 9:28, 37

MOUNT HOR

1. One of the stops in the Wilderness Wanderings - Numbers 21:4; 33:37

2. Aaron died here - Numbers 20:22-29; 33:38-39; Deuteronomy 32:50

MOUNT MERON (JARMAG)

1. 3,962 feet high

2. Before the Six-Day War, it was the highest mountain in Israel

MOUNT SINAI (JEBEL MUSA)

1. Also known as Mount Horeb

2. 7,362 feet above sea level

3. 2,349 feet above the monastery

4. At the ascent (*Siket Abas Basha*), it consists of 1,700 steps up

5. At the descent (*Siket Sidna Mousa*), it is 3,400 steps down

6. The Burning Bush - Exodus 3:1-6; 17:6; 33:6; Deuteronomy 1:2, 6, 19; 4:10, 15; 5:2; 9:8; 18:16; 29:1; I Kings 8:9; 19:8; II Chronicles 5:10; Psalm 106:19; Malachi 4:4

7. The camp of Israel - Exodus 16:1; 19:1-2; Leviticus 7:38; 25:1; 26:46; 27:34; Numbers 1:1, 19; 3:1, 4, 14; 9:1, 5; 10:12; 26:64; 28:6; 33:15, 16; Deuteronomy 33:2

8. God came down upon Mount Sinai - Exodus 19:11; Nehemiah 9:13; Psalm 68:8, 17; Acts 7:30, 38

9. Three times Moses ascended this mountain

   a. First - Exodus 19:3-6

   b. Second - Exodus 19:16-32:16 (19:18, 20, 23; 24:16; 31:18)

   c. Third - Exodus 34:1-35 (2, 4, 29, 32)

10. Mentioned in Deborah's Song - Judges 5:5

11. Elijah fled from Jezebel - 1 Kings 19:8-18

12. Used allegorically by Paul - Galatians 4:24-25

MOUNT TABOR

1. 1,994 feet above sea level

2. 1,400 feet above the plain

3. It marked the boundary of three tribes

    a. Zebulun on the west - Joshua 19:12

    b. Issachar on the south - Joshua 19:22

    c. Naphtali on the north - Joshua 19:34

4. Fortified by Israel under Barak - Judges 4:6, 12, 14

5. The brothers of Gideon were killed - Judges 8:18

6. Mentioned in Psalm 89:12

7. In the Prophets: Jeremiah 46:18; Hosea 5:1

8. Fortified during both the First and Second Temple Periods

9. Catholic site of the Mount of Transfiguration

10. Fortified by Josephus in the First Jewish Revolt

11. Place of pilgrimage since the fourth century

12. By the sixth century, there were three churches on the mount

13. Eleventh century - Another church and monastery built and continuously inhabited by eighteen monks

14. Tancred, the Crusader Prince of Galilee, built a fortress on the summit in 1099 and turned it over to the Order of the Benedictines who held it until 1187

15. Taken by Mameluke Sultan Baybars in 1263 and remained in ruins

16. In 1631, The Order of the Franciscans were allowed to return and built a monastery in 1873

17. A Greek Orthodox monastery was added in 1911

18. A Franciscan church and hostel called *Casa Nova* was added in 1925

NAARAN - NAARAH

1. Border city of the Tribe of Ephraim - Joshua 16:7; I Chronicles 7:28

2. During the Hasmonean Period, it was called Shelomi after Salome Alexander

3. Archelaus took water from there for his plantations (Josephus)

4. During the Roman Period it was a Jewish city in counterpart to pagan Jericho

5. Benjamin of Tudela - Poor relationship between it and Jericho

6. Contains an ancient sixth century synagogue with a mosaic floor which included the signs of the Zodiac and Daniel in the Lion's Den

NABI MUSA

1. Multidomed structure built in 1269 by the Mameluke Sultan Beibars (Baybars)

2. The minaret was built in 1500

3. Became the traditional Moslem tomb of Moses

NAHARIYYAH

1. A modern city founded in 1934 by German Jews

2. The name is based on the Hebrew word for "river" and refers to the Gaaton River that flows through the center of the city

3. During the War of Independence, it was cut off from the rest of the country and contact was maintained by sea in small boats

4. Today it is the capital of western Galilee with a population of 31,000 and a popular resort town for Israelis

NAZARETH (E-NASIRA)

1. Although it has existed since the Canaanite Period, it is not mentioned in the Old Testament

2. At the time of Jesus, it was a small village of 120-150 people

3. Home of Joseph and Mary - Luke 1:26-28; 2:4, 39

4. Home of Jesus - Matthew 2:23; 4:13; 21:11; 26:71;
Mark 1:9, 24; 10:47; 14:67; 16:6; Luke 2:39-40, 51; 4:34; 18:37; 24:19; John 18:5, 7; 19:19; Acts 2:22; 3:6; 4:10; 6:14; 10:38; 22:8; 26:9

5. City of disrepute - John 1:45-46

6. Jesus returned here on two occasions - Luke 4:16-30;
Matthew 13:54-58 (Mark 6:1-6)

7. In the Roman and Byzantine periods, it was a Jewish city with a large population of Messianic Jews

8. It remained largely an isolated town until the Crusader Period during which time many churches and religious centers were established

9. In the twelfth century, the Archbishopric of all Galilee was moved from Beth Shean to Nazareth

10. After the fall of the Crusader Kingdom, the churches and religious centers went into a decline with some being destroyed, some falling into disrepair and some totally abandoned

11. During the long Moslem rule, Greek Orthodox continued to live there and there was a small number of pilgrims from the west that would visit

12. Nazareth began to flourish again in the 18th and 19th centuries during the Ottoman Turkish Period primarily due to the renewed interest by the western world in biblical studies and archaeology

    a. Nazareth had a building boom, especially the Christian institutions

    b. The Templers (German Christians) paved a road from Haifa Bay to Nazareth to facilitate pilgrim travel and later this road was extended to Cana and Tiberias

    c. At the end of the Ottoman Turkish Period, Nazareth achieved the status of a city and became the first of four cities in the Land to which a mayor was appointed

13. During the British Mandate, Nazareth became the Seat of Government for the Galilee District resulting in further building and further renewing of Christian institutions

14. During the War of Independence, Nazareth became the command post of Fawzi el-Kaukji's Arab Liberation Army from which he tried to capture surrounding Jewish settlements

15. Israel captured Nazareth in Operation Dekel on July 16, 1948 - The day after Ben Gurion ordered Israeli troops to avoid desecrating churches and monasteries and even gave an "open fire" order on any soldier found looting in the city

16. Today, it is the largest Arab city in the State of Israel numbering 60,000 - Comprising both Moslem and Christian Arabs and divided into nine quarters

    a. Catholic Quarter

    b. Greek Orthodox Quarter

    c. Moslem Quarter

    d. Six Mixed Quarters

17. It is a city of a number of churches

    a. Basilica of the Annunciation

        (1) Encompasses previous Byzantine Churches built in 427

        (2) Rebuilt by Crusaders

        (3) Present one built in 1955 and 1969; it is now the largest church in the Middle East

    b. Basilica of Jesus the Youth - Built in 1906-1923 by the French Salesian Order in the thirteenth century French Gothic style

    c. Chapel of Our Lady of the Fright - Franciscan marking Mary's fear when Jesus was about to be thrown off the cliff

    d. Mary's Well - By tradition, this is where Gabriel spoke to Mary

    e. Saint Gabriel's Church of the Annunciation - Greek Orthodox Church built in the Crusader Period and rebuilt in 1769

    f. *Mensa Christi*: The Franciscan Church of the Resurrection Supper - Built in 1861

    g. Saint Joseph's Church of the Carpenter Shop - From the sixth century rebuilt by the Crusaders; rebuilt in the present form in 1914

    h. The Greek Catholic Synagogue Church - The sixth century

    i. The Ladies of Nazareth Convent - Built in Gothic style

    j. Anglican Church - The second Protestant Church to be built in the Holy Land after Christ Church in Jerusalem

    k. Carmelite Convent - Built in 1907 in a European style

    l. Coptic Church of the Annunciation - Built in 1952

    m.   Greek Orthodox Bishopric - Residence of the Bishop built in 1863 and surrounded by a church and monastery

    n.   Qasr El-Mutran Greek Orthodox Church - Built in 1862

    o.   Maronite Church (Church of Saint Anthony) - Lebanese Christian Church built in 1774

    p.   Convent of the Sisters of Jesus - Built in 1897

    q.   Sisters of the Annunciation

    r.   Synogogue Church - Crusader Church built over the supposed synagogue of Jesus' day

18. *Har Kedumim*, The Mountain of the Leap

    a.   Hebrew Name: The Mountain of the Ancients - Because of the discovery of Neanderthal remains designated as "The Galilee Man"

    b.   Catholic Name: Based on the tradition that from here Jesus leaped to Mount Tabor to escape the mob

NEIN

The widow's son was raised back to life - Luke 7:11-17

NEOT KEDUMIM

1. The only Biblical Landscape Reserve in the world

2. Contains the plants, flowers and trees of the Bible on 625 acres of recreated biblical landscapes

NIMROD (KALAT-A-SUBEIBE) - L'ASIBEBE

1. Tradition: Burial place of Nimrod

2. Crusader fort overlooking Banyas and controls the mountain route from Damascus to Tyre

3. Built between 1130-1140 by Ranier of Brus on behalf of the Crusader king to guard against Moslem invasion from Damascus

4. The Crusaders called it *L'Asibebe*, which accounts for the Arab name

5. The fortress was captured by the Moslems in 1132 but retaken by the Crusaders in 1139

6. Taken by the Moslems in 1156 who greatly expanded on the Crusader fortress

7. Destroyed in 1219 by the Sultan of Damascus to keep it from falling into Crusader hands again

8. Between 1228-1230, the Ayyubids refortified it and their ten inscriptions are visible to this day

9. In 1260, Mameluke Sultan Baybars took control of the fortress and built a citadel

10. During the 14th-16th century, it served as a political prison by the Damascus Government

11. It has been abandoned ever since

Nitzana (Auja el-Hafir)

1. A Nabatean-Byzantine fortress on the ancient Spice Route where the road branches to Sinai and Egypt on one side and to the west and north on the other

2. Contains the remains of two churches from the fifth and seventh centuries

3. The Nitzana Papyri were found in the fifth century church - An important source of information of the Byzantine and Early Arab Periods in the Negev

4. The present building on top of the tel is the remains of the Turkish-German Administrative Center built during World War I when the allies were preparing to invade Sinai

Ophna

1. City of the Tribe of Benjamin - Joshua 18:24

2. It later became known as the Mountain of Gophna and served as the main refuge for the Maccabees, especially after two events

   a. After Modiin

   b. After Beth Zecharias

Ophrah (Taiba)

1. A city of the Tribe of Manasseh - Judges 6:11, 15

2. Gideon received his call - Judges 6:11-24

3. Gideon's shrine was built - Judges 8:22-27

4. Gideon was buried - Judges 8:32

5. The seventy sons of Gideon were killed - Judges 9:1-5

Ophrah (Taibeh)

1. City of the Tribe of Benjamin - Joshua 18:23

2. One of the areas of the maneuvering of Saul against the Philistines - I Samuel 13:17

3. One of the cities taken by Abijah from Jeroboam - II Chronicles 13:19

4. The city Jesus retired to after the resurrection of Lazarus - John 11:54

Pekiin

1. In the second century A.D., it was the hiding place of Rabbi Shimon Bar Yochai and his son Elazar and where, according to tradition, he wrote the *Zohar*

2. Only town in the Land of Israel that has never been without Jews

3. Today, it is a mixed town with Moslems, Druze, Christians and one Jewish family. The Druze are the majority, numbering about 11,000, representing thirty clans

THE PLAIN OF GINOSAR (GENNESARET)

1. Measures five miles long and two miles wide

2. Separates Upper and Lower Galilee in the east

3. Gave the Sea of Galilee one of its names (Gennesaret) - Luke 5:1

4. Where Jesus went after walking on the sea - Matthew 14:34; Mark 6:53-55

THE PLAIN OF ONO

1. Given to the Tribe of Benjamin - I Chronicles 8:12

2. Area developed after the return from Babylon - Ezra 2:33; Nehemiah 7:37; 11:35

3. Known for its craftsmen - Nehemiah 11:35

4. Involved in the conspiracy against Nehemiah - Nehemiah 6:2-4

5. Today, the town of Rosh Ha-Ayin is found there, settled by Yemenite Jews making Yemenite jewelry - So again, it is known for its craftsmen

POOLS OF SOLOMON

1. Once believed to be the Solomonic pools mentioned in Ecclesiastes 2:6 and Song of Solomon 4:12

2. Earliest possible date is the Hasmonean Period

3. Herod used this to supply water for the Herodium and most likely it originates from the Herodian Period

4. Pontius Pilate repaired these pools and used them to supply water for Jerusalem

5. Measurements

    a. Upper Pool - 380 x 229 x 25

    b. Middle Pool - 423 x 230 x 39

    c. Lower Pool - 582 x 207 x 50

QUMRAN

1. Possibly referred to as the City of Salt - Joshua 15:62

2. Archaeology has shown that there was Jewish settlement here as early as the eighth century B.C. and may have been among Uzziah's towers in the wilderness - II Chronicles 26:10

3. In New Testament times, it was the site of the Essene Community

    a. First arrived in the second century B.C.

    b. In 31 B.C., it was destroyed by an earthquake and abandoned

    c. It was rebuilt during the reign of Archaelaus (4 B.C. - A.D. 6)

4. The Essene Community was destroyed by the Romans in A.D. 68

5. Last known residents were a Roman garrison stationed here during the Bar Cochba Revolt (A.D. 135)

6. The Dead Sea Scrolls were found here in 1947

RAMA (ER RAM)

1. City of the Tribe of Benjamin - Joshua 18:25

2. Area of the home of Deborah - Judges 4:5

3. One option for overnight lodging for the Levite and his concubine - Judges 19:13

4. Home of Samuel - I Samuel 1:1, 19; 2:11; 7:17; 15:34; 16:13

5. Israel made its request for a king - I Samuel 8:4-5

6. One of the places where David fled for refuge from Saul - I Samuel 19:18-21; 20:1

7. Saul pursued David to Rama - I Samuel 19:22-24; 22:6

8. Samuel buried - I Samuel 25:1; 28:3

9. Baasha's attempt to fortify the city caused a war with Asa and Ben Hadad - I Kings 15:16-21

10. Stones used by Baasha to fortify Rama were used by Asa to build Geba and Mizpah - I Kings 15:17-22; II Chronicles 16:1-6

11. Destroyed by Sennacherib - Isaiah 10:29

12. Jeremiah was released by the Babylonians - Jeremiah 40:1

13. Rebuilt after the return from Babylon - Ezra 2:26; Nehemiah 7:30; 11:33

14. In the Prophets: Jeremiah 31:15; Hosea 5:8

15. Mentioned in Matthew 2:18

RAMA OF GALILEE

1. Sits on the dividing line between Upper and Lower Galilee

2. Border city between the Tribes of Asher and Naphtali - Joshua 19:29

3. City of the Tribe of Naphtali - Joshua 19:36

RAMALLAH

1. Name means "the Hill of God"

2. 2,930 feet above sea level

3. May have been the site of the Hill of God where the Spirit of Jehovah came upon Saul - I Samuel 10:5-6

4. Today it is a mixed Christian and Moslem Arab city of 24,000

RAMLEH

1. Arabic word meaning "sand"

2. Built in A.D. 716 by the Umayyad Caliph Suleiman, son of Abd el-Malik, the builder of the Dome of the Rock - The only town built by Arabs that did not exist before and replaced Lod as the capital of the province

3. Water was brought in by aqueducts from Gezer and Aphek (Antipatris)

4. During the Crusader Period, a church was built here which is now the Great Mosque of Ramleh

5. The Franciscan Church and Hospice was built here in 1396

6. Napoleon stayed here during his invasion in 1799 and after he left the Moslems slaughtered the Christians

7. The White Tower is 100 feet tall and was built by Mameluke Sultan Kalaun in 1318 in the center of a caravanesarai built by Caliph Suleiman in 715

8. The large underground water cistern was built by the Umayyads about 740

9. In the War of Independence, it served as a base for Arab forces blocking the road to Jerusalem from Tel Aviv until captured by Israeli forces in Operation Dan in July 1948

REPHIDIM (FIRAN)

1. One of the sites of the encampment of Israel in the wilderness - Exodus 17:1-7; 19:2; Numbers 33:14-15

2. Scene of the Amalekite War - Exodus 17:8-16

3. Site of Paran where Nadab the Edomite fled from Solomon - I Kings 11:18

RIMMON (RAMMOUN)

1. Refuge of the 600 Benjaminites who survived the Anti-Benjaminite War - Judges 20:45-47

2. They began to get their wives - Judges 21:13-15

RIMMON (RUMMANA)

1. A city of the Tribe of Zebulun - Joshua 19:13

2. A Levitical City - I Chronicles 6:77

ROSH HANIKRA

1. Arabic Names

   a. *A-Nawakir*, The Grottos

   b. *Ras-A-Nakura* - Source of the Hebrew name

2. The southern end of the Ladders of Tyre with 225 foot high cliffs of a chalky mountain range

3. Noted for its labyrinth caves - Formed by sea action against the soft white chalk and measuring a total length of about 600 feet

4. Alexander the Great hewed a tunnel here to create a passage way for his army to get through in 323 B.C.

5. During World War I, the British paved a road making it accessible for motor vehicles

6. During World War II, the British dug a 750 foot tunnel for its railway, connecting Haifa with Beirut

7. In March 1948, the Palmach blew up the railway bridge in the grotto to avoid an invasion by the Lebanese Army

8. Today, part of the Israeli-Lebanese border, with the Lebanese border post located 1½ miles north of Rosh Hanikra

9. The cable car ride to the caves is the shortest in the world, taking less than a minute

ROSH PINNA

1. The first Jewish colony in Galilee built in 1878-1882 providing tobacco and silk from silkworms

2. The name comes from Psalm 118:22, meaning "the chief cornerstone"

3. Later it was abandoned for years and then resettled

SAFED

1. It is Israel's highest city at 2,750 feet above sea level; 3,400 feet above Sea of Galilee

2. The origin of Safed begins only in the Middle Ages and by the 16th century it became the capital of Galilee

3. In 1140, the Crusaders built a castle here which was sold to the Templars in 1168

4. Captured by Saladin in 1180

5. The Templars regained it in 1240

6. Captured by Mamelukes under Baybars in 1266

7. Under the Ottoman Turks, it became the capital of a mamlaka

8. Home of famous Cabalists such as Isaac Luria and Joseph Caro, the author of the Shulchan Aruch

9. Nearby is the tomb of Rabbi Shimon Ben Yohai

10. In 1578, the first printing press ever in Asia was set up here and the first book printed in Hebrew occurred here

11. In 1738, an earthquake killed 4,000 residents

12. In 1833, it was destroyed by the Druze

13. In 1837, it was totally destroyed by an earthquake in which 5,000 people, mostly Jews, were killed

14. In 1948, it was occupied by 12,000 Arabs and 1,700 Jews and was one of the three strategic cities of Galilee

    a. In the course of the fighting, 120 members of the Haganah were able to sneak in with the Davidka

    b. The city fell to Jewish control on May 11, 1948

15. It is still a city of the Cabalah and today also serves as one of Israel's artist colonies

16. Today, the population is about 20,000 strong

17. Several leading rabbis are buried in Safed

    a. Rabbi Leib Ba'al Hayisurim

    b. Rabbi Yitzhak Luria Ben Shlomo (Ha'ari) (1534-1752)

    c. Rabbi Yosef (1488-1575)

    d. Nearby Safed

        (1) Honi Hame'agel (First Century B.C.) - Hatzor Haglilit

        (2) Benaiyahu Ben Yehuda (1000 B.C.) - Biriya

18. Things to see

    a. Davidka

    b. The Citadel

    c. Ancient Synagogues - From the Middle Ages

    d. Artist's Colony

SAMARIA - SEBASTE (SEBASTIYA)

1. The city has its origin when Omri bought the Hill of Shemer - I Kings 16:24-28

2. The capital of the majority of the kings of Israel

    a. Omri - I Kings 16:23-28

    b. Ahab - I Kings 16:29-22:40 (16:24, 28, 29, 32; 18:2; 20:1, 10, 17, 34, 43; 21:18; 22:10, 37, 38)

    c. Ahaziah - I Kings 22:51-II Kings 1:18 (1:2, 3; 22:51)

    d. Jehoram - II Kings 3:1-27 (1, 6); 8:28-9:26

    e. Jehu - II Kings 9:30-10:36 (10:1, 12, 17, 35, 36)

    f. Jehoahaz - II Kings 13:1-9 (1, 6, 9)

    g. Jehoash (Joash) - II Kings 13:10-14:16 (13:10, 13; 14:14, 16)

    h. Jeroboam II - II Kings 14:23-29 (23)

    i. Zechariah - II Kings 15:8-12 (8)

    j. Shallum - II Kings 15:13-16 (13, 14)

    k. Menahem - II Kings 15:17-22 (17)

    l. Pekahiah - II Kings 15:23-26 (23, 25)

    m. Pekah - II Kings 15:27-31 (27)

    n. Hoshea - II Kings 17:1-6 (1, 5, 6)

3. Served as the royal court of Ahab and Jezebel - I Kings 16:29-31; 21:18

4. Ahab built the temple to Baal - I Kings 16:32-33

5. Elijah gave his message and prophecy of coming drought - I Kings 17:1

6. Elijah's prophecy fulfilled with Samaria - I Kings 18:2

7. Ahab built his ivory palace - I Kings 22:39

8. Jehoshaphat visited Ahab in Samaria - II Chronicles 18:2

9. The site of the war between Ahab and Ben Hadad -
I Kings 20:1-43 (1, 10, 17, 34, 43)

10. Home of Micaiah the Prophet - I Kings 22:9-10

11. One of the cities of Elisha's circuit - II Kings 2:25; 5:3; 6:20

12. Elisha brought the Syrians who tried to kill him to Samaria -
II Kings 6:19-20

13. Besieged by the Syrians in Elisha's day but failed -
II Kings 6:24-7:20 (6:24, 25; 7:1, 18)

14. Family of Ahab was destroyed in this city - II Kings 10:11-17 (1, 12, 17)

15. Ahaziah, King of Judah, hid from Jehu in Samaria - II Chronicles 22:9

16. The destruction of Baal worship - II Kings 10:18-28

17. Area from which the army of Israel smote cities of Judah -
II Chronicles 25:13

18. Jehoash brought the vessels of the Temple to Samaria -
II Kings 14:11-14 (14); II Chronicles 25:24

19. The army of Samaria took Judean captives to Samaria and then
released them - II Chronicles 28:8, 15, 19

20. Destroyed by Shalmenezer - II Kings 17:1-6; 18:9-10, 34

21. Home of the priest who moved to Bethel to teach the new
inhabitants of Samaria - II Kings 17:28

22. The men who came from here to Gedaliah were killed by Ishmael -
Jeremiah 41:5

23. In the Prophets:
Isaiah 7:9; 8:4; 9:9; 10:9, 11; 36:19; Jeremiah 23:13; 31:5; 41:5;
Ezekiel 16:46-55; 23:4, 33; Hosea 7:1; 8:5, 6; 10:5, 7; 13:16;
Amos 3:12; 4:1-3; 6:1; 8:14; Obadiah 19; Micah 1:1-9 (1, 5, 6)

24. Served as the capital of a province under Assyria, Babylonia and Persia

25. Destroyed by Alexander the Great in 331 B.C., who rebuilt it as a
Greek city

26. Destroyed by John Hyrcanus in 107 B.C.

27. Rebuilt by Alexander Yannai and settled with Jews

28. Further expanded by Pompey in 63 B.C.

29. Rebuilt by Herod the Great and renamed Sebaste in honor of
Augustus Caesar, Sebaste being Greek for Augustus - 27 B.C.

30. Herod married and killed his wife, Mariamne and her two sons here

31. Possibly the city where Philip preached - Acts 8:5, 9, 14

32. Destroyed in A.D. 70 in the First Jewish Revolt

33. Rebuilt by Emperor Septimus Severus (193-211)

34. Declined under by the Byzantines

35. Destroyed by the Arabs in 636

36. Rebuilt by the Crusaders where it became a large and important city

37. With the reconquest by the Arabs, it became the small village it remains to this day

38. One of several places claiming to have the head of John the Baptist

SASA

1. It is Israel's highest kibbutz settled by American immigrants

2. It is 2,685 feet above sea level

SDE BOKER

1. Negev Desert kibbutz founded in 1952

2. Meaning: Cowboy Field - Settling the Israeli "west"

3. Final home of David Ben Gurion, who joined the kibbutz after retiring from political life

4. He died here in 1973 and where he is buried - The path to the grave is modeled after a desert wadi

5. Home of the Sde Boker College - Research into desert biology, agriculture and architecture

6. Things to see

   a. Ben Gurion's Cabin, where he lived out his life, containing some original artifacts and his library

   b. The graves of David and Paula Ben Gurion

SEPPHORIS/TZIPPORI (SAFFOURIYIEH) - DIOCAESAREA - LE SEPHORIE

1. Major city of the Mishnaic - Talmudic (Roman and Byzantine) Period - The most mentioned city in rabbinic literature except for Jerusalem

   a. Already existed in the First Temple Period but not mentioned in the Old Testament

   b. First mention comes from 103 B.C.; from the records of Ptolemy Lathyrus's campaign against Alexander Yannai

2. Josephus called it "the Ornament of all Galilee" and frequently mentioned it but it was never mentioned in the New Testament

3. In 55 B.C., Gabinus, the Proconsul of Syria, made it the district capital of Galilee

4. In 37 B.C., it surrendered to Herod the Great who attacked it in a snow storm

5. Once the largest city in Galilee, it was rebuilt by Herod the Great and made the capital of the province

6. When the city rioted at the death of Herod in 4 B.C., Quintilius Varus, the Legate of Syria, destroyed the city and sold the people into slavery

   a. Revolt led by Yehudah ben Hezekiah who conquered Herod's army and took over the royal arsenal

   b. Varus, with a large army, conquered and destroyed the city

   c. It was then turned over to Herod Antipas

7. When Herod Antipas became the ruler of Galilee, he rebuilt and fortified the city in 3 B.C. and called it *Autocratoris*, Independence

   a. The city's population was about 30,000

   b. It was only three miles from Nazareth, its satellite, with a population of four hundred

   c. Here, Antipas lived until he built and moved to his capital to Tiberias

   d. Water was gathered from the springs of Nazareth and channeled to Sepphoris by aqueducts. The northern aqueduct empties the water into a pool and the southern into an underground reservoir which had a capacity of five hundred cubic meters

8. In the First Jewish Revolt (A.D. 66-70), the city supported Vespasian and avoided destruction - They also minted coins with inscriptions referring to the city as Eirenopolis, meaning "City of Peace"

9. After the Bar Cochba Revolt, the city became Gentile and was renamed Diocaesarea - But it became Jewish again by the third century

10. Home of Rabbi Judah Hanasi

    a. The codifier of the *Mishnah* for the last seventeen years of his life

    b. He died here but, at his request, he was buried in Beth Shearim

11. One of the homes of the Sanhedrin after the Bar Cochba Revolt before it moved to Tiberias and it had eighteen synagogues and several rabbinic academies

    a. The Synagogue of Gophna

    b. The Babylonian Synagogue

    c. The Synagogue of the Tarsians

12. Was the home of several great rabbis: Rabbi Halafta, Rabbi Elazar Ben Azarya, Rabbi Yosi Ben Halafta, Rabbi Yochanan and Resh Lakish

13. It is the burial place of Rabbi Yehudah Nessiah, the grandson of Judah Hanasi

14. In A.D. 351, the Gallus Revolt broke out in the city but was put down without its destruction

    a. Revolt against Constantine who tried to impose Christianity on the Jews through Joseph of Tiberias

    b. Put down by Gallus

15. In A.D. 363, the city was destroyed by an earthquake but rebuilt again at the end of the fourth century

16. Had a large population of Messianic Jews

    a. In A.D. 325, a Jewish believer, Joseph of Tiberias, tried to build a church here but did not succeed

    b. Later in the Byzantine Period, though the Jews were still the majority population, there was a church there with bishops

    c. Inscription on a lintel: "archisynagogue" followed by the Greek letters *chi* and *rho* - The classic letters representing "Jesus Christ"

17. During the Arab Period, the city began to decline

18. During the Crusader Period, it was named *Le Sephorie*

    a. During this period, it was only a small town with a Crusader Church and Crusader Fortress

    b. From this city, the Crusader Army set out against Saladin in 1187 and were defeated at the Horns of Hattin

19. In the 18th century, it became the stronghold of Dahr el-Omar, the Bedouin ruler of Galilee who fortified and rebuilt the castle

20. The Arab town of Saffouriyieh became a base for Arab gangs attacking Jewish settlements during the Arab riots of 1936-1939 and the War of Independence (1948) until it was conquered in the Dekel Campaign

21. Rabbinic explanation of its name: Why is it called Tzippori? Because it is perched on top of the mountains like a bird (*tzippor*) (*B. Megillah* 6a)

22. The Tel and Things to See

    a. The acropolis rising 400 feet above fields contains the cities of the fourth-fifth centuries

    b. East of the acropolis is the Roman city with its fifth century Byzantine renovations

    c. Strongly influenced by Hellenism, it had a theater and statues of Prometheus and Pan were found

    d. Coin found with the following inscription: "Diocaesarea, the holy city, city of shelter, loyal friendships and alliance between the Sanhedrin and the Senate of the Roman people."

    e. There are thirteen mosaic floors dating from the fifth and sixth centuries

    f. There are eighteen Jewish ritual baths

    g. The Theater - Built in the latter half of the first century in the shape of an amphitheater, it remained in use through the Byzantine Period and seated 4,000 people

    h. The Saint Anne Monastery - Based on the tradition that the parents of Mary, Joachim and Anna lived here

    i. Crusader Church - Contains inscriptions taken from a synagogue which stood here during talmudic times

    j. The Residential Quarter - Also called "The Jewish Quarter," it was used by Jews from the Hasmonian to the end of the Roman Periods as attested by the ritual baths

    k. The Citadel - Built by the Crusaders on Byzantine remains and reused during the Turkish Period with the renovations

    l. Two water aqueducts carrying water from various springs into a reservoir measuring 541 feet long and 32 feet high

m. The Roman Villa and the Dionysian Mosaic Floor - From the third century, it contains multi-colored mosaic floors with scenes of the life of the wine-god, Dionysius and what is now called "the Mona Lisa of Galilee"

n. The Colonaded Road - One of the main streets of Sepphoris from the Roman Period and may have been the cardo for the city

o. The Nile Mosaic - On the floor of a large building depicting the festivals of Egypt when the Nile reached its flood stage

SHAALVIM (SALBIT)

1. City of the Tribe of Dan - Joshua 19:42

2. Retained by Canaanites - Judges 1:35

3. Home of Eliahba, one of David's mighty men - II Samuel 23:32

4. In the Second Solomonic District - I Kings 4:9

SHAAR HAGAI (BAB EL-WAD)

1. It was one of the three bottlenecks on the main road to Jerusalem that was blocked by the Arabs in 1948

2. It was this blockade that required the building of the Burma Road

3. The Khan at the entrance to the pass was built in 1869 and owned by Jews

   a. Original name: *Malon Bab el-Wad*

   b. Later: Judean Hills Hotel

   c. Moses Montifiore stayed overnight in 1875 on the way to Jerusalem

   d. With the coming of the railroad and the automobile, it fell into disuse

SHARUHEN (TEL EL-FARIA)

1. In Egyptian records, it is mentioned by Ahmose and Thutmose III

2. The last stronghold of the Hyksos, finally defeated by the Egyptians

3. City of the Tribe of Simeon - Joshua 19:6

4. At times it was heavily Philistine

SHECHEM - NEAPOLIS (NABLUS) (TEL BALATA)

1. In Egyptian records, it is mentioned in the Execration Texts and the El Amarna Letters

2. Abraham passed through this city and built an altar - Genesis 12:6

3. Jacob purchased some land in this area for his altar - Genesis 33:18-20

4. The Dinah incident occurred here - Genesis 34:1-31; Acts 7:16

5. Jacob buried the idols brought by his wives - Genesis 35:4

6. Part of the area where Joseph searched for his brothers - Genesis 37:12-14

7. Border city between Ephraim and Manasseh - Joshua 17:7

8. City given to the Tribe of Ephraim - Joshua 21:20-21; I Chronicles 7:28

9. City of Refuge - Joshua 20:7; I Chronicles 6:67

10. Levitical City - Joshua 21:21

11. The covenant renewed - Joshua 24:1-28 (1, 25)

12. The bones of Joseph were buried - Joshua 24:32-39

13. Gideon's concubine bore Abimelech - Judges 8:31

14. Abimelech was made king of Shechem - Judges 9:1-21 (1, 2, 3, 6, 7, 18, 20)

15. The Abimelech War broke out - Judges 9:22-57 (23, 24, 25, 26, 31, 34, 39, 41, 46, 47, 49, 57)

16. Mentioned in the directions given to Benjaminites - Judges 21:19

17. Rehoboam split the kingdom - I Kings 12:1-20; II Chronicles 10:1-5

18. Jeroboam's first capital - I Kings 12:25

19. Men from this city were killed by Ishmael - Jeremiah 41:5

20. In the Psalms: 60:6; 108:7

21. In 125 B.C., it was captured by John Hyrcanus who destroyed the Samaritan Temple

22. A.D. 72 - Rebuilt by armies of Vespasian and Titus and renamed Neapolis

23. Birthplace of Justin Martyr

24. Called Nablus with Arab Invasion in 636 - Corruption of Neapolis

25. Destroyed in 1927 by an earthquake

26. During the War of Independence, it became a base for Iraqi troops

27. Taken by Israel in the Six-Day War

28. Today

   a. Largest Arab city in the country with a total population 121,000

   b. 120,000 Moslems, 750 Christians and 250 Samaritans

29. Things to see

   a. Jacob's Well

      (1) In an unfinished, Russian Orthodox Church; the building of which was interrupted by the Communist Revolution of 1917

      (2) The well is 115 feet deep

   b. Tombs of Joseph, Ephraim and Manasseh - Marked as such only since the Byzantine Period

SHILOH (KHIRBET SAILUN)

1. The second stop of the Ark of the Covenant and its home for 200 years - Joshua 18:1; Judges 18:31; I Samuel 1:3; 2:14; 4:3

2. Seven of the tribes received their tribal divisions - Joshua 18:1-19:51 (18:8, 9, 10; 19:51)

3. Levitical Cities were all assigned - Joshua 21:1-2

4. Because of the Ark of the Covenant, it became a place of pilgrimage - Judges 21:19

5. The Transjordanian Tribes returned to their possessions - Joshua 22:9

6. The place where the Cisjordanian Tribes gathered together to war against the Transjordanian Tribes - Joshua 22:12

7. Remaining wives for the Benjaminites were taken - Judges 21:19-23

8. The virgins of Jabesh Gilead brought to Shiloh for the Benjaminites - Judges 21:12

9. Home of Eli - I Samuel 2:12-14; I Kings 2:27

10. Hannah prayed for a son - I Samuel 1:1-19 (3, 9)

11. Samuel was raised and received his call - I Samuel 1:24-28 (24);2:18-3:21

12. The Ark of the Covenant was lost to the Philistines and Shiloh destroyed and in ruins for 150 years - I Samuel 4:1-18 (3, 4, 12)

13. Home of Ahijah the Priest - I Samuel 14:3

14. Rebuilt by Jeroboam and had continued occupation until the Middle Ages

15. Home of Ahijah the Prophet - I Kings 11:29; 12:15; 14:2; 15:29; II Chronicles 9:29; 10:15

16. Jeroboam's wife made her request for the life of her son - I Kings 14:1-16 (2, 4)

17. Probably destroyed by the Philistines in the Battle of Aphek

18. It became known as a heap of ruins - Psalms 78:60; Jeremiah 7:12, 14; 26:6, 9

19. Men from here were killed by Ishmael - Jeremiah 41:5

20. Rebuilt in the return from Babylon - I Chronicles 9:5

21. In Arabic the valley outside Shiloh is known by two names:

   a. *Marj el-Id ('Aid)*, The Valley of the Feast

   b. *Marj el-Banat*, The Valley of the Daughters

22. Remains of two Byzantine churches from the fifth-sixth century

SHIVTA - SOBATA (SUBEITA)

1. One of the three Nabatean-Byzantine cities in the Negev

2. History extends from the third century B.C. to the seventh century

3. Taken by Rome in A.D. 106

4. City did not have a city wall but the houses and courtyard walls were built in a continuous line giving it the appearance of a wall interrupted by nine streets, each street having a gate

5. Remains

   a. Three Churches - Each with three apses

      (1) The Southern Church - The oldest of the three

      (2) The Middle Church

      (3) The Northern Church - The youngest of the three

   b. Wine Press

   c. Stable House

   d. Pool House

   e. The Double Pools

   f. The Governor's House

SHUNEM (SULAM)

1. City of the Tribe of Issachar - Joshua 19:18
2. The camp of the Philistines against Saul - I Samuel 28:4
3. Home of Abishag, David's nurse - I Kings 1:3, 15; 2:17, 21-22
4. Home of the Shunammite woman - II Kings 4:12, 25, 36
5. Elisha had his prophet's chamber - II Kings 4:8-10
6. Raised the Shunammite's son - II Kings 4:32-37
7. The Shunammite's land was restored - II Kings 8:1-6
8. Home of the bride of Solomon in the Song of Solomon - 6:13

SICHNIN (SACKNIN)

1. Important city of the talmudic period
2. Had a strong presence of Messianic Jews; among the most famous was Jacob of Sichnin

SOCOH-SHARON

1. Played a major role in Egyptian campaigns prior to Israelite conquest
2. Part of the Third Solomonic District - I Kings 4:10

SOCOH-SHEPHELAH

1. Given to the Tribe of Judah - Joshua 15:35
2. Philistine army camp against Israel - I Samuel 17:1
3. Fortified by Rehoboam - II Chronicles 11:7
4. Taken by the Philistines in the days of Ahaz - II Chronicles 28:18

SODOM AND GOMORRAH

1. Border of Canaanite territory - Genesis 10:19
2. At one time, it was known for its fertility - Genesis 13:10
3. The home of Lot - Genesis 13:11-13
4. Part of the area of the invasion of the kings - Genesis 14:1-24
5. The famous judgment occurred here - Genesis 18:16-19:28

6. Became a comparison for other judgments and calamities - Deuteronomy 29:23; 32:32; Isaiah 1:9-10; 3:9; 13:19; Jeremiah 23:14; 49:18; 50:40; Lamentations 4:6; Amos 4:11; Zephaniah 2:9; Matthew 10:15; 11:23-24; Mark 6:11; Luke 10:12; 17:29; Romans 9:29; II Peter 2:6; Revelation 11:8

7. To be rebuilt in the Millennial Kingdom - Ezekiel 16:46-56

8. In the vicinity, there is Mount Sodom

   a. Arabic: *Jebel Usdum*, Mountain of the Salt

   b. 3 x 5 miles

   c. 742 feet above the Dead Sea

SYCHAR

1. Part of the area that Jacob purchased from Shechem - Genesis 33:18-20

2. The burial place of Joseph - Joshua 24:32

3. Incident between Jesus and the Samaritan woman - John 4:4-42

4. Jacob's Well

   a. Tradition since A.D. 333

   b. Original - 105 feet

   c. Stones cast in - 75 feet

TAANACH (TINNIK)

1. Guarded the Tanaach Pass

2. The king was killed by Joshua - Joshua 12:21

3. City of the Tribe of Manasseh - Joshua 17:11; I Chronicles 7:29

4. Levitical City - Joshua 21:25

5. Retained by the Canaanites - Joshua 17:12; Judges 1:27

6. Part of the battle against Sisera - Judges 5:19

7. Part of the Fifth Solomonic District - I Kings 4:12

8. Disappeared from history after the fall of the First Temple

9. The Taanach Letters were discovered here - Twelve cuniform tablets from the fifteenth century B.C.

TABGHA - HEPTAPEGON - EIN SHEVA

1. Name comes from the Greek heptapegon meaning "Seven Springs"

2. It was a fisherman suburb of Capernaum

3. Traditional site of the feeding of the 5,000 - Mark 6:30-44

4. Earliest report of this tradition comes from the pilgrim, Lady Egeria, in 383

5. Remains of three Byzantine churches commemorating three events

   a. The Church of the Miracles of the Loaves and Fishes

   b. The Church of Saint Peter - Peter appointed the Chief of the Apostles and so also called the Church of the Ascendancy - John 21:15-23

   c. The Sermon on the Mount

6. *Mensa Christi* - Where Jesus prepared breakfast for His disciples - John 21:1-14

   a. Meaning: The Table of Christ

   b. Originally built in the fifth century

   c. During the Crusades, it was destroyed and rebuilt

   d. Destroyed by Moslems in 1263

   e. Present church built by the Franciscans in 1933

7. The Church

   a. Egeria reports that a church existed around the altar where the loaves were laid - This church was built around 350 probably by a Jewish believer named Joseph, who built a number of churches on New Testament holy sites

   b. The above, Syrian style church, was replaced by a Byzantine style church with all its mosaic in 480

      (1) Inscription names Patriarch Martyrios of Jerusalem as the builder

      (2) He was formally a monk in Egypt which helps to explain the mosaic floor for it reflects the fauna and flora of the Nile Delta Region

   c. The church was destroyed in the Persian Invasion of 614 and the site remained hidden for 1300 years

   d. The Byzantine Church and its mosaics were discovered again in 1892 and a provisional church was built over it in 1932-1936

   e. In 1980-1982, the new present church was built incorporating the ancient foundation and the mosaics

   f. The church and land are now the property of the Catholic Association for the Holy Land and in the care of the Benedictine Monks of the Dormition Abbey of Jerusalem

TEKOA (TUQU)

1. The origin is in I Chronicles 2:24; 4:5

2. City of the Tribe of Judah - I Chronicles 4:5

3. The wise woman of Tekoa convinced David to invite Absalom to return - II Samuel 14:1-20 (2, 4, 9)

4. Home of Ira, one of David's mighty men - II Samuel 23:26; I Chronicles 11:28; 27:9

5. Fortified by Rehoboam - II Chronicles 11:6

6. The army of Jehoshaphat passed by here on the way to Berachah and this is where Jehoshaphat prayed - II Chronicles 20:20

7. Fire signal town for Jerusalem's defenses - Jeremiah 6:1

8. Inhabitants of this city helped rebuild the wall - Nehemiah 3:5, 27

9. It was the home of Amos the Prophet - Amos 1:1

TEL AVIV

1. A new city established in 1909

2. Name chosen to combine the old (*tel*) and the new (*aviv* - spring)

3. Once the largest city of Israel but now superseded by Jerusalem

4. Today, the city itself has a population of 350,000 but with the greater metropolitan area, it is over a million strong. Among these are:

   a. Rishon Letzion - 168,000

   b. Holon - 164,000 (this town contains a Samaritan Synogogue; the only place Samaritans are found within the State of Israel)

   c. Bnei Brak - 129,000

   d. Bat Yam - 140,000

   e. Petach Tikvah - 154,000

5. Things to see

   a. Shalom Tower

   b. Dizengoff Street

   c. Diaspora Museum

TEL HAI

1. Originally founded in 1907 as an agricultural settlement on land purchased by Baron de Rothschild in 1893

2. In 1917, it was settled by a group led by Joseph Trumpeldor

3. In March 1920, it was attacked by Arabs and he was killed along with five men and two women - His last words were: "It is good to die for one's country"

4. The incident showed that for Israel to be established it would have to be by blood and fire

5. Source of the motto: "By blood and fire Judah fell, by blood and fire Judah will rise"

6. Led to area falling under British rather than French rule and so ultimately it was included in the border of Israel

7. The city of Kiryat Shmoneh (the town of the eight) is named after them - Built on the area from which the Arabs began their attack

8. It contains the museum of the underground movement

9. Contains the cemetery of *Hashomer* - An early Jewish defense organization preceding the *Haganah*

THEBEZ (TUBAS)

Abimelech killed - Judges 9:50-57; II Samuel 11:21

TIBERIAS

1. Built by Herod Antipas in A.D. 20 in honor of Caesar Tiberias

2. The Jews refused to live here because it was built over a graveyard - So it was primarily a Gentile city in Jesus' day

3. The only biblical reference to this town is found in John 6:23

4. Often gave its name to the Sea of Galilee - John 6:1; 21:1

5. After the Bar Cochba Revolt failed, the Sanhedrin was moved here from Sepphoris and Beth Shearim

   a. By Jewish tradition, Rabbi Shimeon Bar Yochai cleansed the city and the cemetery over which it stood of all ritual impurity (A.D. 135-145)

   b. This allowed Jews to move into the city and the Jewish population reached around 25,000

   c. Became a center of Jewish learning for several centuries

   d. It became one of the four holy cities along with Jerusalem, Hebron and Safed

6. The *Gemara* of the *Jerusalem Talmud* and the *Masorah* (the Hebrew punctuation of the biblical text) were fixed here

7. During the reign of Constantine, a Jewish believer named Joseph built Galilee's first churches. Jewish opposition to his evangelistic efforts led to his moving to Beth Shean

8. The Persian Invasion of 614

   a. The Jews sided with the Persians against the Byzantines

   b. Benjamin of Tiberias raised a Jewish army of 20,000 to support the Persians killing many Byzantine Christians and destroying the churches built by Joseph and others

   c. In the reconquest by the Byzantines in 628, many Jews were killed or converted - The Byzantine Emperor himself baptized Benjamin of Tiberias

9. Fell to the Moslems in 637 who made it the capital of Galilee and turned it into a major textile and tapestry center

10. Destroyed in 748-9 and again in 1033 by a series of earthquakes and population dwindled

11. Served as the capital of the Galilee under the Crusaders who rebuilt the city in 1099; moving it north of the Roman-Byzantine site to the present city center

12. Destroyed and devastated by the Arabs under Saladin in 1187 as the Crusaders were expelled

13. Fell to the Mamelukes in 1247

14. In 1560, the Turks under Suleiman the Magnificent gave the area to Don Joseph Nassi and Donna Garcia, Portuguese Morannos, who rebuilt the walls and brought in industry - Then the Jews moved in

15. Jews left after one generation due to Arab attacks and Turkish anarchy

16. The city remained largely a ruin until 1595 when a Lebanese Druze War Lord named Fakhr-a-Din arrived

   a. Turned Tiberias into a private kingdom that, at various times, included Samaria, Galilee, the Golan Heights, Lebanon and the Coastal Plain

   b. Supported by the French, he invited both Jews and Christians to settle in Tiberias

   c. The city enjoyed decades of peace and prosperity until he was defeated by the Turks in 1635

   d. The city again fell into decadence

17. In 1740, the Turks turned the governorship of Tiberias over to a bedouin named Daher-el-Omar

   a. Invited both Jews and Christian to settle there

   b. Jews return in 1740 under Sephardic Rabbi Chaim Abulafia who arrived from Turkey

   c. Rebuilt the city walls and the Crusader Fortress which withstood an 85-day siege of the Army of Damascus in 1742

   d. Turks resented his growing influence and had him killed in 1775

   e. Turkish rule resumed

18. Walls were destroyed in the earthquake of 1759

19. Chassids arrive from Europe in 1777

20. City was ruled by the Egyptian Ibrahim Pasha - 1830-1840

21. In 1837, it was destroyed by an earthquake but the Jews rebuilt the city

22. By 1917, the Jews were the majority population

23. During the British Mandate Period, it was a mixed city of Jews and Arabs. The first Jewish mayor was elected in 1928 but was assassinated in the Arab riots of 1938 creating continuous friction until the War of Independence

24. In 1947, there was a mass exodus of its Arab population and, on April 28, 1948, it was one of the three strategic cities of Galilee taken by the Jews and the first mixed Arab-Jewish city to be liberated

25. It lies about 600 feet below sea level and it is today a major resort city

26. Leading rabbis are buried here

   a. Rabbi Yochanan Ben Zakkai (A.D. 70)

   b. Rabbi Akiba (50 - 135 A.D.)

   c. Rabbi Jeremiah ben Abba - Talmudic rabbi

   d. Rabbi Kahanah - Third century talmudic rabbi

   e. Rabbi Moishe Ben Maimon (*Rambam*) or Maimonides (1135-1204)

   f. Rabbi Meir Ba'al Haness - Second century talmudic rabbi but this site was first identified as his burial place in 1210

g. Rabbi Isaiah ben Abraham haLevi Horowitz (1565-1630) - Author and head Ashkenazi Rabbi of Jerusalem

h. Rabbi Moshe Chaim Luzzato (*Haramhal*) (1707-1746) - Mystic rabbi from Italy

i. Rabbi Chaim Abulafia (1660-1744)

j. Rabbi Nachman of Horodenka (1780) - Helped establish the Chassidic Community of Tiberias

k. Rabbi Menachem Mendel of Vitebsk (1730-1788) - Established the Chassidic community

l. Rabbi Israel ben Shmuel of Shklor (1839) - Brought followers of Vilna Gaon to Tiberias

27. Present population - 38,000

28. Things to see

a. The Archaeological Garden - The Greek inscription on the mosaic floor reads: "Proklies, son of Crispus founded"

b. Roman-Byzantine Crusader fortifications

c. Crusader-Turkish Castle - The present form of the citadel was built in 1745 by Chulabi, the son of Daher el-Omar and now mostly an art gallery

d. The Crusader Church

e. The El Omri Mosque: The Great Mosque of Tiberias - Built by Sheik Daher el Omar in 1743

f. Saint Peter's Church - Twelfth century Franciscan church rebuilt in 1870, enlarged in 1903 and restored in 1944

g. Tiberias Museum of Antiquities - In the *Jami el Bahr* (*Al Bahri*) Mosque built in 1880 on a Crusader site

h. The Greek Orthodox Monastery built in 1862 over remains from 342-422 and later Crusader remains

i. Etz Chaim Synagogue - Built in 1950 over the remains of previous synagogues dating from 1740 (destroyed by an earthquake), 1759 (destroyed by an earthquake in 1837) and 1847 (destroyed by a flood in 1934)

j. The Karlin-Stolin Synagogue - Hasidic Synagogue named after two Lithuanian towns where the founder, Rabbi Aaron ben Jacob (1736-1772), lived

k. HaSenyor Synagogue - Built in 1837 by Rabbi Chaim Shmuel haCohen known as the Senyor

l. The Hotel Tiberias/Meyuchas Youth Hostel

(1) Built in 1896 as the largest hotel in Galilee

(2) Under the British Mandate, it served as the local headquarters of the British Army

      (3) When the British left, it was taken by Arab forces

      (4) In a fierce battle, it was taken by the Jewish forces on April 17, 1948 and became the turning point for the Battle of Tiberias

      (5) Converted into a youth hostel in 1971

  m. Saint Andrews Church - Scottish Missionary Hospital in 1894; now a Scottish hospice

  n. Mater Ecclesiae Center

      (1) Built by Catholics in 1908 and was the first building outside the city wall and used as a girls' boarding school and a hospice

      (2) During World War I it was used as a hospital

      (3) Today it is an American Catholic-run study center for nuns

  o. Ancient City Walls

  p. The Lakeside Promenade

  q. The Byzantine Church of Mount Bereniki

      (1) Hill named after Berenice - Daughter of Agrippa I and sister of Agrippa II

      (2) Not known what the church commemorates

      (3) Emperor Justinian extended the city wall by about two miles to incorporate the church

      (4) Damaged in the earthquake of 749

      (5) Rebuilt during Moslem rule and used until the end of the Crusades

      (6) Became a private home under Mamelukes

      (7) Destroyed by an earthquake in 13th-14th century

  r. The Roman Baths and Cardo

  s. Rabbi Yochanan's (180-279) *Beit Midrash* - Where he worked on *Mishnah*

  t. "The Galilee Experience" - a multi-screen presentation of the history of Galilee

TIRZAH

1. The king was killed by Joshua - Joshua 12:24

2. Third capital of Israel under Jeroboam - I Kings 14:17

3. Capital of Israel under Baasha - I Kings 15:21, 33; 16:1-7 (6)

4. The capital city under Elah - I Kings 16:8-14 (8, 9)

5. The capital under Zimri - I Kings 8:15-20 (15, 17)

6. Site of the first two years of Omri's reign - I Kings 16:23

7. Home of Menahem, one of the kings of Israel - II Kings 15:14, 16

8. Beauty is commented on by Solomon - Song of Solomon 6:4

VALLEY OF AJALON/AYALON (CITY: YALU)

1. Site where the moon stood still - Joshua 10:12
2. City given to the Tribe of Dan - Joshua 19:42
3. Later, it became a city of the Tribe of Benjamin - I Chronicles 8:13
4. Levitical City - Joshua 21:24; I Chronicles 6:69
5. The city was retained by the Amorites - Judges 1:35
6. Saul smote the Philistines - I Samuel 14:31
7. It marked the end of the Saul and Jonathan Philistine War - I Samuel 14:31
8. Fortified by Rehoboam - II Chronicles 11:10
9. Taken by the Philistines in the days of Ahaz - II Chronicles 28:18
10. Judah Maccabee defeated the Greeks under Nicanor on the way to Jerusalem
11. Roman forces under Titus gathered here to begin their siege of Jerusalem in A.D. 68
12. Jews of Jerusalem settled here after A.D. 70 but when it joined the Bar Cochba Revolt, it was destroyed in A.D. 135
13. During World War I, the British fought the first battle here for control of Jerusalem
14. In 1948, as a result of the Battle of Latrun, it became a "no-man's land" between Israel and Jordan
15. In 1967, it fell totally under Jewish control

VALLEY OF BETH HAKEREM

This valley divides Upper and Lower Galilee in the west

VALLEY OF DOTHAN

1. Joseph was sold to the Midianites - Genesis 37:17-28 (17)
2. Elisha and the encounter with the Syrian Army took place here - II Kings 6:12-18 (13)

VALLEY OF ELAH

The conflict between David and Goliath occurred here - I Samuel 17:1-58; 21:9

VALLEY OF IPHTAEL - VALLEY OF BETH NETOFA

1. Given to the Tribe of Zebulun - Joshua 19:14
2. Marked the border for the Tribe of Asher - Joshua 19:27
3. Known as Azochis during the Greek and Roman periods
4. Site of the city of Cana of Galilee

VALLEY OF JEZREEL

1. Largest valley of Israel
2. Part of the Via Maris

3. Names

    a. The Valley - Joshua 17:16; I Chronicles 10:7

    b. Jezreel - Judges 6:33; Joshua 17:16

    c. Esdraelon - The Greek form of Jezreel

    d. Armageddon - Revelation 16:16

4. The valley had seven entrances and each entrance had fortified cities

    a. The Pass from Acco: Achshaph and Harosheth Hagoyim - (Kishon Pass)

    b. The Pass from the Lake: Mount Tabor - (Tabor Pass)

    c. The Descent from Samaria: Jezreel and Ein Ganim (Jenin Descent)

    d. The Beth Shean Pass: Beth Shean - (Jezreel Pass)

    e. The Megiddo Pass: Megiddo

    f. The Yokneam Pass: Yokneam

    g. The Taanach Pass: Taanach

5. Retained Canaanite control until the time of Deborah and Barak - Joshua 17:16

6. Camp of the Midianites - Judges 6:33

7. Part of Ishbosheth's rule - II Samuel 2:8-9

8. Scene of several biblical battles

    a. Barak and the Canaanites - Judges 4:12-16; 5:19-22

    b. Gideon and the Midianites - Judges 7:19-23

    c. Saul and the Philistines - II Samuel 28:4

    d. Josiah and Pharaoh Necho - II Kings 23:29-30; II Chronicles 35:25; Zechariah 12:11

9. In the Prophets: Hosea 1:5; 2:22

10. The first Jewish settlement in the valley was Merhavia, established in 1911, followed by Nahalal in 1921

11. Those who made battle here

    a. Thutmose III

    b. Ramses II

    c. Nebuchadnezzer

    d. Sargon

    e. Sennacherib

    f. Pharaoh Necho

    g. Alexander the Great

    h. Titus

    i. Richard I

    j. Saladin

     k.   Napoleon

     l.   Allenby - His victory here over the Turks gave him the title: Lord Allenby of Megiddo

VALLEY OF REPHAIM

1. Marked the northern border of Judah - Joshua 15:8

2. Marked the southern border of Benjamin - Joshua 18:16

3. The camp of the Philistines - I Chronicles 11:15

4. David defeated the Philistines on two occasions - II Samuel 23:13; I Chronicles 14:9

     a.   First - II Samuel 5:17-21

     b.   Second - With the miracle of the mulberry trees - II Samuel 5:22-25

5. In the Prophets: Isaiah 17:5

VALLEY OF SOREK

1. The incidents of Samson and Delilah - Judges 16:4-20

2. The Ark of the Covenant returned to Israel via this valley

3. The Roman legions went by way of this valley to attack Bar Cochba at Betar

4. A Jewish legend says that the blood flowed to the sea via the Valley of Sorek after the fall of Betar

VALLEY OF TIMNA

1. The Valley - Semicircular and about 35 square miles

     a.   North: Mount Milhan (235 feet) and Mount Etek (270 feet)

     b.   West: Mount Berech and Mount Maaleh Berech (285 feet)

     c.   South: Mount Gadna and Mount Hahlil (135)

     d.   East: It is open

2. Contains layers of rock composed of sandstone, dolomite, lime and marl

3. The center of the valley contains Mount Timna, composed of dark cleft block of plutonium rock of granite and syenite

4. Major area of copper mining from ancient times - Over 10,000 mining shafts have been found

5. Copper mining began in the Calcolithic Period about 3500 B.C.

6. The 19th and 20th Dynasties of Egypt mined the area in the 14th-12th century B.C.

     a.   Often used Midianites and Kenites as workers

     b.   Remains of a Semitic Temple for Midianites and Kenites

     c.   Remains of an Egyptian Temple to the goddess Hathor (for Egyptian workers) was located here; a copper serpent was found

7. Contrary to the modern name of "Solomon's Pillars" located here, there is no biblical or archaeological evidence that Solomon or any other Israelite kings mined here

8. Romans also mined here as did the Arabs and, recently, the Israelis

9. Main source of the Eilat Stone today

10. The Valley Today and Things to See

    a. It is a nature preserve (Timna Park)

    b. Contains a man-made lake (Timna Lake)

    c. Contains ancient inscriptions and drawings (graffiti)

        (1) Painting of chariots, hunters with bows and arrows and animals from the 13th-11th century B.C.

        (2) Wall drawing of Raamses III offering gifts to the goddess Hathor

    d. Has unusual geological formations

        (1) Solomon's Pillars - Sandstone cliffs carved by natural erosion

        (2) The Mushroom - Caused by natural erosion

        (3) The Arches

    e. Archaeology

        (1) The Temple of the Goddess of Hathor built during the reign of Seti I from the 14th century B.C.

        (2) The Ancient Copper Mines - Since 4000 B.C.

        (3) The Smelting Works - From the 14th and 12th century B.C.

        (4) Sacred Temple - Semitic Kenite Temple

        (5) Slaves Hill

VALLEY OF YAVNEEL
A valley given to the Tribe of Naphtali - Joshua 19:33

VALLEY OF ZEPHATHAH
Where Asa defeated the Ethiopians - II Chronicles 14:9-10

WILDERNESS OF PARAN

1. Route of the invasion of the kings - Genesis 14:6

2. Ishmael was raised after his expulsion from the home of Abraham - Genesis 21:21

3. Part of the Wilderness Wanderings - Numbers 10:12; 12:16-13:29; Deuteronomy 1:1; 33:2

4. From this area the twelve spies were sent out - Numbers 13:3-20

5. Refuge of David from Saul - I Samuel 25:1

6. Route of the flight of Hadad the Edomite from Solomon - I Kings 11:17-18

7. In the Sinai Campaign of 1956, the war began here

WILDERNESS OF ZIN

1. From this area the twelve spies were sent - Number 13:21

2. Part of the area of the Wilderness Wanderings - Numbers 20:1; 27:14; 33:36; Deuteronomy 32:51

3. Miriam died here - Numbers 20:1

4. The incident of the Waters of Meribah occurred here and Moses was forbidden to enter the Land - Numbers 20:2-13; Deuteronomy 32:51

5. Israel's request to Edom was made from here - Numbers 20:14-21

6. It marked part of the southern border of the Land - Numbers 34:3-4

7. It marked part of the southern border of the Tribe of Judah - Joshua 15:1, 3

YAD MORDECAI

1. A kibbutz founded in 1943 and named after Mordecai Anilewitz, the leader of the Warsaw Ghetto Revolt

2. In 1948, it held the Egyptian advance for six days but then was taken by the Egyptians and later retaken

3. These six days allowed the newborn state to arm itself for war

YANOAH (YANUH)

1. One of the cities taken by Tiglath Pileser III - II Kings 15:29

2. Today an Israeli Arab village

YARKON RIVER

1. Originates from the springs of Aphek and Rosh Ha-Ayin and flows into the Mediterranean Sea

2. Separates the Plain of Sharon from the Philistine Plain

3. Marked the border between the Tribe of Dan and the Tribe of Ephraim - Joshua 19:46

YARMUK RIVER

1. A river that runs for about 45 miles and empties into the Jordan River south of the Sea of Galilee

2. Marked the border between Bashan and Gilead

3. Marked the border between the Tribes of Manasseh and Gad

4. In 1948, it marked the border between Syria and Jordan

5. Since 1967, it has marked the border between Israel (Golan Heights) and Jordan

6. Never mentioned in Scripture

7. In A.D. 636, the Moslems invaded the Land through the Yarmuk River Valley and defeated the Byzantine Army on August 20, 636 thus conquering the Land

8. The Turks built the Haifa-Damascus Railroad in 1905 and crossed the Yarmuk River by a bridge

   a. During World War I, Lawrence of Arabia tried to destroy the bridge but failed

   b. In 1946, it was one of ten bridges destroyed by the *Palmach* (The Night of the Bridges Operation) to pressure the British to leave the Land without killing British soldiers)

YAVNE

1. It is the Jabneel of Joshua 15:11 and marked the northern border of Judah

2. It became Philistine but was defeated and destroyed by Uzziah - II Chronicles 26:6

3. In 147 B.C., at the Battle of Yavne, Jonathan and Simeon Maccabee defeated the army of Demetrius II under Appolonias

4. Rabbi Yochanan ben Zakkai founded the center of Judaism after A.D. 70

5. Began to decline after the Bar Cochba Revolt

6. Became Moslem with the Arab conquest

7. During the Crusader Period, it was fortified and renamed Ybellin

8. Important city in the Mameluke Period

9. During the Ottoman Turkish and the British Mandate Periods, it became a small town

10. In the War of Independence, it became a base for Arab forces until taken by Israeli forces

YAVNE YAM

In 163 B.C., Judah Maccabee vanquished the Greeks here for planning to drown the Jews

YEHIAM - CASTLE JUDIN (QAL'AT JEDIN)

1. It was a Crusader fortress built by the Knights Templars in 1191 for the protection of Acco and named Castle Judin - Built on the ruins of Roman and Byzantine remains

2. It was given to the German Order of Teutonic Knights in 1208 who greatly strengthened the fortifications

3. Destroyed by Mameluke Sultan Baybars in 1265

4. In the 18th century, was renovated by a local ruler named Sheik el-Hussein

5. Used by the Bedouin Sheikh, Daher el-Amar, who gained control over the Galilee but was abandoned after him

6. The kibbutz, on whose grounds the castle is located, was founded in 1946 and used as a stronghold by the kibbutzniks during the War of Independence

7. The Yehiam Convoy

    a. Seven armored supply trucks trying to relieve the siege of Yehiam were attacked by a force of 500 Arabs on March 27, 1948

    b. A total of 47 (out of 90) Israelis were killed trying to resupply Yehiam from Nahariyyah

    c. The kibbutz withstood all enemy attacks until all of western Galilee was liberated in May 1948

YODEFAT (KHIRBET JIFAT)

1. The Jotbah of II Kings 21:19 and the birthplace of Meshulemeth, the wife of Manasseh and the mother of Amon, the king of Judah

2. It marked Josephus' last stand in the battle for Galilee

    a. Vespasian besieged the city for 47 days - 40,000 Jewish defenders against 60,000 Roman soldiers

    b. City fell July 1, 1967

    c. Women enslaved

    d. 15,000 men killed

    e. 2,000 sent to build Corinthian Canal

    f. Josephus and forty of his soldiers hid in a cistern. While he wanted to surrender to the Romans, the others voted for suicide. The order was decided by lot and Josephus, by manipulating the straws, was able to pick the last. After the other forty were killed, he surrendered

3. It was settled again by Jews during the Byzantine Period and then disappeared from history

YOKNEAM

1. It guarded the Yokneam Pass

2. The king was killed by Joshua - Joshua 12:22

3. City given to the Tribe of Zebulun - Joshua 19:11

4. Levitical City - Joshua 21:34

5. Part of the Fifth Solomonic District - I Kings 4:12

YOTVATA

One of the spots of the Wilderness Wanderings - Numbers 33:33-34; Deuteronomy 10:7

ZERED RIVER - WADI EL-HASA

1. It marked the border between Moab and Edom - Deuteronomy 2:13-14

2. Part of the Israelite encampment - Numbers 21:12; Deuteronomy 2:13-14

ZIGLAG (TEL ESH-SHARI'AH) - TEL SERA

1. City of the Tribe of Judah - Joshua 15:31; I Chronicles 4:30

2. Inhabited by the Tribe of Simeon - Joshua 19:5

3. Served as David's exile headquarters - I Samuel 27:6; 30:1; I Chronicles 12:1

4. Many Jews joined David's forces while he was at Ziglag - I Chronicles 12:1, 20

5. The Amalekites destroyed Ziglag and David avenged it - I Samuel 30:1-31 (1, 14, 26)

6. David heard of Saul's death and killed the Amalekite - II Samuel 1:1-27; 4:10

7. Rebuilt after the return from Babylon - Nehemiah 11:28

ZORAH (TEL TZARA)

1. Mentioned in the El Amarna Letters

2. Its origin is given in I Chronicles 2:53

3. Border city of Judah - Joshua 15:33; I Chronicles 4:2

4. Given to the Tribe of Dan - Joshua 19:41

5. Home of Manoah, the father of Samson - Judges 13:2

6. Area of the activities of Samson - Judges 13:25

7. Samson was buried here - Judges 16:31

8. Eventually the spies of Dan came from here and the inhabitants went to settle at Laish - Judges 18:2, 8, 11

9. Fortified by Rehoboam - II Chronicles 11:10

10. Rebuilt in the return from Babylon

Jordan
The Modern State

I. GENERAL INFORMATION

A. THE TERRITORY

The modern nation of Jordan comprises four ancient territories: Gilead, Ammon, Moab and Edom.

Today, the country is divided into five districts called *Muhafazahs*: Irbid, Amman, Balqa, Karak and Ma'an. Amman is the capital of the nation.

Jordan has a land area of 56,823 square miles. It is almost completely land-locked being bordered by Syria, Iraq, Saudi Arabia and Israel. Its only outlet to the sea is Aqaba on the Red Sea where it has about ten miles of coastline.

B. HISTORY

In 1918, the Ottoman Turkish Empire came to an end and in 1920 the League of Nations established the Mandate for Transjordan.

On May 25, 1946, Transjordan became an independent monarchy under King Abdallah. When the Jordan Legion captured the West Bank in 1948, it was annexed and the name of the country was changed to the Hashemite Kingdom of Jordan in April 1950.

King Abdallah was assassinated in Jerusalem on July 20, 1950 and succeeded by King Talal. King Hussein ascended the Throne of Jordan in 1953 and ruled until his death in 1998. His son, King Abdallah II, is now the ruler of Jordan.

C. POPULATION

The population of Jordan is about 4.2 million with two million living in Amman. About sixty percent is urbanized; 37 percent is rural and three percent are Bedouin. The peasant population of the northwest is believed to be descendants of the Amorites and Ammonites. The Bedouin of the east number about 140,000 divided among the following tribes: Majah, Beni Attiyah, Al Is, Al Sirhan and Beni Khaled. There is also a Circassian population of about 3,000. The Palestinian population numbers about 1,200,000.

Eighty percent of the population is Sunni Muslim. The majority of the remaining twenty percent are mostly Christian and centered in and around Amman. It is made up of Roman Catholics, Greek Orthodox and Protestants.

Besides Amman, the major cities are (population figures from the census of 1979):

1. Zarga - 215,687
2. Irbid - 112,954
3. Salt - 32,866
4. Kerak - 11,805
5. Ma'an - 11,308
6. Aqaba - 26,986

D. THE DESERT CASTLES

In addition to the cities and towns listed in this study-guide, Jordan contains a number of castles in the desert built by the Caliphs of the Umayyad Dynasty (eighth century) where they went for hawking, hunting and horse racing during the day with the enjoyment of hot baths at night accompanied with music and dance. They were also part of extensive agricultural and trade communities resulting from the ability to harness water. Some were built on earlier Roman remains from the second century A.D. The desert castles include:

1. Qasr el-Hallabat
2. Qasr el-Azraq
3. Qasr Hamman esh Sarkh
4. Qasr el-'Amra
5. Qasr el-Kharana
6. Qasr et Tuba
7. Qasr el-Mushatta
8. Qasr Mushaoh
9. Qasr 'Ain es-Sil
10. Muwaqqar
11. Bayir
12. Qastal

There are also the remains of Roman forts that were not rebuilt as Umayyad castles and these include:

1. Qasr Aseikhin
2. Qasr 'Uweinid
3. Deir el-Kahf

Jordan
The Specific Places

THE ABARIM MOUNTAINS

1. The mountain range of Moab where Mount Nebo and Pisgah are located

2. One of the stopping places of Israel in their march to the Promised Land - Numbers 33:47-48

3. Area from which Moses saw the Land and died - Numbers 27:12-14; Deuteronomy 32:48-52

4. In the Prophets: Jeremiah 22:20

ADAM (DAMIYA)

The place where the Jordan River was stopped while Israel crossed into the Promised Land - Joshua 3:16

AMMON

From the Jabbock River in the north to the Arnon River in the south - Numbers 21:24

1. Northern section known as the Mishor, a root meaning "Tableland"

    a. Also called the Tableland of Moab - Deuteronomy 3:10

    b. Part of the Transjordanian conquest of Israel - Joshua 13:9, 16

    c. Area of Balaam's prophecies - Numbers 23-24

    d. Moses was buried nearby - Deuteronomy 34:6

2. The origin of the Ammonites - Genesis 19:38

3. Taken by Israel - Numbers 21:24; Deuteronomy 3:11; Joshua 12:2

4. Sections will always belong to Ammon - Deuteronomy 2:19, 37

5. Half of the territory was given to the Tribe of Gad - Deuteronomy 3:16; Joshua 13:10, 25

6. Along with Moab, it oppressed Israel - Judges 3:13

7. Defeated by Jephthah - Judges 10:6-12:3

8. Subdued by Saul - I Samuel 11:1-11; 12:12; 14:47

9. Subdued by David - II Samuel 8:12, 17; I Chronicles 18:11

10. Home of one of David's mighty men - I Chronicles 11:39

11. Revolted against David and was defeated - II Samuel 10:1-19; I Chronicles 19:1-20:3

12. Capital was besieged and destroyed in the Uriah incident - II Samuel 11:1-12:31

13. Solomon built a temple for the god of Ammon - I Kings 11:1, 5, 7, 33; II Kings 23:13

14. The mother of Rehoboam was from Ammon - II Chronicles 12:13

15. It warred against King Jehoshaphat - II Chronicles 20:1-23

16. Home of the mother of Zabad, one of the killers of Joash - II Chronicles 24:26

17. Subdued by Jotham - II Chronicles 27:5

18. Subdued by Uzziah - II Chronicles 26:8

19. Raided Judah in the days of Jehoiakim - II Kings 24:2

20. Involved in the conspiracy in the murder of Gedaliah: Ishmael sent by King Baalis - Jeremiah 40:11-41:15

21. Tobiah came from there - Nehemiah 2:10, 19; 4:3; 13:1-9

22. Tried to influence the returnees from Babylon against rebuilding - Nehemiah 4:7

23. Jews intermarried with Ammonites - Ezra 9:1; Nehemiah 13:23

24. Anti-Israel - Psalm 83:7

25. In the Prophets: Isaiah 11:14; Jeremiah 9:26; 25:21; 27:3; 49:1-6; Ezekiel 21:20, 28; 25:1-10; Daniel 11:41; Amos 1:13-15; Zephaniah 2:8-9

26. Finally brought to an end by Judah Maccabbee

THE ARABAH PROPER

1. 110 miles long, 6-12 miles wide

    a. Begins at 1,292 feet below sea level

    b. After 62 miles, it rises to 650 feet above sea level

    c. Highest point above sea level is at Jebel er Rishe

    d. After another 48 miles, it descends to sea level

2. Borders

    a. The mountains of Edom on the east which change colors during the day from light pale in the morning to pink, red and purple in the evening

    b. The Negev Hills in the west made up of limestone and flint ridges

3. Area of the battle of the five kings against the four - Genesis 14:1-12

4. Cities of the Arabah destroyed - Genesis 19:1-29

5. Part of the Wilderness Wanderings - Deuteronomy 1:1; 2:8

6. Part of the area that Joshua took over - Joshua 11:16; 12:1-3

7. Taken by Israel - Deuteronomy 1:7; 3:10, 17; 4:49

8. Eastern border of the Land - Joshua 18:18

9. David defeated the Syrians - II Samuel 8:13

10. David defeated the Edomites - I Chronicles 18:10-13; Psalm 60: superscription

11. Route of the Queen of Sheba

12. Amaziah defeated the Edomites - II Kings 14:7; II Chronicles 25:11

ARBILA (IRBID)

1. One of the ten cities of the Decapolis

2. Now the most northern city of Jordan

AR-MOAB (RABBA) - AREOPOLIS

1. Original inhabitants were a race of giants called the Emim - Deuteronomy 2:9-11

2. They were dispossessed by the Moabites - Deuteronomy 2:9

3. Border city for the Moabites - Numbers 21:13-15

4. Taken from the Moabites by Sihon and the Amorites - Numbers 21:26-28

5. Part of journey of Israel to the Promised Land - Deuteronomy 2:18, 29

6. In the Prophets - Isaiah 15:1

7. Called Rabbath-Moab by the Greeks

8. The Romans called it Areopolis

9. Contains the remains of a temple dedicated to Diocletian and Maximianus

ARNON RIVER (WADI EL-MUJIB)

1. Served as the border between Ammon and Moab - Numbers 21:13; 22:36

2. Taken by Israel - Numbers 21:13-28; Deuteronomy 2:24-37; 3:1-17; 4:48; Judges 11:13, 22-26

3. The City of Moab where Balaam and Balak met was at this border - Numbers 22:36

4. The southern point of the Tribe of Reuben - Deuteronomy 3:16; Joshua 13:16

5. It served as one of the Israelite encampments - Deuteronomy 2:24-36; Numbers 21:13-26; Judges 11:18

6. The southern limit of what Hazael took from Jehu - II Kings 10:32-34

7. In the Prophets - Isaiah 16:2; Jeremiah 48:20

AROER (ARA'IR)

1. Taken by Moses - Deuteronomy 2:36; 3:12; 4:48; Joshua 12:2; 13:9

2. Given to the Tribe of Gad - Numbers 32:34; Joshua 13:25

3. It was a border town with the Tribe of Reuben - Joshua 13:16

4. Claimed by Jephthah against Ammonite claim - Judges 11:26

5. Where Jephthah defeated the Ammonites - Judges 11:33

6. Part of Joab's census - II Samuel 24:5

7. Smitten by Hazael - II Kings 10:33

8. In the Prophets - Isaiah 17:2; Jeremiah 48:19

9. Destroyed by the Assyrians and Babylonians

10. Occupied by Nabateans

11. Destroyed by Romans in A.D. 106

ATAROTH (ATARUZ)

1. Taken by Moses - Numbers 32:3

2. Given to the Tribe of Gad - Numbers 32:34

3. Mentioned in the Mesha Stele as a city fortified by Omri, the King of Israel

BAAL-MEON (MA'IN)

1. Meaning: "Baal of the Waters"

   a. Contains hot mineral springs

   b. Used by Herod the Great for his ailments

2. Given to the Tribe of Reuben - Numbers 32:38; Joshua 13:17; I Chronicles 5:8

3. In the Prophets - Ezekiel 25:9

4. Mentioned in the Mesha Stele

BETH HARAM [HARAN] (TEL ARRAMAH)

Given to the Tribe of Gad - Numbers 32:36; Joshua 13:27

BOZRA-PETRA

1. Identification

   a. Identified by some to be modern Buseira

   b. Identified by others to be Petra - Nearby is the Arab site of Butzeira, which retains the name

2. Bozrah

   a. Home of Jobab, one of the kings of Edom - Genesis 36:33; I Chronicles 1:44

   b. Famous for its sheep - Micah 2:12

   c. The place of Israel's future refuge - Micah 2:12-13

   d. The place of the Second Coming - Micah 2:12-13; Isaiah 34:1-7; 63: 1-6

   e. Destined for eternal destruction - Jeremiah 49:13, 22; Amos 1:12

3. Petra - "The rose red city half as old as time" (Dean Burgon)

   a. Extensively occupied for one thousand years - 500 B.C.-A.D. 500

   b. Originally settled by Edomites

  c. The Nabatean Period - 312 B.C. - A.D. 106

    (1) The city as it stands now is mostly Nabatean - An Arab tribe

    (2) It was attacked by the Seleucids under Antigonus in 312 B.C. but they were repelled by only a few Nabateans in the *siq*

    (3) It withstood Pompey's attack in 63 B.C. and another Roman attack about 25 B.C.

    (4) At its height, it is estimated that 20,000-30,000 people lived here

  d. The Roman Periods - 106-395

    (1) The Romans were able to take it without fighting by cutting off its water supply

    (2) In A.D. 131, Hadrian visited here and named it Adriana Petra

    (3) Occupied and flourished as a Roman city until about A.D. 200 - Trajan built a new road connecting Syria with the Red Sea that passed by Petra

    (4) In the fourth century, trading patterns began to change causing its decline

  e. The Byzantine Period - 395-636

    (1) During the Byzantine Period, many of the tombs were converted into churches

    (2) Petra became the seat of a bishopric

    (3) By the time the Arab Invasion arrived, only a few Bedouins were living here

  f. The Crusaders arrived in 1101 and the city had a short lived revival

  g. With the expulsion of the Crusaders, it disappeared from history

    (1) Ruled for a short while by Saladin's brother, Al Adil

    (2) Ruled by An Nasir in 1229

    (3) Ruled by Mameluke ruler Izzidin Ahek in 1253

    (4) The last Moslem leader to visit was Sulten Baybars in 1276 who only passed by

  h. Rediscovered in 1812 by an Anglo-Swiss explorer, John Louis Burckhardt, who, disguised as an Arab, found it

 4. Wadi Musa - Town outside of Petra

  a. Location of *Ain Musa*, The Spring of Moses

  b. Name is based on the Arab tradition that this is where Moses struck the rock

  c. Contains the ruins of *Li Vaux Moyse* - A Crusader fortress built by Baldwin I in 1127

    (1) Besieged unsuccessfully by the Egyptians in 1158

    (2) Finally taken by the Arabs in 1188-1189

5. Suburbs of Petra - With similar but less impressive remains of that of Petra

   a. *Siq el-Barid* - Known as "Little Petra," it also contains a narrow passageway and cliff-carved buildings

   b. *El-Beidha* - Neolithic (among the oldest in the Middle East) and Nabatean remains

   c. *El-Sabrah* - Contains remains of temples and barracks used by soldiers or miners and a small theatre seating between 500-800 people

6. Things to see

   a. The *Siq* - The Petra Pass

      (1) Approximately 1¼ mile in length leading into the city

      (2) The cliffs on each side reach as high as four hundred feet

      (3) Was the only entry and exit for the city

      (4) A channel was cut into the cliff which carried water into Petra from Ain Musa in addition to the two springs within the city

      (5) It was paved with limestone blocks paid for by Herod the Great and Harith IV; parts of which are still visible

      (6) Could be dangerous - On April 8, 1963 a flash flood killed 28 people

      (7) A dam has now been built to divert the water during flash floods so as not to endanger the tourists

      (8) Still visible are the ruins of the Triumphal Arch in honor of Emperor Adrianus at the entry which was still intact until 1896

   b. *El Khazneh* (The Treasury) or *Khazneh Fara'un* (The Pharaoh's Treasury)

      (1) 130 feet high

      (2) 92 feet wide

      (3) The urn (eleven feet high) on top has many bullet marks from shootings by those who believed that Pharaoh hid his treasure in it

      (4) Believed by some to have been used as a temple to the goddess Al-Uzza

      (5) Believed by others to be the Tomb of King Harith IV (85-84 B.C.)

   c. The Roman Amphitheater

      (1) First built in the early first century A.D., it was enlarged after A.D. 106 when the Romans took the city

      (2) Seats about three to four thousand people (by some estimates, seven to eight thousand)

      (3) Destroyed some Nabatean structures in order to be built

      (4) Believed to be built by Harith IV and modified by Malik II and remodeled by the Romans

      (5) Destroyed by an earthquake in A.D. 363

d. The High Place of Sacrifice - The Attuf Ridge

   (1) The Obelisk Ridge - Two, twenty feet high Obelisks about one hundred feet apart and which are bedrock representing Nabatean deities: Dushara and Al Uzza

   (2) The Place of Sacrifice

      (a) Best preserved high place from biblical times

         i. Ritual immersion pool

         ii. *Al-Madhbah* - The place of sacrifice measuring 48 by 21 feet

         iii. Altar - Where the blood was shed

         iv. Drains - To catch the blood from the altar

         v. *Mense Sacra* - Five inch high platform for bloodless offerings

      (b) Both animal and human

e. *Qasr el-Bint*, The Temple of the Daughter, or *Qasr bint Fara'un*, The Temple of the Daughter of Pharaoh

   (1) Built between 40-30 B.C.

   (2) To the goddess al-Uzza or the god Dushara

   (3) Overlooks the Arabah from four thousand feet high

   (4) Originally thought to be Roman but now assumed to be Nabatean

      (a) Begun by Obodas III

      (b) Completed by Aretus IV

   (5) Has an altar in front

f. The *Umm el-Biyara*

   (1) Rises about 3,500 feet above sea level

   (2) Massive cliff rocks from which some believe that ten thousand Edomites were thrown to their death

   (3) Has Edomite remains on top

   (4) Contains eight huge bell-shaped Edomite cisterns which explain the Arabic name: Mother of Cisterns

   (5) Believed by some to be the biblical Sela

g. The Temanos Gate - Roman arched monumental gateway that led to the Sacred Temanos complex and the *Qasr el-Bint*

h. The Collonaded Street - Built by the Romans after A.D. 106, it was the north-south *cardo maximus* for the city

i. The Necropolis - the Turkamaniya Graves

j The *ed-Deir*, The Monastery, Temple

    (1) The largest of the rock-carved monuments

        (a) 165 feet wide

        (b) 148 feet high

        (c) Entrance is 26 feet high

        (d) The inside chamber measures 38 feet by 33 feet

        (e) The urn on top is thirty feet

    (2) Overlooks the Arabah from four thousand feet high

    (3) Used as a temple

k. The Street of the Facades - Over forty monumental facades with three dominant ones located in the outer *Siq* just inside Petra

    (1) Some are tombs

    (2) Some are debated whether they are tombs or homes

l. The Nymphaeum - Public water fountain built where two wadis meet: Wadi Musa and Wadi Mataba

m. The Three Markets - Known as Trojan's Market

    (1) The Upper Market

    (2) The Middle Market

    (3) The Lower Market

n. The Royal Palace

o. The Temple of Atargatis

    (1) Also called the Temple of the Winged Lions

    (2) Atargatis was the Nabatean version of Venus

p. The Great Temple

q. The Propylaea - Steps that led into the Great Temple

r. *El Habis* - A sheer-sided rock with the remains of a crusader fort

s. The Columbarium - Tiers of niches for cinerary urns or pigeons - Exact use is unknown

t. The Convent Group - A set of monuments that may have had an unknown religion purpose

u. The Hermitage - Caves believed to be occupied by hermits during the Byzantine Period

v. The Faroun Pillar - Part of the temple complex but the exact significance is unknown

w. The Lion Monument

    (1) Fifteen feet sized beast which was the symbol of the goddess Al Uzza

    (2) Used as a fountain for pilgrims

x. The Ma'aiseret Ridges - It has many varieties of monuments, tombs and high places

y. Pharoah's Column - The only remains of what once was a Nabatean Palace

z. The tombs or temples or dwelling places of Petra (debated which they are)

   (1) The Urn Tomb

       (a) Believed by some to be the Tomb for King Malchios III; built around A.D. 70

       (b) Used as a church in 447

       (c) Also called *Al-Mahkamah*, Royal Court of Justice

   (2) The Corinthian Tomb - Combination of Hellenism and Nabateanism architecture and dedicated to King Malkus II

   (3) The Palace Tomb

       (a) The largest of the royal tombs - Three stories high

       (b) Believed by some to be the Tomb of Rabbel II and his family, the last of the Nabatean kings

   (4) The Governor's Tomb - *Qasr al-Hakim*, The Grave of the Ruler

       (a) Inscription identifies it to be the Tomb of Sextus Florentinus

       (b) He was the Roman Governor of Arabia in A.D. 127

       (c) In his will, he instructed that he be buried in Petra

   (5) The Silk Tomb or the Rainbow Tomb - Bands of brilliant multi-colors

   (6) The Renaissance Tomb

   (7) The Tomb of the Roman Soldier

   (8) The Garden Tomb - Actually the Garden Temple

   (9) The Obelisks Tomb - Greek and Nabatean inscriptions date this to the reign of Malichos II (A.D. 40-71)

   (10) The Snake Tomb

   (11) The Lion Tomb - Actually the Triclinium where banquets were held to honor the dead

   (12) The *Bab el-Siq* Triclinium - 35 feet square

   (13) The Unfinished Tomb - Shows the manner by which Petra monuments were made

   (14) The Broken Pediment Tomb - Nabatean

   (15) Al Najr Tomb - Roman

   (16) The Carmine Tomb - Multi-colored tomb of purplish red with streaks of blue and white

   (17) The Turkamaniya Tomb - The only one which contains Nabatean inscriptions

   (18) The Mughar El Nasara Tombs

     (a) Tombs of Christians who lived in Petra

     (b) Nasara - Arabic for Nazareth

     (c) Has crosses on the wall and believed to be a ghetto for Christians

   (19) The Tomb of the Seventeen Tombs

   (20) Tomb of Uneishu

     (a) Inscription stating this was the brother of Shaq ilat - Probably Shaqilat II

     (b) Used as a royal tomb for thirty years

BUSEIRA

Believed by some to be Bozrah

DEAD SEA

1. It has a number of names given in the Scriptures

 a. The Salt Sea - Genesis 14:3; Deuteronomy 3:17

 b. The Eastern Sea - Joel 2:20; Ezekiel 47:18

 c. The Former Sea - Zechariah 14:8

 d. The Sea of the Arabah - Deuteronomy 3:17; II Kings 14:25

 e. Arabic

  (1) Bahr Lut, Sea of Lot

  (2) Bahr el-Mivet, Dead Sea

 f. Greek and Roman - Lake Asphatites

2. The basic measurements

 a. 48 miles long

 b. 11 miles wide - Average 9½ miles

 c. 124 miles around

 d. 189 square miles on the surface

 e. It is 1,292 feet below sea level

 f. It is 1,319 feet deep

 g. The bottom is 2,600 feet below sea level

3. Divided by The Lishon (the "Tongue") which, in biblical times, crossed over the entire Dead Sea and divided it in two, though today it only protrudes about 2/3 of the way

4. Area of the battle of the five kings against the four - Genesis 14:1-12

5. Border of the Transjordanian Tribes - Deuteronomy 3:17; Joshua 12:3

6. When Israel crossed the Jordan River, its waters were cut off from entering the Dead Sea - Joshua 3:16

7. It marked the southern and eastern border of the Land of settlement - Numbers 34:3, 12

8. Taken by Israel - Joshua 12:3

9. Beginning of the southern border - Joshua 15:2

10. East border of the Tribe of Judah - Joshua 15:5

11. East border of the Tribe of Benjamin - Joshua 18:19

12. The southern border of the Land was restored under Jeroboam II - II Kings 14:25

13. In the Kingdom, the Dead Sea waters will be healed and will have and contain life - Ezekiel 47:6-12

14. Today it is very rich in minerals

   a. Potassium chloride - 2 billion metric tons

   b. Magnesium bromide - 980 million metric tons

   c. Sodium chloride - 11 billion metric tons

   d. Magnesium chloride - 22 billion metric tons

   e. Calcium chloride - 6 billion metric tons

   f. Gypsum - 81 million metric tons

DIBON (DHIBWAN)

1. Took part in the War of Sihon against Israel - Numbers 21:30

2. One of the stopping points of Israel's march to the Promised Land - Numbers 33:45-46

3. A city given to the Tribe of Reuben - Joshua 13:9, 17

4. But it was rebuilt by the Tribe of Gad - Numbers 32:3, 34

5. In the Prophets: Isaiah 15:2; Jeremiah 48:18, 22

6. The Meshe Stele, also called the Moabite Stone, was discovered here in 1868

   a. Mentions Omri, King of Israel

   b. Mesha, King of Moab, is mentioned in II Kings 3:4-5

EDOM

1. From the Zered River in the north to the Red Sea in the south

2. The origin of the Edomites - Genesis 25:30; 32:3; 36:9; I Chronicles 1:43-54

3. Settled by the descendants of Esau - Genesis 36:1-43

4. Took note of the Red Sea crossing - Exodus 15:15

5. Refused passage to Israel in the Wilderness Wanderings - Numbers 20:14-23; 21:4; 33:37; Judges 11:17-18

6. Part of Balaam's prophecy - Numbers 24:18

7. A border of the Promised Land - Numbers 34:3; Joshua 15:1, 21

8. Part of Deborah's prophecy - Judges 5:4

9. Subdued by Saul - I Samuel 14:47

10. Home of Doeg - I Samuel 21:7; 22:9, 18, 22; Psalm 52: superscription

11. Subdued by David - II Samuel 8:14; I Chronicles 18:11-13

12. Solomon controlled the port area - I Kings 9:26; II Chronicles 8:17

13. Solomon intermarried with Edomites - I Kings 11:1

14. Revolted against King Solomon - I Kings 11:14-22

15. Joined Israel and Judah against Moab - II Kings 3:8-26

16. Had no king but a deputy - I Kings 22:47

17. Revolted against Judah in the time of Joram - II Kings 8:20-22; II Chronicles 21:8-10

18. Joined the Ammonites and Moabites in the war against Jehoshaphat - II Chronicles 20:10, 23

19. Defeated by Amaziah - II Kings 14:7, 10; II Chronicles 25:11-19

20. Judah worshipped the gods of Edom - II Chronicles 25:20

21. Defeated Judah under Ahaz - II Chronicles 28:17

22. Jews returned from Edom to Mizpah - Jeremiah 40:11

23. In the Psalms - 60:superscription, 8-9; 83:6; 108:9-10; 137:7

24. In the Prophets -
    Isaiah 11:14; 34:1-15; 63:1; Jeremiah 9:26; 25:21; 27:3; 40:11; 49:7-22; Lamentations 4:21-22; Ezekiel 25:12-14; 32:29; 35:15; Daniel 11:41; Joel 3:19; Amos 1:6, 9-12; 2:1; 9:12; Obadiah; Malachi 1:4

25. The Edomites later moved into the Negev and the area was renamed Idumea

26. Herod the Great was Idumean

EILAT (AILAH) (AQABA)

1. It was often mentioned with the town of Ezion Geber - Deuteronomy 2:8; I Kings 9:26; II Chronicles 8:17

2. It was one of the stopping points in the Wilderness Wanderings - Deuteronomy 2:8

3. It served as a Solomonic port - II Chronicles 8:17-18

4. It was rebuilt and restored to Judah under Azariah or Uzziah - II Kings 14:22; II Chronicles 26:2

5. Taken by Rezin, king of Assyria - II Kings 16:6

6. In Roman times, the Roman Tenth Legion was stationed there

7. Was the base of a Jewish tribe with whom Mohammad made a treaty

8. During the Moslem Period, it was a crossroads for pilgrimages to Mecca from Egypt, Africa and the Israeli Coast

    a. Main Road: *Dareb el-Haj*, The Pilgrim's Way

    b. Minor Road: *Dareb el-Aza*, The Gaza Way

9. Conquered by Crusaders in 1116 by King Baldwin I with a small force of 40 knights

    a. This action separated the two large Moslem centers of Cairo and Damascus

    b. Moslems wishing to make a pilgrimage to Mecca had to pay a toll tax

    c. Baldwin also built a fortress here; later reused by the Mamelukes

10. Reconquered by Saladin in 1170 after he transported parts of ships on camel back by way of the *Dareb el-Haj*

11. In 1182, Reynald de Chatillon, the Crusader ruler of Transjordan, tried to do the same but, after an initial success, the venture ended with the death of all the knights

12. The fort was built by Sultan Nasir about 1320 and rebuilt by the last of the Mameluke Sultans, Qanush el-Ghuri, in 1505

13. Area was largely abandoned except by Bedouins until the late Turkish Period

14. Taken by the British in World War I by Lawrence of Arabia

15. In 1925, it became part of the Emirate of Transjordan

16. Modern Eilat, now a city in Israel, was built around an old Police Station called Umm Rashrash

17. Biblical Eilat is now Aqaba in Jordan

    a. Originally the Arab name was Ailah

    b. In the 15th century, the name was changed to Aqaba

18. Aqaba Today

    a. It is Jordan's most southern city

    b. Serves as Jordan's only port with access to the Indian and Pacific Oceans

19. Things To See

    a. The Crusader Castle - Now a museum

    b. Ezion Geber - Tel Khalaifah

    c. Wadi Rum

ELEALEH (EL 'AL)

1. Taken by Moses - Numbers 32:3

2. Given to the Tribe of Reuben - Numbers 32:37

3. In the Prophets - Isaiah 15:4; 16:9; Jeremiah 48:34

4. Important site during the Roman and Byzantine Periods

EZION GEBER (TEL KHALIFEH)

1. One of the stops in the Wilderness Wanderings - Numbers 33:35-36; Deuteronomy 2:8

2. Port city for the ships of Solomon - I Kings 9:26-28 (10:11, 22); II Chronicles 8:17-18

3. Port for the ships of Jehoshaphat and here they were broken - I Kings 22:48; II Chronicles 20:35-37

GEDARA (UMM QEIS)

1. One of the ten cities of the Decapolis

2. It was the capital of a district called Gedaritis which included Perea

3. Controlled an area that included Gergasa - Matthew 8:28; Mark 5:1; Luke 8:26

4. Though located in Gilead on the other side of the Yarmuk River, its harbor was located at Tel Samra (Haon) on the Sea of Galilee

5. The city's history began in the Hellenistic Period and it became a major city for Greek poets, playwrights, philosophers, satirists and orators, including the following:

    a. Meleagros - First century B.C. poet

    b. Menippos - Third century B.C. satirist

    c. Philademos - First century B.C. epicurean philosopher who was a teacher of Virgil and Horace

    d. Apsines - Third century A.D. orator

    e. Theodros - First century A.D. orator who founded a school of rhetoric in Rome and became the private tutor of Emperor Tiberius

6. First built as a military outpost by the Ptolemies of Egypt, it was conquered by the Seleucid King Antiochus the Great in 218 B.C.

7. Taken by the Hasmonean, Alexander Yannai, in 98 B.C. after a ten-month seige

8. Taken for Rome by Pompey in 65 B.C. who also had the city rebuilt

9. It became one of the seats of the five Jewish Councils set up by Gabinius

10. The Emperor Augustus Caesar gave it to Herod the Great in 30 B.C.

11. After Herod's death, it became part of the Province of Syria and marked the border between Galilee and Southern Syria

12. It was destroyed by Vespasian

13. It was rebuilt at the end of the first century A.D. and reached its peak in the second century from which most of its ancient structures date

14. Pleasure seekers who went to the hot baths of Hammat Gader would stay at the higher elevated Gedara since it was considerably cooler

15. In the third century, two Christians, Zacharias and Alpheios, suffered martyrdom in the reign of Diocletian

16. During the Byzantine Period (fourth-seventh centuries), it flourished and served as an episcopal seat

17. Taken in the Moslem invasion in A.D. 636, it was part of the main route of pilgrimage from Damascus to Mecca and Medina

18. After the earthquakes of the seventh and eighth centuries, it went into a long period of decline

19 In the Crusader Period, it was only a small village

20. Contains the remains of three theaters, a temple, a colonnaded street and basilica

21. Things to see

    a. The Eastern Necropolis - The site of three well-preserved and marked Greco-Roman tombs with Latin or Greek inscriptions

        (1) Tomb of Quintus Publius Germanus and Aulus Germanus Rufus

        (2) Tomb of Lucius Sentius Modestus

        (3) Tomb of Chaireas, son of Chaireas, grandson of Demetrius, "built in the year 154" - Equivalent to A.D. 90-91

    b. Acropolis Hill - The city center during the Hellenistic-Roman Period

        (1) Now occupied by the Ottoman Turkish village of el-Melab; built at the turn of the century

        (2) Village was built along the street division of the ancient city and reused many of the same stones

    c. Two theaters - Built of black basalt rock

    d. The Basilical Terrace - A paved plaza from the Byzantine Period measuring about 300 feet by 100 feet and served as the atrium of a Byzantine Church

    e. Vaulted shops on the Roman Street: *Decumanus Maximus*

    f. The Nymphaeum - Public fountain

    g. Public Baths - Two bath complexes

    h. The North Mausoleum - Dated A.D. 355-356

    i. The Underground Mausoleum - Built during the Roman Period and reused during the Byzantine Period with two sphinx statuettes at the entry

    j. City walls and gate

    k. The Hippodrome - Outside the wall

    l. The Monumental Arch - Unknown to whom

GERESA (JERASH OR JARASH)

1. Founded in the Hellenistic Period by Greek soldiers and known as "Antioch on the Chrysorrhoas"

2. Earliest historical reference to this city is from Josephus who mentions an event that dates to the second century B.C.

3. Taken by Alexander Yannai (103-76 B.C.)

4. After the conquest of Pompey in 63 B.C., it became one of the ten Greek cities of the Decapolis

5. Much of the present remains date from the first and second century A.D. especially under Trajan (98-117) and Hadrian (135) - The golden age of Geresa

JORDAN: THE SPECIFIC PLACES

6. The city reached its peak in the third century and was granted the status of a Roman colony - But then its decline began

    a. Given the status of a Roman colony by Caracalla (211-217) and renamed: Colonia Aurelia Antoniniana

    b. But this action only temporarily slowed its decline

7. It was christianized and temporarily reused in 350 and then many churches were built and pagan temples destroyed or converted into churches

    a. Between A.D. 400-600, thirteen churches were built - Nine in the sixth century alone and seven under Emperor Justinian (527-565)

    b. The Jews were expelled in 531

    c. The last church was built in 611 by Bishop Genesius

8. The Byzantine revival ended with the Persian Invasion (614-628)

9. The Arab Conquest in 635 completed the decline of the city

    a. Many churches continued to be used but in 720 Caliph Yazid II ordered all images destroyed leading to the destruction of many mosaic church floors

    b. The earthquake of 747 virtually brought the city to an end

10. It was not a center during the Crusader Kingdom

11. Circassians, settled in the region by Turks at the end of the nineteenth century, often used the stones of Geresa for private building

12. It was rediscovered by a German traveler named Ulrich Jasper Seetzen in 1808

13. Things to see

    a. Hippodrome - For horse and camel racing and seated 15,000 spectators about A.D. 130

    b. South Gate - Original gate replaced at the time of Hadrian

    c. North Gate - Built in A.D. 115 by C. Claudius Severus, the Legate of Emperor Trajan, who built the road from Geresa to Pella

    d. Temple of Zeus - Built in A.D. 166

    e. Temple of Artemis - Built in A.D. 150

    f. North Theater - Also called the Odeom; originally built around A.D. 165 and used as an Odeom until the fifth and sixth century

    g. South Theater - Built during the reign of Domitian (A.D. 81-96); seating over 3,000 people

    h. West Baths - Built in the second century

    i. East Baths

    j. Synagogue Church - A church built into a previously existing synagogue in 530

    k. Church of Saints Peter and Paul - Built 540

l. Cathedral - Built 350-375 with stones taken from the Temple of Dyonysius

m. Church of Saint Theodorus - Built 494-496

n. Church of Saints Cosmus and Damian - Built 529-533

o. Church of Saint John the Baptist - Built 529-533

p. Church of Saint George - Built 529-533

q. Church of the Apostles, Prophets and Martyrs - Built between 461-465

r. Viaduct Church - Built in 565

s. Procopius Church - Built in 526-527

t. South Tetrapylon - Marks the intersection of the south decumanus

u. North Tetrapylon - Dedicated to Julia Domma, the Syrian wife of Emperor Septimus Severus (A.D. 193-211)

v. Triumphal Arch - Built in A.D. 129 in honor of Emperor Hadrian

w. The Forum or the Oval Piazza - Oval shaped and built in the first century. 240 feet at its widest with 56 Ionic columns still standing

x. The *Cardo Maximus*, Street of the Columns - 360 columns on each side

y. City Walls - Over 10,000 feet around encircling about 210 acres

z. Nymphaeum: Double water fountain built in A.D. 191

aa. North Bridge - Connected two sides of the city across the river flowing through the city

bb. South Bridge - Over the Chrysorhoas River

cc. The Church of Bishop Genesius - The last church built in 611

GILEAD

1. Name comes from a root meaning "rugged land"

2. From the Yarmuk River in the north to the Jabbock River in the south

3. Area of the flight of Jacob from Laban - Genesis 31:21, 23, 25

4. The buyers of Joseph came from here - Genesis 37:25

5. Area taken and settled by the Transjordanian Tribes - Numbers 32:1-42; Deuteronomy 2:36; 3:10, 15-16; 4:43; Joshua 12:1-6; 13:11; 22:9, 13, 15, 32

6. Part of the area was given to the Tribe of Manasseh - Numbers 32:39-40; Joshua 13:31; 17:1-6; I Chronicles 27:21; Psalm 60:7; 108:8

7. Another part was given to the Tribe of Gad - Numbers 32:33-36; Joshua 13:24-28; I Chronicles 5:14-16; 6:80

8. Area of Ramoth, a City of Refuge - Joshua 20:8; 21:38

9. Members of the Tribe of Reuben also settled here - I Chronicles 5:1-10

10. Settled by the family of Jair - I Chronicles 2:21-23

11. Part of the area that Moses saw - Deuteronomy 34:1

12. Did not participate in Barak's revolt - Judges 5:17

13. Where the fearful went after leaving Gideon - Judges 7:3

14. Home of Jair, one of the judges of Israel - Judges 10:3-5

15. Home of Jephthah, one of the judges of Israel - Judges 11:1; 12:7

16. Ephraim defeated here under Jephthah - Judges 12:4-7

17. Participated in the Anti-Benjaminite War - Judges 20:1

18. Part of the Saul and Jonathan Philistine War - I Samuel 13:7

19. Saul's body was brought here and burned and the bones buried - I Samuel 31:11-13

20. Ishbosheth ruled over the northern tribes of Israel from here - II Samuel 2:8-10

21. The war between David and Absalom occurred here - II Samuel 17:24-19:10

22. Home of Barzillai - II Samuel 17:27; 19:31; I Kings 2:7; Ezra 2:61; Nehemiah 7:63

23. Included as part of David's census - II Samuel 24:6

24. Home of some of David's men of valor - I Chronicles 26:31

25. The northern section was part of the Sixth Solomonic District - I Kings 4:13

26. The southern section was part of the Twelfth Solomonic District - I Kings 4:19

27. Home of Elijah the Prophet - I Kings 17:1

28. Area where Ahab was killed at Ramoth Gilead - I Kings 22:1-36

29. Where Jehu was anointed King of Israel - II Kings 9:1-15a

30. Area taken by Hazael from Jehu - II Kings 10:32-33

31. Participated in Pekah's revolt against Pekahiah - II Kings 15:25

32. Taken by Tiglath Pileser III - II Kings 15:29

33. Famous for its medical balm - Jeremiah 8:22; 46:11

34. The goats of Gilead - Song of Solomon 4:1; 6:5

35. In the Prophets: Jeremiah 22:6; 50:19; Ezekiel 47:18; Hosea 6:8; 12:11; Amos 1:3, 13; Obadiah 19; Micah 7:14; Zechariah 10:10

36. Area of Perea of the New Testament

HESHBON (HISBAN)

1. Capital of Sihon, King of the Amorites, who warred against Israel and was defeated - Numbers 21:21-35; Deuteronomy 1:4; 2:24-37; 3:2, 6; 4:46; 29:7; Joshua 9:10; 12:2, 5; Judges 11:19-22; Nehemiah 9:22

2. Given to the Tribe of Reuben - Joshua 13:10, 17, 21

3. Border city with the Tribe of Gad - Joshua 13:26-27

4. Levitical City - Joshua 21:39; I Chronicles 6:81

5. Famous for its fish pools - Song of Solomon 7:4

6. In the Prophets - Isaiah 15:4; 16:8-9; Jeremiah 48:2, 34, 45; 49:3

7. When the Jews were taken into Assyrian Captivity under Sargon II, it was reoccupied by the Moabites

8. Taken by the Babylonians in 588 B.C.

9. Taken by Hasmonian, Alexander Yannai

10. Herod the Great built a fort here to protect Perea

11. Taken by Placidus, a Roman general under Vespasian, and renamed Esbus

12. Christianized in the Byzantine Period

13. Moslemized in the Arab Conquest

JABBOCK RIVER - NAHR EZ ZARQA

1. Enters Jordan at Succoth (South) and Adam

2. Border between Gilead and Ammon - Numbers 21:24; Deuteronomy 3:16; Joshua 12:2

3. Jacob crossed this river - Genesis 32:22

4. It was part of the Israelite Conquest - Numbers 21:24; Deuteronomy 2:37; Joshua 12:1-6; Judges 11:13, 22

5. Border between the Tribes of Gad and Reuben - Deuteronomy 3:12, 16

JEBEL HARUN

1. The highest mountain in Mount Seir

2. The Moslem Tomb of Aaron

3. Originally a Greek Christian Shrine; it was moslemized in the thirteenth century by Sultan Qalamun

4. Present structure built in 1459

5. Every year a goat is sacrificed here to commemorate the sacrifice of Isaac

JORDAN RIVER

1. From Mount Hermon to the Dead Sea
   a. 150 miles by air and 310 miles in actual flow
   b. Descending from 3,000 feet above sea level to 1,300 feet below
   c. The longest river in the Promised Land

2. The river has four sources
   a. Banyas (Hermon)
   b. Dan
   c. Baragit (Iyon Valley - Tanur)
   d. Hatzbani (Senir)

3. Served as the Canaan border and a general border throughout history - Numbers 22:1; 26:3, 63; 31:12; 35:10, 14; Deuteronomy 1:5; 2:29; Joshua 2:10; 9:10; 12:1, 7; 20:8; 23:4; I Chronicles 26:30

4. Marked the eastern border of the Land - Numbers 34:12

5. Jacob crossed this border into the Land of Canaan - Genesis 32:10

6. Included in what the twelve spies spied out - Numbers 13:29

7. Area of Israelite encampment before crossing it - Numbers 33:48-50; 35:1; 36:13; Deuteronomy 1:1

8. It marked the tribal border between the Cisjordanian and Transjordanian Tribes - Numbers 32:5, 19, 21, 29, 32; 34:15; Deuteronomy 3:22; 4:41-49; Joshua 1:14-15; 13:8, 23, 27, 32; 14:3; 17:5; 18:7; 22:4, 7, 25; 24:8; Judges 11:13, 22; I Chronicles 6:78; 12:15, 37

9. Moses was forbidden to cross the Jordan - Deuteronomy 3:27; 4:21-22; 31:2

10. Israel was told to cross the river - Numbers 33:51; 35:10; Deuteronomy 12:10; 4:26; 9:1; 11:30-31; 27:2, 4, 12; 30:18; 31:13

11. Joshua ordered to cross the river - Joshua 1:2, 11

12. The men of Jericho searched to this limit for the two spies - Joshua 2:7

13. The Jordan River parted when Joshua crossed - Joshua 3:1-17 (1, 8, 11, 13, 14, 15, 17); 7:7; 24:11; Psalm 114:3, 5

14. Twelve stones were taken out of the Jordan after the crossing to commemorate the event - Joshua 4:1-24 (1, 3, 5, 7, 8, 9, 10, 16, 17, 18, 19, 20, 22, 23)

15. News of the crossing of the Jordan River spread throughout the Land - Joshua 5:1; 9:1-2

16. It marked the border for seven tribes

    a. Western border of Reuben - Joshua 13:23

    b. Western border of Gad - Joshua 13:27

    c. Eastern border of Judah - Joshua 15:5

    d. Eastern border of Ephraim - Joshua 16:1, 7

    e. Eastern border of Benjamin - Joshua 18:12; 19-20

    f. Eastern border of Issachar - Joshua 19:22

    g. Eastern border of Naphtali - Joshua 19:33-34

17. After the taking of the Land, an altar was set up by the river by the 2½ Transjordanian Tribes - Joshua 22:10-11

18. Ehud the Judge guarded the fords of the Jordan - Judges 3:28

19. Mentioned in Deborah's song - Judges 5:17

20. Gideon the Judge also guarded the fords of the Jordan - Judges 7:24

21. Gideon crossed the Jordan in pursuit of the Midianites - Judges 7:25; 8:4

22. The Ammonites crossed the river to oppress Israel - Judges 10:8-9

23. Jephthah guarded the fords of the river against Ephraimites using the test of Shibboleth - Judges 12:5-6

24. Some Jews of the Cisjordan crossed the river during the Philistine oppression - I Samuel 13:7; 31:7

25. Crossed by Abner in his flight from Joab - II Samuel 2:29

26. David crossed the river in pursuit of the Syrians - II Samuel 10:17; I Chronicles 19:17

27. David crossed the river in flight from Absalom - II Samuel 17:16, 22; I Kings 2:8

28. Absalom crossed this river - II Samuel 17:24

29. David crossed the Jordan River again when he returned from the war against Absalom - II Samuel 19:15-43 (15, 17, 18, 31, 36, 39, 41); I Kings 2:8

30. Border of those loyal to David after Sheba's revolt - II Samuel 20:2

31. Joab crossed the river for the census - II Samuel 24:5

32. Elijah was fed by the ravens by the river - I Kings 17:3-5

33. Elijah parted the Jordan - II Kings 2:6-8

34. Elisha parted the Jordan - II Kings 2:13-14

35. Naaman healed after dipping seven times in the Jordan - II Kings 5:8-14

36. The limit to where the Syrians were pursued - II Kings 7:15

37. The border of Hazael's conquests - II Kings 10:33

38. In the Poetic Books - Job 40:23; Psalms 42:6; 114:3, 5

39. In the Prophets - Isaiah 9:1; Jeremiah 12:5; 49:19; 50:44; Ezekiel 47:18; Zechariah 11:3

40. The ministry of John the Baptist - Matthew 3:1-6; Mark 1:4-5; Luke 3:2-3; John 1:28; 3:26

41. Jesus baptized - Matthew 3:13-17; Mark 1:9-11; Luke 3:21-22

42. In the ministry of Jesus - Matthew 4:15, 25; 19:1; Mark 3:8; 10:1; Luke 4:1; John 10:40

43. The eastern border of the Millennial Israel - Ezekiel 47:18

JORDAN VALLEY

1. Extends from the Sea of Galilee to the Dead Sea

2. Distance of seventy miles

3. 4-14 miles wide

4. The Zor

   a. 100-150 feet lower than the main valley

   b. 600 feet to two miles wide

5. River bed, lying within the Zor, is 90-200 feet wide

6. Fed by other rivers

   a. From east: Yarmuk and Jabbock

   b. From west: Nahr Jalud and Wadi Faria

7. Place where Lot settled - Genesis 13:10-11

8. Israelite encampment before crossing the Jordan River -
   Numbers 31:12; 33:50; 35:1; Deuteronomy 1:1

9. Part of the area that Moses was allowed to see - Deuteronomy 34:3

10. Area of Jewish settlement - Deuteronomy 4:46, 49

11. Involved in the defeat of Ai - Joshua 8:14

12. Part of the northern confederacy against Joshua - Joshua 11:2

13. Defeated and taken by Joshua - Joshua 11:6-8

14. Eastern part of it was given to Gad - Joshua 13:27

15. The route for murderers of Ishbosheth - II Samuel 4:7

16. Solomon made his furniture for the Temple - I Kings 7:46;
    II Chronicles 4:17

17. Area where Elijah hid - I Kings 17:3-5

18. Area of John the Baptist's ministry - Matthew 3:5; Luke 3:3;
    John 1:28

19. Zedekiah was captured here - II Kings 25:4-5; Jeremiah 39:4-5; 52:7-8

20. A section of it known as The Pride of the Jordan was once the abode
    of many lions: The Zor - Jeremiah 12:5; 49:19; 50:44; Zechariah 11:3

21. In the Psalms: 42:6

THE KING'S HIGHWAY

1. The main road running north-south from Damascus to the Red Sea
   and along the western edge of the Hill Country of the Amorites

2. The route of the invasion of four kings against the five - Genesis 14:1-6

3. The highway Moses wanted to use but could not -
   Numbers 10:14-21; 21:21-23; Deuteronomy 2:26-30

KIR (KARAK)

1. Capital of Moab - Isaiah 15:1

2. Also known as

   a. Kir Heres - Jeremiah 48:31, 36

   b. Kir Haraseth - II Kings 3:25; Isaiah 16:7, 11

3. Defeated by Jehoshaphat - II Kings 3:21-27 (25)

   a. Mesha had revolted against Israel after Ahab's death

   b. Jehoram, King of Israel, went to war against Moab; Jehoshaphat,
      King of Judah, allied himself with Israel

   c. In the process, Mesha sacrificed his eldest son on the city wall to
      Chemosh, god of Moab (I Kings 3:26)

4. Destroyed in 646 B.C. by Ashurbanipal, King of Assyria

5. Occupied by Nabateans until about the second century B.C.

6. During the Greek Period, it was an important city renamed Kharkha

7. Christianized during the Byzantine Period

8. After the Arab conquest, it was abandoned

9. It was rebuilt as a fortress during the Crusader Period by Payen, the cupbearer of King Fulk, in 1136 and it became a district capital called Crac des Moabites or La Pierre du Desert of the Province of Oultre Jourdain

10. When Karak was under Renaud de Chatillon, it was attacked by Saladin in 1183 and 1184 but each time he was forced to withdraw

11. Karak finally fell (after Saladin's death) to Saladin's brother, Al'Adil

12. The fortress was enlarged in 1263

13. Karak became a bone of contention between the Ayyubids of Syria and the Mamelukes of Egypt; changing hands more than once

14. After the Turkish Conquest in 1517, the city began to lose its importance

15. In 1894, it became a regional capital of a Turkish Sanjak

16. It continued as a regional capital after World War I

LABAN
Mentioned as being part of the area where Moses spoke the words of Deuteronomy - Deuteronomy 1:1

MACHAERUS (MAKHWAR OR MEKAWIR)
1. First built by the Hasmonean, Alexander Yannai (103-76 B.C.)

2. Destroyed by Gabinius in 67 B.C.

3. Rebuilt and became one of the three main fortresses of Herod the Great

4. The place where Herod Antipas beheaded John the Baptist

5. Captured by the Zealots in A.D. 66; it again fell to the Romans in A.D. 70 under Bassus who destroyed it

MAHANAIM (KHIRBET EL-MAHNEH)
1. Here, the angels of God met Jacob on his way back to the Land - Genesis 32:2

2. Given to the Tribe of Gad - Joshua 13:26

3. It was one of Gad's border cities with the Tribe of Manasseh - Joshua 13:29-30

4. Levitical City for the Tribe of Gad - Joshua 21:38

5. Capital of Ishbosheth, the son of Saul - II Samuel 2:8, 12, 29

6. Place to where David fled from Absalom - II Samuel 17:24, 27; I Kings 2:8

MEDEBA (MADABA)

1. Taken by Israel from Sihon, King of the Amorites - Numbers 21:30

2. Given to the Tribe of Reuben - Joshua 13:9, 16

3. Ammonite city in David's day which participated in the war against David - I Chronicles 19:7

4. In the Prophets: Isaiah 15:2

5. Attacked by the Maccabees (Jonathan and Simon) after a Nabatean family that ruled the city ambushed and killed Yochanan Maccabee

6. Captured after a six-month siege by John Hyrcanus in 110 B.C. and held until Alexander Yannai (76 B.C.)

7. It later became a Nabatean city

8. It flourished in the Roman and Byzantine Periods and became part of the Province of Arabia

9. The site of a number of early Christian martyrs during the reign of Diocletian

    a. Zenon of Zizya, a Roman army officer, along with his servant, Zena

    b. Theodore of Belga and his five friends: Julian, Eubolos, Malkamon, Mokimos and Salamon

10. Byzantine records list the names of many bishops over several centuries

11. Destroyed in the Persian Invasion of A.D. 614

12. After the Arab Conquest it was abandoned - Especially after the earthquake of A.D. 747

13. In 1880, two thousand Christians from Karak settled there and later they were joined by other Christians and Moslems - This became the origin of the modern city

14. The discovery of many Byzantine mosaics caused the modern city to be called the City of Mosaics

15. Location of the sixth century Byzantine Madaba Map

    a. Discovered in 1890

    b. A map of the Middle East from the Byzantine period containing about 150 place names

    c. The focus is on Jerusalem and the Church of the Holy Sepulchre

MOAB

1. From the Arnon River in the north to the Zered River in the south - Numbers 21:13-15; Judges 11:18

2. The origin of the Moabites - Genesis 19:37; I Chronicles 1:4

3. Hadad the Edomite smote Midian in the Field of Moab - Genesis 36:35

4. Took note of the Red Sea Crossing - Exodus 15:15

5. Moab's refusal to allow Israel to pass through forced Israel to walk around their land - Numbers 21:11-30; Deuteronomy 2:9, 11, 29; Judges 11:15, 18; II Chronicles 20:10

6. Israel camped in the Fields of Moab -
   Numbers 26:1-63; 31:12; 33:44-50; 35:1; 36:13

7. Hired Balaam to curse Israel - Numbers 22:1-24:17; Joshua 24:9-10

8. Israel's sin in Moab - Numbers 25:1

9. Moses died in the Land of Moab - Deuteronomy 34:1-8

10. Members of the Tribe of Judah had possessions in Moab -
    I Chronicles 4:22

11. Some Benjaminites were born there - I Chronicles 8:8

12. Oppressed Israel - Judges 3:12-30; Joshua 13:32; I Samuel 12:9

13. Israel worshipped the gods of Moab - Judges 10:6

14. Not claimed by Israel - Judges 11:15-25

15. The family of Naomi went to live here and it was the home of Ruth -
    Ruth 1:1-22; 2:2, 6, 21; 4:3, 5, 10

16. Subdued by Saul - I Samuel 14:47

17. David hid his family here during his flight from Saul - I Samuel 22:3-5

18. Subdued by David - I Chronicles 18:1-2; II Samuel 8:2, 12

19. Benaiah, one of David's mighty men, killed men of Moab -
    II Samuel 23:20; I Chronicles 11:22

20. One of David's mighty men came from here - I Chronicles 11:46

21. Solomon's intermarriage and worship - I Kings 11:1, 7, 33;
    II Kings 23:13

22. Rebelled against Israel after the death of Ahab - II Kings 1:1

23. Warred with Judah and Israel - II Kings 3:4-27

24. Warred against Jehoshaphat - II Chronicles 20:1-23

25. Home of the mother of Jehozabad, one of the killers of Joash -
    II Chronicles 24:26

26. Raided Israel in the days of Joash - II Kings 13:20

27. Raided Judah in the days of Jehoiakim - II Kings 24:2

28. From here, the Jews returned to Mizpah - Jeremiah 40:11-12

29. Jews intermarried with the Moabites - Ezra 9:1; Nehemiah 13:23

30. In the Psalms - 60:8; 83:6; 108:9

31. In the Prophets -
    Isaiah 11:14; 15:1-16:14; Jeremiah 9:26; 25:21; 27:3; 40:11; 48:1-47;
    Ezekiel 25:8-11; Daniel 11:41; Amos 2:1-2; Micah 6:5; Zephaniah 2:8-9

MOUNT NEBO (JEBEL NABA)

1. Reaches about 3,400 feet above sea level; contains two peaks

   a. Northern Peak: Mount Pisgah (Siyagha)

   b. Southern Peak: Mount Nebo (el-Mekhayyat)

2. Closely associated with Pisgah - Deuteronomy 34:1

3. One of the stopping points in Israel's march toward the Promised Land - Numbers 33:47

4. Given to the Tribe of Reuben - Numbers 32:3, 38

5. The place from which Moses saw the Land and where he died - Deuteronomy 32:48-52; 34:1-6

6. In the Prophets: Isaiah 15:2; Jeremiah 48:1, 22

7. Contains the remains of a fourth century Byzantine church: *Siyagha* - The Memorial of Moses' View

   a. Enlarged in the sixth century

   b. In the seventh century, the Chapel of the Virgin Mary was added to the basilica

8. Contains the remains of subsequent Byzantine churches as late as the seventh century, including a baptistry and a diaconicon (where deacons prepared consecrated vessels) and a mosaic floor dated in 531

9. The ancient town of Nebo is located at the nearby Khirbet el-Mekhayyat - Contains the largest mosaic floor ever found in Jordan dating from the sixth century

10. Mount Nebo today has two main structures

    a. The Franciscan Monastery - Built in 1932

    b. The Sanctuary of Moses

MOUNT SEIR (SHERA)

1. A long north and south mountain range stretching the whole land of Edom

2. The original inhabitants were the Horites - Genesis 12:6; 36:20, 21, 30; Deuteronomy 2:12, 22

3. Part of the area conquered by the four kings - Genesis 14:6

4. Became the possession of Esau and the Edomites who disposed the Horites - Genesis 32:3; 33:14, 16; 36:8, 9; Deuteronomy 2:5; Joshua 24:4

5. Mentioned in the Oracles of Balaam - Numbers 24:18

6. Mentioned in the Wilderness Wanderings - Deuteronomy 1:2, 44; 2:1, 4, 5, 8, 12, 22, 29

7. Mentioned in the Song of Moses as being part of the area of the Second Coming - Deuteronomy 33:2

8. Border of the area conquered by Joshua - Joshua 11:17; 12:7

9. Mentioned in the Song of Deborah - Judges 5:4

10. Five hundred Simeonites raided Mount Seir and destroyed the remnants of the Amalekites - I Chronicles 4:42-43

11. Participated in the invasion of Judah in the days of Jehoshaphat - II Chronicles 20:10, 20-23

12. Smitten by Amaziah, King of Judah - II Chronicles 25:11-14

13. In the Prophets: Isaiah 21:11; Ezekiel 25:8; 35:2, 3, 7, 15

NIMRIM (SHUNAT NIMRIN)

1. The waters were to be dried up - Isaiah 15:6

2. The waters were to become desolate - Jeremiah 48:34

PELLA (TABAQAT FAHL)

1. The original ancient name was Pihilum or Pahel

2. Settled as early as the Neolithic Period

3. First mentioned in the Execration Texts of the 19th century B.C.

4. Mentioned in the Tel Amarna Letters

5. Mentioned in Papyrus Anastasi

6. Strategically located on a trade route connecting with Scythopolis (Beth Shean) and the Mediterranean Sea on the west and Jaresh (Gerasa) and the Kings Highway on the east

7. Destroyed by Babylon in 586 B.C. and remained uninhabited for three centuries

8. Rebuilt as a city during the Hellenistic Period

9. Taken by Antiochus the Great in 218 B.C.

10. Destroyed by Alexander Yannai in 83-82 B.C. when the residents refused to convert to Judaism

11. Rebuilt by Pompey and the city began to develop as a major city of the Roman world

12. Became one of the ten cities of the Decapolis

13. The city where Jewish believers fled to in A.D. 66

14. After the revolt, many stayed behind helping to turn the city into a strong Christian city during the Roman and Byzantine Periods - There are remains of at least four churches containing a mixture of both Jewish and Christian symbols

15. The city reached its peak in the fifth and sixth centuries A.D. with a population of 25,000

16. Captured in the Moslem Invasion in 635 but the city was still half Christian into the ninth century

17. Suffered some major destruction in the earthquake of A.D. 747

18. Began a long period of decline in the ninth and tenth centuries until it was reduced to a small village of about 200; its history ends in the sixteenth century

PENUEL (TEL EL-TAHAB)

1. Where Jacob wrestled with the Angel - Genesis 32:24-31

2. Gideon broke down its tower and killed its men due to its failure to help him - Judges 8:8-9, 17

3. Became one of the capitals of Jereboam I - I Kings 12:25

PETRA (SEE BOZRAH)

PISGAH

1. Closely associated with Mount Nebo - Deuteronomy 34:1

2. One of the stopping points on Israel's march to the Promised Land - Numbers 21:20

3. Taken by Israel from the Amorites - Deuteronomy 4:47-49; Joshua 12:1-3

4. One of the places from which Balaam tried to curse Israel - Numbers 23:14

5. It marked a border point between the Tribes of Reuben and Gad - Deuteronomy 3:17

6. It was given to the Tribe of Reuben - Joshua 13:20

7. The place from where Moses saw the Land and where he died - Deuteronomy 3:27; 34:1-6

QAL'AT AT EL-RABADH

1. Located near modern Aijlun and reaching 3700 feet above sea level

2. Castle-fort built during the Ayyubid Dynasty by General Iz al-Din Osman Ibn Munakid (a cousin of Saladin) in 1184-1185 in order to impede Crusader expansion from the west and south

3. Enlarged by Aybek Ibn Muazzam in 1214-1215

4. It next came under the control of Saladin Yussuf Ibn Ayub, the ruler of Haleb in Syria

5. With the expulsion of the Crusaders, it became an administrative headquarters

6. Captured by the Tartars (Mongols) in 1260 and it was laid waste but they were driven out the same year by the Mamelukes under Baybars

7. Restored by Iz al-Din Aybk, when he begame governor of the region

8. With the beginning of the Ottoman Turkish Period (1517) it was manned by fifty soldiers

9. Served as a relay station for sending messages between Cairo and Baghdad either by signal fires or homing pigeons

10. Largely abandoned by the 1800's - When the Swiss explorer Jean Lewis Burckhardt visited the fortress, he reported that it was being used as a private home by the Barakat family

11. Parts were destroyed in the earthquakes of 1837 and 1927

RABBAH OR RABBATH OF AMMON (AMMAN) - PHILADELPHIA

1. Capital city of the Ammonites - Deuteronomy 3:11

2. Contained the large bed of iron of Og, King of Bashan - Deuteronomy 3:11

3. Became an Ammonite border city with the Tribe of Gad - Joshua 13:25

4. Fought against by the army of David and taken by Joab and all this was also in connection with the sin of Bathsheba and the murder of Uriah - II Samuel 11:1-25; 12:26-31; I Chronicles 20:1-3

5. Home of Shobi who provided food for David in his flight from Absalom - II Samuel 17:27-29

6. In the Prophets - Jeremiah 49:2, 3; Ezekiel 21:20; 25:5; Amos 1:14

7. During the Hellenistic Period, it was rebuilt and renamed Philadelphia - Named after Ptolemy II Philadelphos (285-247 B.C.)

8. Taken by the Seleucids under Antiochus III in 218 B.C.

9. It joined the Decapolis in 63 B.C.

10. Taken by the Nabateans in 31 B.C.

11. Retaken by Herod the Great in 30 B.C.

12. It became part of the Roman Province of Arabia in A.D. 106 and rebuilt on a grand scale

13. Conquered in the Moslem Invasion in A.D. 635

14. In the Byzantine Period, it was the seat of the Bishopric of Petra and Philadelphia

15. It actually declined into a small village with no history for a millennium and in the 15th century it was called "a pile of ruins"

16. In 1878, it was resettled with Circassians by the Turkish Sultan Abdul Hamid and began to grow again

17. In 1922, it became the capital of Transjordan and in 1950 of Jordan

18. The modern city

   a. Located 3,000 feet above sea level

   b. Spread over seven hills

   c. It has a population of about 1¾ million

19. Things to see

   a. The Roman Theater - Built between A.D. 169-177 to accommodate six thousand people

   b. The Odeam - A smaller theater from the second century A.D.

   c. The Roman Nymphaeum

   d. The Acropolis or Citadel Hill - Site of the biblical city

      (1) Temple of Hercules - Erected in honor of Emperor Marcus Aurelius (A.D. 161-180)

      (2) Byzantine Church

      (3) Al-Qasr - Built between A.D. 720-750, it was the governor's residence during the Umayyad Dynasty

   e. The Jordan Museum of Antiquities

   f. The Museum of Jewelry and Costumes

   g. The Folklore Museum

Ramoth-Gilead (Ramtha) (Tel er-Rumeit)

1. Part of the Sixth Solomonic District - I Kings 4:13

2. Major area of conflict between Israel and Syria and where King Ahab was killed - I Kings 22:1-40; II Chronicles 18:1-34

3. Place where King Joram of Israel was wounded by the Syrians - II Kings 8:28-29; 9:14-15; II Chronicles 22:5-6

4. Place where Jehu was anointed the King of Israel - II Kings 9:1-13

Red Sea

1. Israelite crossing from Egypt - Exodus 13:18; 14:1-31; 15:4, 22; Numbers 33:8; Deuteronomy 11:4; Joshua 2:10; 4:23; 24:6; Judges 11:16; Nehemiah 9:9-11; Psalms 106:7, 9, 22; 136:13, 15; Acts 7:36; Hebrews 11:29

2. One of the borders of the Promised Land - Exodus 23:31

3. Area of the Wilderness Wanderings - Numbers 14:25; 21:4; 33:10-11; Deuteronomy 1:1, 40; 2:1

4. King Solomon's ships - I Kings 9:26

5. Part of Armageddon - Jeremiah 49:21

Sela (Sila)

1. City of Edom

2. Border point for Amorite control - Judges 1:36

3. Taken by Amaziah, King of Judah, who killed 10,000 Edomites by throwing them off a cliff and renamed it Joktheal - II Kings 14:7; II Chronicles 25:11-12

4. In the Prophets: Isaiah 16:1; 42:11; Jeremiah 49:16; Obadiah 3

Shobak

1. Crusader Fortress called Mont Real or Mons Regalis built in 1115 by Baldwin along the King's Highway halfway between Kir and Petra

2. Conquered in 1189 by Saladin

3. Restored by the Arabs in the fourteenth century

Succoth (Deir Alla)

1. One of the places where Jacob stayed for a while before returning to the Land - Genesis 33:17

2. Given to the Tribe of Gad - Joshua 13:27

3. Refused to help Gideon in his pursuit of the Midianites and was punished for it - Judges 8:4-9, 14-16

4. Area where work was done on items for the Solomonic Temple - I Kings 7:46; II Chronicles 4:17

5. In the Psalms: 60:6; 108:7

6. Here, an Aramaic tablet was found containing prophecies of Balaam, son of Beor (same as the one in the Bible), identifying him as the head of the Deir Alla Sanctuary

TEMAN (TUWANA)

1. Named after a grandson of Esau - Genesis 36:11, 34

2. Home of Eliphaz, one of Job's friends - Job 2:11

3. Home of Husham, King of Edom - Genesis 36:34; I Chronicles 1:45

4. In the Prophets - Jeremiah 49:7, 20; Ezekiel 25:13; Amos 1:12; Obadiah 9; Habakkuk 3:3

TOPHEL (TAFILA)

1. Mentioned as being in the area where the words of Deuteronomy were spoken - Deuteronomy 1:1

2. Contains a Crusader fortress

UMM EL-JIMAL

1. Meaning: "Mother of Camel"

2. A Nabatean-Byzantine city built of black basalt

3. First established in the first century B.C. by the Nabateans with many open spaces to accommodate caravans and with the unique Nabatean ways of gathering water since it had no natural water source

4. Taken by the Romans in the second century A.D. and the Northwest Gate was built by Emperor Commodus (A.D. 180-192)

5. Surrounded by a wall with six gates built in the second century and rebuilt in the fourth century

6. In the Byzantine Period it became a major Christian center; it has the remains of fifteen churches

   a. The earliest church is the Church of Julianus built in 345

   b. The Cathedral - Built 557

   c. The West Church - Best preserved church

   d. The Numerianos Church

   e. The Claudianus Church

   f. The Double Church

   g. The Church of Masechos

   h. Other unnamed churches

7. Things to see

   a. Remains of fifteen churches

   b. The Gate of Commodus

   c. The Praetorium - From 371

   d. The Barracks - Originally built for that purpose but later became a monastery

WADI RUM

1. Beautiful and mountainous desert territory made famous by Lawrence of Arabia

2. Controlled by the Desert Patrol, it has both a Nabatean fort and a Desert Patrol fort

3. Graffiti left by passing caravans over centuries dating as far back as the fourth millennium B.C.

YARMUK RIVER

1. A river that runs for about 45 miles and empties into the Jordan River south of the Sea of Galilee

2. Marked the border between Bashan and Gilead

3. Marked the border between the Tribes of Manasseh and Gad

4. In 1948, it marked the border between Syria and Jordan

5. Since 1967, it has marked the border between Israel (Golan Heights) and Jordan

6. Never mentioned in Scripture

7. In A.D. 636, the Moslems invaded the Land through the Yarmuk River Valley and defeated the Byzantine Army on August 20, 636, thus conquering the Land

8. The Turks built the Haifa-Damascus Railroad in 1905 and crossed the Yarmuk River by a bridge

   a. During World War I, Lawrence of Arabia tried to destroy the bridge but failed

   b. In 1946, it was one of ten bridges destroyed by the *Palmach* (The Night of the Bridges Operation) to pressure the British to leave the Land without killing British soldiers

ZARETHAN (TEL SAIDIYAH)

1. Near the place where the Jordan River was stopped when Israel crossed - Joshua 3:16

2. Near the place where Solomon made many of the vessels for the Temple - II Chronicles 4:17

ZERED RIVER - WADI EL-HASA

1. It marked the border between Moab and Edom - Deuteronomy 2:13-14

2. Part of the Israelite encampment - Numbers 21:12; Deuteronomy 2:13-14

GLOSSARY OF TERMS

Aelia Capitolina: The name given by the Emperor Hadrian to his Romanized city of Jerusalem after the Bar Cochba Revolt was crushed in A.D. 132.

Akiba: A Jewish rabbi and martyr who resided in Israel in the second century. Akiba laid the basis of the Mishnah by beginning the systemization of Jewish Oral Law.

Alexander Yannai: (126-76 B.C.) Hasmonean King of Judea and High Priest from 103-76 B.C. Under Yannai, Judea experienced massive territorial expansion including control of coastal Israel, the territory east of Jordan, Decapolis and Golan.

Aliyah: Immigration (Hebrew). Means ascent or spiritual going up. It presently represents the ingathering of the exiles, a fundamental aspiration of Zionism and the State of Israel.

Amarna Letters: Correspondence between Egyptian vassals in Canaan and the last two Pharoahs of the eighteenth dynasty in the 14th Century B.C. found at Tel el Amarna.

Aramaic: A Semitic language of the Arameans later used in southwest Asia (as by the Jews after the Babylonian Exile)

Aravah (Arabah): Wilderness (Hebrew). The desert plain which is formed by the Syro-African Rift Valley between the Jordan River and the Gulf of Eilat.

Ashkenazi Jews: Jewish people from Polish and Germanic extraction.

Ayyubids: Moslem rulers of the Holy Land in the Second Moslem Period (A.D. 1187 A.D. 1250).

Bacchides: A Syrian general and governor of the Seleucid territories west of the Euphrates (2nd century B.C.). Engaged in many battles with the Jews to secure the Seleucid hold on Jerusalem and Judea and eventually accepted peace with Jonathan.

Bar Cochba: The name of a Jewish resistance hero who led a revolt against Rome in A.D. 132.

Basalt: A black, volcanic rock. The local building material of villages around the Sea of Galilee.

Basilica: Royal (Greek-*basilikos*). A Church building designed like a colonnaded, royal hall.

Bedouins: Nomadic Arabs of the Arabian, Syrian or North African deserts.

Bronze Age: A period of human culture characterized by the use of bronze tools and held to begin in Europe about 3500 B.C. and in western Asia and Egypt somewhat earlier.

Cabalism: The study of the Jewish Cabalah (Jewish writings which read hidden, mystical meanings into the Scriptures.)

Caravanesarais: Lodging places in eastern countries for camel caravans.

Cestius Gallus: Roman Governor of Syria, appointed by Nero in A.D. 63. Attacked Jerusalem in A.D. 66 and besieged the Temple Mount but withdrew days later.

Channukah: The Jewish Festival of Lights commemorating the lighting of the Temple lampstand after the reconsecration of the temple under the Maccabees in 165 B.C.

Circassian: Coming from the western Caucasus.

Cisjordanian: Lands west of the Jordan River.

Cleopatra: Daughter of Ptolemy XI Auletes and Queen of Egypt from 48 B.C. until her suicide in 31 B.C.

Crypt: An underground vault or room often a burial place under the floor of a church.

Decapolis: A large territory south of the Sea of Galilee, mainly to the east of the Jordan but including Beth-Shean to the west, consisting of ten, Greek speaking, Gentile cities that formed a league for trade and mutual defense against the Semitic tribes.

Execration Texts: Lists of Egyptian "curses" against Canaanite kings dating from 1900 B.C.

Fatimids: The Shi'ite Muslim Dynasty which ruled in Egypt, North Africa and the Near East. Ancestry is traced back to Fatima, the daughter of Mohammed. Under the Fatimids, the Jews enjoyed a reasonable degree of tolerance, security and prosperity.

Hadrian: (A.D. 76-138) Emperor of Rome during the second Jewish Revolt. Established the series of defensive fortifications that historically marked the end of Roman territorial expansion.

Haganah: Defense (Hebrew). Jewish Defense League-which was formed between 1910 and 1920 to defend early Jewish settlers and which resisted the British during the Mandate Occupation of the Holy Land. It formed the basis of the Israeli Army in 1947.

Hasidic: Pertaining to a Jewish mystical sect founded in Poland about 1750 in opposition to rationalism and ritual laxity.

Hashomer: Guard (Hebrew). Israeli Socialist political movement, noted for the founding of Kibbutzim.

Hasmoneans: Collective name given to the descendants of Simon Macabee, one of the Macabee brothers who initiated the Maccabean Revolt of 168 B.C., and who fathered a dynasty of Jewish priest/kings in Judaea prior to the Roman conquest in 64 B.C.

Hellenistic: Pertaining to Greek culture and religion.

Herod the Great: The Roman appointed King of Judea from 37-4 B.C., married to a Hasmonean princess. Constructed theaters, amphitheaters, hippodromes throughout Judea and began rebuilding the Temple in Jerusalem.

Hyksos: A foreign line of Semitic "shepherd kings" who ruled Egypt from about 1720 B.C. to 1560 B.C. Some scholars believe that the last of the Hyksos dynasty coincided with the arrival of Joseph's family in Egypt: hence their sympathetic welcome and Joseph's emancipation.

Josephus: A Jewish historian and Pharisee of both royal and priestly lineage, who obtained favor with the Roman Emperor Vespasian and recorded much of the history of the first century A.D.

Karaite Jews: One of a stricter group of Jews adhering to the literal interpretation of Scripture as against the Oral Law and rejected Rabbinic Judaism.

Khan: An inn or rest house.

Khwarizmians: Referring to those who supposedly practice a syncretistic form of Judaism, that began before the Arab Conquest with the people of Khorezm, which is on the lower course of the Amu Darya River, south of the Aral Sea.

Maccabee: "Hammerer" (Hebrew). The name given to the heroes of the Jewish revolt against the Greeks in 168 B.C.

Madaba Map: A mosaic map of Byzantine Jerusalem and the Land of Israel found at Madaba in Jordan.

Maktesh: Crater (Hebrew).

Mamluks (Mamelukes): A military force of former Circassian slaves who became the rulers of Egypt and who ruled the Holy Land from A.D. 1250 - A.D. 1517.

Mark Antony: Roman orator, triumvir and soldier who served under Gaius Julius Caesar. At the outbreak of the civil war between Caesar and Pompey, Antony was appointed Caesar's commander in chief. After Caesar's assassination he ruled the eastern portion of the Triumvate Roman Empire. He committed suicide upon false report of his lover, Cleopatra's, death.

Messianic Jew: A Jew who recognizes that Jesus is the Messiah.

Mishnah: To repeat, teach, learn (Hebrew - *shanah*). The Jewish Oral Law, codified into its final form in A.D. 220.

Monophysite: One who holds that Jesus had just one composite nature.

Nabateans: An Arab people located in Petra. They occupied agricultural settlements south of Hebron as well as in Edom and Moab between the 6th and 4th Centuries B.C. By NT times their territory stretched from the Mediterranean and the Red Sea right across eastward to the Euphrates.

Neolithic: Of or relating to the latest period of the Stone Age characterized by polished stone implements.

Omayyad: See Umayyads.

Ostraca: Pieces of pottery tile used for writing.

Ottomans: The Turkish Empire founded by Othman. The Ottoman Turks defeated the Mamluks and ruled the Holy Land from 1517 until 1917.

Paleolithic: Of, relating to, or being the second period of the Stone Age, which is characterized by rough or crudely chipped stone implements.

Palmach: The "Commando" section of the Haganah.

Patriarchate: *Nasi* (Hebrew). During the Talmudic Period, the term applied to a rabbinic dynasty that excercised authority over the Jews in the Land of Israel under Rome

Pharisees: A Jewish sect of NT times noted for strict observance of rites and ceremonies of the Written Law and for insistence on the validity of the Oral Law.

Pompey: (106-48 B.C.) A Roman general who subdued the Jews and captured Jerusalem.

Ptolemies: Name of 15 kings of Egypt comprising the Macedonian or XXXI Dynasty, which ruled from 323-30 B.C.

Sadducees: A Jewish sect at the time of Jesus that consisted largely of a priestly aristocracy and that rejected doctrines not in the law.

Saladin: Sultan of Egypt and Syria from 1138-1193. Overthrew the Fatimids in 1171 and became the first Ayyubid Sultan of Egypt and Syria in 1175. His Muslim armies defeated the Christian forces near Tiberias in 1187 and his capture of Jerusalem led to the Third Crusade.

Sargon II: Ruler of Assyria from 722-705 B.C.

Selucids: Seleucia was founded by Seleucus in 301 B.C. as the new west capitol of Antioch. The Seleucid domain was spread over most of Asia Minor and ruled Syria for 250 years until suspended by the Romans. The Jews were caught in the middle of the Seleucids' struggle with Egypt over Israel.

Sennecherib: Assyrian King from 705-681 B.C. The originator of great public works including the construction of canals and watercourses and the erection of a palace at Ninevah.

Sephardic Jews: Jewish people of Spanish and Portuguese extraction.

Sicarri: A murderous band of Jewish knifemen in the NT period.

Talmud: (Hebrew) The fundamental code of Jewish civil and canon law comprising the *Mishnah* and its commentary, the *Gemara*.

Tel: (Arabic) - An ancient mound consisting of layers of debris, each representing a different period of habitation.

Terebinth: A small tree related to the sumac that yields an oleoresin.

Tiglath Pileser III: King of Assyria 745-727 B.C.

Titus: Roman Emperor, son of Vespasian. He fought under his father's command during the Jewish rebellion in Israel. He succeeded his father as General of the Roman army and captured Jerusalem in A.D. 70.

Transjordan: Lands to the east of the Jordan River.

Umayyads: Moslem rulers of the Holy Land in the First Moslem Period (A.D. 538 - A.D. 750).

Unicameral: Having only one house of government.

Vespasian: Roman Emperor from A.D. 69-79. In A.D. 66, he began a campaign against the Jews in Judea, which was completed by his son, Titus.

Via Maris: The Way of the Sea (Latin) - A major trading route connecting Egypt with Mesopotamia which passed along the Mediterranean Coast and across northern Israel.

Wadi: (Arabic) A dried up river bed, liable to flash flooding in the rainy season.

Yeshivah: A Jewish educational establishment: a school or seminary for training rabbis.

Yom Kippur: (Hebrew) Day of Atonement.

Zohar: One of the most important Cabalistic texts, being an allegorical interpretation of the Five Books of Moses.

Zoroastrian: An ancient dualistic religion founded by Zoroaster (or Zarathustra) set forth in the Zen d-Avestra, and still adhered to by the Guebres in Iran and the Parsees in India.

SCRIPTVRAL REFERENCE

Index

A

B

C

D

ן

ן

K

L

M

Y

Z